Building Literacy With Love

A Guide for Teachers and Caregivers of Children Birth Through Age 5

Building Literacy
With Love

A Guide for Teachers and Caregivers of Children Birth Through Age 5

BETTY S. BARDIGE

AND

MARILYN M. SEGAL

ZERO TO THREE
PRESS
Washington, D.C.

Published by

 2000 M St., NW, Suite 200, Washington, DC 20036-3307
(202) 638-1144

Toll-free orders (800) 899-4301, *Web:* http://www.zerotothree.org
The mission of the ZERO TO THREE Press is to publish authoritative research,
practical resources, and new ideas for those who work with and care about infants,
toddlers, and their families. Books are selected for publication by an independent
Editorial Board. The views contained in this book are those of the authors and do not
necessarily reflect those of ZERO TO THREE: National Center for Infants, Toddlers
and Families, Inc.

Cover design: John Hubbard
Text design and composition: Seven Worldwide Publishing Solutions

Library of Congress Cataloging-in-Publication Data

Bardige, Betty Lynn Segal.
  Building literacy with love: a guide for teachers and caregivers of children from
  birth through age 5 / Betty Bardige and Marilyn Segal.
    p. cm.
  ISBN 0-943657-82-2
  1. Language arts—Study and teaching (Preschool)—Activity programs.
I. Segal, Marilyn M. II. Title.
  LC149.B264 2005
  372.6--dc22

                                                                    2004022329

10 9 8 7 6 5 4 3 2 1
ISBN 0-943657-82-2
Printed in the United States of America
Photo credits: Lorraine Breffni: 94, 127, 226, 274, 352, 358; Sarah Merrill: 6;
Marilyn Nolt: 21, 48, 145, 150, 170, 179, 213, 338
Suggested citation:
Bardige, B. S., & Segal, M. M. (2005). *Building literacy with love: A guide for teachers and
caregivers of children birth through age 5.* Washington, DC: ZERO TO THREE Press.

Table of Contents

Foreword

This is an important book. Many parents and caregivers do not know how children become literate. Most adults do not remember how they learned to read and write, much less what happened that made the development of these skills interesting and meaningful. Often adults think literacy begins when children start school and teachers teach reading. They assume that learning to recognize letters and then how to combine them into words is the key. They do not know that reading and writing involve complex cognitive and affective skills that depend on a myriad of experiences and integrate thinking, feeling, and communicating.

Building Literacy With Love is important because it outlines the skills, concepts, and processes intrinsic to learning to read and write, and the experiences that adults can provide for children to help them learn. This is a down-to-earth, practical guide for understanding literacy.

Many people find it surprising that the path to literacy begins in infancy. Yet it is true. Over the past 20 years, we have gained new insights into how children develop and learn. This research shows a strong link between early care and education and later learning. Luckily, young children come into the world ready to learn. They are born with a natural inclination to use their abilities to figure out the world around them. The research shows clearly that we do not need to force children to learn; they are ready to learn as a part of their developmental equipment. In just a few short years, the typical child learns to love and be loved, to manipulate and categorize objects, to speak her family's language, to move in space, and a million other things.

But children do not learn these things by themselves. They learn them because their families and caregivers provide them with opportunities, encourage their explorations, and share their delight in their discoveries and achievements.

Reading and writing are skills that depend on an interest in socializing and knowledge of speech, characteristics that are ideally developed in the earliest caregiver–child relationships. Children are not automatically able to use adults as sources of information, support, and enjoyment. This is only the case if the primary caregivers set the stage. It is from interactions with caregivers that infants get a sense of well-being and an interest in social engagement. It is through the love and responsive care babies receive that they learn to engage socially and to communicate with others.

Building Literacy With Love is an important book because it points out the importance of relationships in children's literacy development and provides practical examples of how to establish the kinds of relationships with individual children that support their development. The critical ingredient is loving and responsive relationships with caregivers—relationships that facilitate the child's exploration of the world, stimulate and support communications between the child and other people, and lead the child to believe that the world is safe, interesting, and meaningful.

While loving relationships are important, they are not all that is needed if children are to become literate. Literacy is based on formal language. There are individual differences in how early and how well children learn to talk with family and friends, but most children need little more than love and responsiveness in order to acquire speech. Unfortunately, home language may not be enough of a foundation for literacy. Children who learn to read and write with the greatest ease are those who attend to and use formal language; they have large vocabularies, relate verbal ideas to experience, understand and use complex sentence structures, and rely less on nonverbal contextual clues to understand, to name a few of the necessary skills. Thus, to learn to read and write easily and well, children need rich and diverse experience with oral and written language. For some children, their home environment provides all they need. Others, because of cultural differences or long hours spent away from home, may need more careful attention to their formal language or programs in schools and centers to build their literacy-specific language experience.

Building Literacy With Love is an important book because it points out how to help children from culturally diverse families and communities gain supportive literacy experiences. With this extra attention and using the strengths of their home culture and language, children can develop the skills and knowledge that underlie literacy.

Helping children become literate requires more than understanding the process, providing supportive relationships, and focusing on language. It also requires specific teaching. Writing and reading are ways of communicating, but they are as not natural as language. Many groups of people who effortlessly communicate with one another do not have a written language, and many children grow up in literate societies without ever learning to read and write. And, even though many children do not need as much careful teaching to learn to read and write as others, all need some instruction and practice to learn.

This book is important because it explains what needs to be taught to children about reading and writing. Teachers and caregivers will find numerous practical and fun activities to promote phonemics, phonetic awareness, alphabetic knowledge, and fluency.

Today, literacy must have a high priority in the lives of young children. We must teach not just some children to be literate, but all children: poor, middle-class, and rich children; black, white, and brown children; typically developing children and children with special needs and handicapping conditions. The window of opportunity for teaching literacy is relatively small and closes early. Although people can learn to read at any age, children who are not reading comfortably and on grade level by the end of third grade are likely to struggle in school and may drop out before the end of high school. That is why this book is so important. With it, adults will see how to provide the experiences that facilitate all children's ability to become literate—with love.

—BARABARA BOWMAN
President emerita,
Erikson Institute,
Chicago

Acknowledgments

Building Literacy With Love began as a grant proposal. In order to improve the school readiness of young children deemed at risk due to poverty, lack of experience with English, or residence in a district with a history of school failure, the U.S. government invested in a small number of demonstration projects. Early Childhood Professional Education grants would provide training activities to help early educators improve their skills at fostering emergent literacy. Nova Southeastern University's (NSU) PARITY project was one of nine projects funded in 2002. Only one of the others included infant–toddler teachers and caregivers.

The PARITY project worked with 67 classrooms in 20 centers and 11 family child-care homes in two Florida counties. Over a 2-year period, directors, teachers, and caregivers took a course in emergent literacy, offered by NSU at its Fort Lauderdale and Tampa Bay sites. Mentors worked intensively with participants to help them implement what they were learning. In addition, the project provided books, furnishings, and other materials for their classrooms and home-lending libraries and supported Story Time events for families.

The instructor's notes developed for the emergent literacy course provided the framework for *Building Literacy With Love.* The partnering centers provided a laboratory for testing and refining many of the practical suggestions that are included in the book. We are grateful to the following NSU staff members for their help in shaping the Emergent Literacy course and providing ongoing feedback on its implementation and application: Hilde Reno, Jesse Leinfelder, Judy Zimmerman, Donna Shreve, and Yvonne Britt helped us define the essential territory to be covered. Donna Shreve and Lorraine Breffni developed a wealth of active learning opportunities for the course participants and helped them to document the changes they made in their classrooms. We especially thank Lorraine Breffni for her classroom photographs. Wendy Masi provided overall direction to the project.

We are grateful to the directors, teachers, caregivers, and parents who were partners in the PARITY project for their eager embrace of the program, creative implementation, and important feedback.

Special thanks go to Christine DiSilvestro for organizing notes, researching citations, and working diligently through many versions of the manuscript.

In addition, we would like to thank Kori Bardige, an early childhood special educator, for providing us with classroom anecdotes, suggested activities and teaching strategies, and key resources. We owe an added debt to Jesse Leinfelder, Lorraine Breffni, Mary Jean Woika, and Yvonne Britt for their careful critiques. The changes that they suggested strengthened the manuscript.

We would also like to thank Emily Fenichel at ZERO TO THREE for her encouragement of this work, her perceptive questions, her insistence upon scientific accuracy and good writing, and her unrelenting focus on the promise, curiosity, and eagerness to learn and connect that are characteristic of all young children.

Finally, we thank the A. L. Mailman Family Foundation, the Children's Services Board of Hillsborough County, the Broward Children's Services Council, the Broward School Readiness Coalition, and Nova Southeastern University for helping to support the PARITY project.

Overview

Teach Me to Read

*Teach me to read, says Justin
So I can be grown-up and smart.
If you say you will, I will try to sit still
And learn all my letters by heart.*

*When I can read, says Justin,
Everything's going to be great.
I will sit at the table and read every label
Before I put food on my plate.*

*When I want my most favoritest story
And everyone says, "Not today!"
I'll go to the shelf and get it myself
And I'll read every page the right way.*

*I will get a big book from the library
And learn something no one else knew.
Then all of the guys will hail Justin the Wise
'Cause they'll be so amazed that it's true.*

—BETTY BARDIGE, *unpublished poem*

Literacy, as 5-year-old Justin realizes, is more than reading back the words on a page. It involves following a story, deducing the meaning of new words, and garnering information. More often than not, it entails emotional engagement such as amusement, empathy, suspense, comfort, or surprise. Literacy also goes beyond reading to include writing, critical listening, speaking, and interpretation of mathematical symbols. It requires the application and integration of prior knowledge and experience, the understanding of underlying concepts, and the recognition of patterns and conventions. It is both the cause and effect of ongoing learning.

Research shows that children who are fluent readers by the end of third grade are likely to do well in school and go on to higher education. Those who continue to struggle—who read too slowly and laboriously to get the overall message or whose small vocabularies and lack of general knowledge make reading to learn a chore—are likely to languish and may not complete high school.

Some children learn to read with little explicit intervention or instruction; they just seem to "pick it up." Some are held back by subtle or serious difficulties with vision, hearing, language, information processing, or social–emotional adjustment. For most, though, learning to read well is a process that takes many years and includes both explicit instruction and lots of playful, self-motivated practice with words, sounds, symbols, stories, and books.

After reviewing the massive body of research on how children learn to read, a panel convened by the National Research Council of the National Academy of Sciences (Burns, Griffin, & Snow, 1999, p. 6) concluded that good readers demonstrate three characteristics:

- They understand the alphabetic system of English to identify printed words,

- They have and use background knowledge and strategies to obtain meaning from print, and

- They read fluently.

The panel (Burns, Griffin, & Snow, 1999, p. 8)further concluded that:

- Research consistently demonstrates that the more children know about language and literacy before they get to school, the better equipped they are to succeed in reading.

- Main accomplishments include:

  - Oral language skills and phonological awareness,

  - Motivation to learn and appreciation for literate forms, and

  - Print awareness and letter knowledge.

- These language and literacy accomplishments are achieved best through activities that are integrated across different developmental areas, that is, cognitive development, fine and gross motor development, social development, and language development.

Most 4- and 5-year-olds are quite capable of learning the letters of the alphabet and the sounds the letters make. But oral language, background knowledge, motivation to learn in general and to learn to read in particular, phonological and print awareness, and appreciation for literate forms are acquired over a much longer period of time. They require lots of experience and practice, through activities that are embedded in children's daily lives. That's why the foundation laid in the early years is so critical.

Laying this foundation begins in babyhood. Once upon a time, people thought that young babies were not very good at seeing or hearing. We now know that this notion is not the case. From the moment of birth, babies tune in to the world around them. They soon learn to recognize their parents' voices and to focus on things that are interesting to watch—especially the faces of their caregivers.

Within the first month, babies learn to associate a sight with a sound and will turn their heads to see who those approaching footsteps belong to or what made that rattling sound. They soon learn to engage in back-and-forth "conversations," cooing and making faces as they respond to their caregivers' overtures and elicit responses to their own. They learn to love, to trust, to count on someone responding to their cries, to predict the effect of their actions. They show interest in things that are "moderately novel"—new, but not too strange. As they gain control over their movements, they begin to explore their environments.

Seeing and hearing, connecting sights and sounds that go together, communicating and conversing, enjoying interaction, and expressing curiosity—these early pursuits are the roots of language and literacy. We must nurture these roots if the flowers are to bloom.

HOW LITERACY EMERGES

I n actuality, reading even the simplest of texts is quite complex. Anyone who wants to read needs to know some basics that most readers take for granted:

- The text carries the meaning.

- Spaces indicate breaks between words.

- The words on the page correspond to spoken words.

- In English, we read from right to left, top to bottom, starting at the front of the book.

- In an alphabetic writing system, the words are made up of letters and letter combinations that correspond to sounds, but in English, a letter (such as *c*, *s*, *g*, or any vowel) can correspond to more than one sound, and different letters or letter combinations (such as *g* and *j*, *c* and *k*, or *x* and *cks*) can correspond to the same sound.

- A capital letter indicates the beginning of a sentence, and a period marks the end.

- The sentences combine to tell a story that is likely to follow a familiar pattern, with a beginning, middle, and end.

- The story is told from a particular point of view that may shift as different characters talk.

A reader also needs to know some specifics, including the sounds that the letters and letter combinations stand for, the meaning and pronunciation of the words, and the grammar of the language that she is reading.

Most children acquire these fundamentals of reading in early childhood. They babble, learn to speak, put words together into sentences of increasing complexity, learn new words and concepts, and use language for a variety of purposes. They listen to stories and come to understand the specialized language that is found in books and other print materials. Children handle (and chew) books, identify pictures, recognize symbols, and learn to follow along as a book is read to them. They repeat familiar actions in pretend play and retell or reenact "stories" from real life, books and movies, and their own imaginations. Children learn songs and nursery rhymes and play with the sounds of words. They learn to recognize and write the letters in their names and, eventually, learn the whole alphabet.

Early, or emergent, literacy refers to these precursors of formal reading. Emergent literacy is not quite the same as "reading readiness." Reading readiness assumes that children must reach a certain level of maturation before they are "ready" to learn to read. That model has not proven to be very useful. Some children teach themselves to read at the age of 3, and others show little interest in learning to read on their own until they are 5 or 6 or even older. Clearly, more than maturation is involved.

Emergent literacy is based, instead, on the premise that literacy is a continuum of abilities that children develop as they learn to use symbols to represent aspects of reality. Thus, a 3-year-old who is pretending to read, holding a book right side up, retelling the familiar story, and turning the pages at roughly the right times is demonstrating a fairly high level of emergent literacy skill. Of course, that child still has a long way to go before she will be reading on her own and deriving meaning, information, and enjoyment from texts that she has not seen before. As children relate to and communicate with their primary caregivers, as they learn and practice spoken language, and as they learn to recognize and create written symbols, they are developing the foundation for formal reading and writing.

THE READING PROCESS

Reading, whether fluent or emergent, involves the bringing together of two processes. The first, which we usually associate with decoding or "sounding out words," involves close attention to the marks on the page and the analysis and interpretation of these symbols in terms of the sounds they stand for. The second process is associated with both literal comprehension and with understanding and appreciation of nuance, style, and significance. It involves bringing in one's own knowledge, experience, and feelings in order to make sense of the text. The two approaches work together. As we identify the words, they evoke meanings and associations. At the same time, our understanding of the text as a whole not only helps us to identify the individual words but also influences how we interpret them.

In a seminal article written in 1998, reading researchers White-hurst and Lonigan describe these processes or approaches as "inside-*out*" and "outside-*in*."

- Inside-*out* refers to the use of alphabet knowledge and text analysis skills, including the understanding of sound and print units.

- Outside-*in* refers to the bringing in of real-world information and concepts as well as knowledge of language and story schema (patterns) that provide the meaning base of literacy.

This 4-year old's "writing" shows his grasp of print concepts. He knows, for example, that words are groups of letters with space in between.

Helping Children Build a Firm Foundation

The inside-*out* and outside-*in* skills needed for literacy rest on four interlocking cornerstones: efficacy, emotional engagement, language, and the social support of family, community, and culture.

Efficacy

All learning, especially for young children, begins with an emotional context. How a child feels is as important as what he thinks. How he feels about himself and about his likelihood of success plays as important a role in his ability to solve problems or master new skills as does what he knows and can do or how he reasons. T. Berry Brazelton, in the preface to *Heart Start: The Emotional Foundations of School Readiness* (ZERO TO THREE, 1992), refers to this belief that a person can make things happen, that her efforts are likely to pay off, as a sense of efficacy. He routinely identifies it in infants before their first birthday. As an example, Brazelton describes a 9-month-old child who pulls himself up to a standing position for the first time. His parents applaud his accomplishment, and the baby beams with pride. According to Brazelton, this baby has developed a sense of efficacy. He has confidence in his ability to succeed and will continue to persist with a challenging task until he accomplishes it. He has learned to expect not only the reward of accomplishment but also the smile and praise that come with it.

Unfortunately, some babies learn to expect failure rather than success. They will make one or two lackluster attempts to meet the challenge; if they are not immediately successful, they will give up trying. Caregivers who provide young children with relatively easy challenges and praise them for meeting the challenges can rebuild feelings of efficacy. As children's new accomplishments are recognized and encouraged, they will develop a positive self-image and will recognize that they can succeed if they really try.

Efficacy is best described by the classic children's book, *The Little Engine That Could* (Piper, Hauman, & Hauman, 1978). In this story, the big, powerful engines all fail to pull the little train over the mountain. They either believe they cannot do it, or they do not care to try. The little engine succeeds because he really wants to, and because he keeps saying to himself, "I think I can."

Emotional Engagement

Young children who have developed a sense of efficacy are eager learners by nature, but their interest in learning particular things is highly dependent on the emotional climate in which that learning takes place. A baby who sees a trusted family member enjoying a new food is much more likely to try it than one whose caregiver makes a face or looks away. A toddler who habitually hears encouraging words is likely to have a larger vocabulary than one who hears more "no's." A 3-year-old who enjoys sitting on an adult's lap and repeating the refrain of a familiar story will ask for that book over and over again. A 4-year-old who likes playing house with her friends may be motivated to "write" a shopping list or make menus for her pretend restaurant. A 6-year-old who loves sports will choose sports stories to read and may even try to read the sports page.

The teacher's job, then, is to establish positive relationships with individual children while also helping children to develop positive relationships with one another. These positive relationships provide children with self-esteem and self-confidence, and a secure base for further exploration. As adults and children get to know one another, teachers can tap into and extend children's interests while also introducing them to new areas for exploration. Whether working with babies or with preschoolers, teachers have daily opportunities to share children's discoveries, introduce them to new areas of experience, and encourage their love of all aspects of literacy.

The individual relationships that teachers, caregivers, and family members establish with children make all the difference—and not just in the present. The quality of these early relationships can have lifelong effects. Empathy, efficacy, self-esteem, security, and eagerness to learn are all grounded in these early relationships.

Language

Language is fundamental to reading; if a person does not understand the language, then the words in a book are just gibberish, even if he can read them. But language is also a fundamental part of both the outside-*in* and inside-*out* domains. Language gives us the labels through which we name and understand our world. It also gives us the capacity to recall events and information; to enter imaginary worlds; and to reason, ask questions, and make predictions. Children who develop facility in using language in these ways can engage with fiction and nonfiction writing and can derive meaning, information, enjoyment, and deep understanding from what they read and from what is read to them.

In the inside-*out* domain, facility with language is also critical. Nursery rhymes, tongue twisters, and word games help children tune in to the sounds of language and the ways in which words are put together. In addition, knowing and using lots of words helps children become familiar with common patterns such as prefixes, suffixes, and roots; plural and past-tense endings; and common and less frequent sound combinations.

Children whose homes or child-care environments are rich in books, interesting things to explore and talk about, and people interested in talking about them develop rich vocabularies and use their words in a variety of complex sentences for a variety of purposes. Children with less responsive people to talk to and less topics to talk about are likely to recognize fewer words and use words in more limited ways. In one study (Morrison, Griffith, & Alberts, 1997), a group of children entering kindergarten showed scores in receptive vocabulary (number of words understood) that ranged from ages 21 months to 10¾ years.

The good news is that children who are slow to develop their vocabularies can expand them over time. Unlike grammar, which is learned most easily in early childhood, vocabulary does not get harder to learn as one gets older. The bad news is that "catching up" to peers with respect to vocabulary size gets harder and harder as time goes on. The gap widens every year because children who develop rich vocabularies by age 3 or 4 tend to increase their vocabularies at a faster pace than children whose vocabularies are more limited. This widening gap should be no surprise. The more words of a sentence or paragraph one understands, the easier it is to pick up new words from the context. Similarly, having a richer vocabulary enables a child to be more expressive—to ask more nuanced questions, make more precise observations, imagine more interesting scenarios, draw on more sources for making analogies, and give and understand more detailed explanations or inferences. Thus, the child's use of richer language accelerates her learning and provides increased opportunities for mastering new words and asking new questions.

The language foundation that preschool children develop as they converse with teachers, family members, and other children can prepare them for school success. Their early caregivers and teachers play critical roles in building this foundation, both directly (through their interaction with children and intentional teaching) and indirectly (through their support of communication among children and their alliances with families).

Many children will be developing this language foundation in two or even three languages. This expanded language foundation is an enormous gift. Children are learning their second language naturally in early childhood—when their brains are particularly primed to pick up sound and grammar patterns—instead of being taught that language in school. They may be more flexible in their thinking because they learn early that the same thing can be labeled in different ways and that different ways of speaking and acting are expected in different contexts. They become sensitive to different points of view and different expectations as they develop the capacity to identify and speak the language of their listener.

Children learn basic concepts most easily in the language in which they feel most comfortable, which is usually the language that their parents speak. But if they will be taught the inside-*out* skills of reading in English, then it is important that they have enough experience with English so they become familiar with its sound patterns and learn the critical mass of vocabulary words that will enable them to understand the beginning reading texts. Catherine Snow, a language and emergent literacy researcher who chaired the National Academy of Sciences panel on preventing reading difficulties, recommends that children who will be taught to read first in English have 2 years of English practice in addition to maintaining their native language.

Social Supports

Children are individuals, but they are also members of many groups, and these groups provide social supports that influence both what and how children learn. Urie Bronfenbrenner (1981), in *The Ecology of Human Development*, introduced his ecological model of human development. This model identifies the critical factors beyond biological makeup that influence the development of a child. Bronfenbrenner conceptualizes the child as the center of concentric circles in which each ring influences those inside of it. The outside ring, which is culture, influences the social and economic context of development, which in turn influences the immediate family environment. This ecological perspective helps us understand the way in which culture, community, and family support emergent literacy.

Considering Bronfenbrenner's model, let's start with the smallest circle: the family. We know from research that what families do with their young children makes a difference in children's emotional development and in their acquisition of language and literacy. Practices such as talking with babies, providing young children with explanations and choices, and reading to children daily have proven to be so important that intervention programs deliberately encourage their adoption, and evaluations of early childhood programs count families' use of these practices as signs of success.

The influence of family goes beyond what family members do directly with the child. The culture of the family also makes a difference, and this family culture is influenced by the outer circles of community and culture. Some families have a culture of literacy. Conversation is constant and covers a wide range of topics. Adults do a lot of reading—not only of books but also of magazines, newspapers, instruction manuals, recipes, maps, and labels. They jot notes, make lists, mark calendars, pay bills, send e-mail, and keep records. They read for pleasure and enjoy learning. Curious children are encouraged to join in—to watch and listen, imitate, ask questions, and try to contribute. Because they enjoy reading, adults pass this enjoyment on to their children. Reading together becomes a treasured activity, one that is likely to occur many times each day, particularly at special times like bedtime. Families might make frequent trips to the library or build their own collections of much-loved children's books.

Other families might engage in less reading and writing, but this limited engagement is counterbalanced by a rich oral tradition.

Children hear complex stories and extended conversations at home and also learn language through music and poetry. They participate in community gatherings and religious events on a regular basis, beginning when they are babies. In this kind of rich linguistic environment, children can acquire large vocabularies and rich, expressive language. They may come to school or preschool lacking intimate familiarity with print, but their facility with words and awareness of their component sounds provides a firm grounding for learning how the alphabet works.

Other families might be more isolated and less verbal. Home may be a quiet place, or a very busy, noisy one. Either way, a young child may not be included in much conversation. Reading, writing, singing, and storytelling might not be frequent or enjoyed adult activities. Reading materials might be largely absent, or they might be kept out of sight or out of reach of young children. In homes like these, parents can be supported to adopt playful parenting habits and consciously create a home culture that supports language and literacy. Even if they are not fluent readers themselves, they can help their children by recounting stories from their own lives; making family scrapbooks; sharing the music that they enjoy; showing interest in their child's discoveries, questions, and accomplishments; and taking advantage of everyday opportunities for building a love of learning.

Beyond the home, young children and their families are supported by their neighborhoods and communities. Here again, vast differences can be found. In some communities, children are part of a "village," in which they are surrounded by people who are concerned about their welfare or available to play with them. These communities may place a stronger emphasis on care and interconnectedness than on independence or one-to-one relationships. Children may spend considerable time in mixed-age groups and derive a sense of security from being part of an extended family or a neighborhood group.

In some neighborhoods high-quality children's books are readily available. They might be obtained from bookstores, libraries with toddler-friendly areas and children's librarians, school-based library programs, or bookmobiles. In addition, pediatricians, home visitors, community-based organizations, and public officials might give away books at public events or as part of their work with families. Other neighborhoods are resource poor. They provide few safe spaces for young families to gather and offer limited access to books and other reading materials.

The widest circle in Bronfenbrenner's model is culture. For many children, of course, culture is not one circle but two or more overlapping ones. And, of course, cultures are always evolving. Nevertheless, some generalizations about differences and similarities in cultural beliefs and attitudes have held up over time. One widely reported area of difference is individualism versus collectivism. Some cultures stress the importance of independence, competitiveness, and individual achievement, whereas other cultures emphasize interdependence, cooperation, and collective goals. Other culturally based differences relate to child-rearing practices. In some cultures, children are encouraged to express their feelings, to engage adults in conversations, and to offer their own opinions. Other cultures stress the importance of obedience and respect for elders. These beliefs are reflected in child-rearing practices that may be associated with language learning and reading success.

Home, community, and cultures also influence children's approaches to social situations and learning opportunities. The way a child learns in school is likely to reflect the way she learns at home. Children from cultures with a strong oral tradition may learn best from dramatic storytelling and from participating in choral or call-and-response activities. Children from families where they are always told what to do may seek direction or permission before doing things on their own and may need help getting started. Children from families that encourage play and invite children to explore are more likely to initiate play activities and are less likely to wait for directions.

Culture can be a central part of a child's identity. When her culture is affirmed, so is she. When a setting or experience reflects or is consistent with her culture, she feels at home. When people behave in ways that the child has come to expect, then she feels secure. In this sense, culture is not only the outer ring of influence but also an important cradle and support for a growing child.

Effective teachers understand these linkages. They provide families with resources and information to help them nurture their children's curiosity and literacy development. At the same time, they take advantage of the resources and information that each family brings and the knowledge that families have about how their children like to learn.

Building Literacy With Love

W e have written this book for teachers, caregivers, and family child-care providers who are working with children between the ages of zero and 5 years. *Building Literacy With Love* presents research on child development and on effective teaching practices, and also provides practical suggestions for implementing research-informed methods and activities in child-care centers and in home-based care. It includes stories from the field (often told in a humorous way to emphasize a point) and resources for practicing teachers.

The various chapters in this book expand on the following ways to build literacy:

- Develop relationships with children that build efficacy, emotional engagement, and language.

- Engage all children in active, playful learning.

- Support children's language development through conversations, intentional teaching, and reading together.

- Help children develop outside-*in* skills and knowledge, including knowledge of how print works, an understanding of written language conventions and story patterns, a rich vocabulary, and a large font of background knowledge.

- Help children develop inside-*out* skills and knowledge, including awareness of sounds and word parts, ability to recognize and name letters, and familiarity with written words.

- Create a classroom (or home) environment that supports all aspects of emergent literacy.

- Use art, music, dance, and drama to enhance emergent literacy.

- Observe and assess individual children and track their emergent literacy progress.

- Encourage programs to develop partnerships with families—partnerships that enrich those programs and help them meet individual children's needs.

• Help families to support their children's language, emergent literacy, and ongoing school success.

In addition, we have written this text with the hope that it will help teachers and child-care providers to enjoy the magic of words and to further appreciate the delightful unfolding of language and literacy that occurs in the children in their care. We hope that you enjoy the journey and that you find the resources useful.

Reflections

Before you read further in this book, take a moment to remember your own emergent literacy experiences. Throughout this text and in your ongoing work with children and families, you will want to draw upon what you have learned through your own experience, including how you feel and what you know. Here are some questions to get you started:

What are your earliest memories of learning to read?

Do you remember books that were read to you or stories that were told over and over? Any special favorites?

Who were the people involved? What did they do to help you feel loved, cared for, interested, and competent?

What was your primary language? Did you also learn in another language? If so, how did you feel about your bilingual experiences?

REFERENCES

Bronfenbrenner, U. (1981). *The ecology of human development: Experiments by nature and design* (2nd ed.). Boston: Harvard University Press.

Burns, M. S., Griffin, P., & Snow, C. E. (Eds.). (1999). *Starting out right: A guide to promoting children's reading success.* Washington, DC: National Research Council.

Morrison, F .J., Griffith, E. M. &. Alberts, D. M. (1997). Nature-nurture in the classroom: Entrance age, school readiness, and learning in children. *Developmental Psychology 33(2): 254–262.*

Piper, W., Hauman, G., & Hauman, D. (1978). *The little engine that could.* New York: Penguin Putnam.

Snow, C. E., Burns, M. S., & Griffin, P. (Eds.). (1998). *Preventing reading difficulties in young children.* Report of the Committee on the Prevention of Reading Difficulties in Young Children, convened by the National Research Council. Washington, DC: National Academy Press.

Whitehurst, G., & Lonigan, C. (1998). Child development and emergent literacy. *Child Development, 68,* 848–872.

ZERO TO THREE. (1992). *Heart start: The emotional foundations of school readiness.* Arlington, VA: ZERO TO THREE: National Center for Clinical Infant Programs.

CHAPTER 2

Building a Social–Emotional Foundation

The Joys of Reading

*Kate is a princess
Up in her tower
Reading and reading
Hour after hour*

*Having adventures
Doing brave deeds.
A pile of books is
All that she needs!*

—BETTY BARDIGE, *unpublished poem*

Like the child in the poem, many of us have experienced the joy of being lost in a book and transported to another realm. The books we love touch our hearts, engage our minds, and fuel our imaginations. They provide us with beautiful language and imagery, characters who become our friends, and thrilling plots that compel our interest. For us, literacy isn't just about being able to read—it's also about love for the written and spoken word and the ability to appreciate and learn from the messages they contain.

Those of us who would foster literacy in young children must begin, then, by fostering a love of learning and a love of literature. To develop this love, we must build the kinds of relationships that affirm children's worth, nurture their curiosity and confidence, and encourage them to share our passions and interests as well as to develop their own.

These relationships provide children with three interrelated attributes that are critical to their development and ongoing learning:

- ***Efficacy***—The confidence that your actions will have predictable effects, that you can make people respond and make things happen, that it is worth trying because it is possible to succeed, and that your success will please the people who are important to you

- ***A secure base for exploration***—A safe haven from which to launch forays into the outside world or take risks to try new things; a base that you can return to when you need reassurance, guidance, or refueling

- ***Social referencing***—Looking to the people you trust for clues about how to approach new experiences. Their reactions let you know what is safe and what is dangerous, what is likely to be pleasant or unpleasant, what is valuable and what is trivial, what is to be avoided and what is worth pursuing.

If we want children to believe in themselves, to be eager and curious learners, and to be interested in what we have to teach, then we need to matter to them and to let them know that they matter to us.

BUILDING RELATIONSHIPS WITH BABIES

T he grounding of learning in relationships begins very early. In fact, the more we learn about babies, the more we come to appreciate the power of early relationships. Babies come into the world utterly dependent on their caregivers. They are wired for connection and therefore are programmed to elicit and respond to love and care.

Young babies respond emotionally to internal sensations such as hunger and to external sights, sounds, smells, and physical sensations. Indeed, one of their biggest challenges is regulating their emotional state. They cannot learn when they are too keyed up—crying, overly excited, agitated and flailing, fearful, or stressed. They also cannot learn when they are tuned out—asleep, depressed, lethargic, droopy, or shut down. Most of their learning occurs during a quiet, alert state when they can focus their attention outside themselves and mobilize their energy for action.

Babies count on adults to help them keep their emotions within bounds—not only to feed them when they are hungry and comfort them when they are upset but also to intrigue and engage them when they are ready to play. This balancing is a subtle dance. As baby and adult get to know each other, the baby gives moment-to-moment cues about what she needs. She may look at the adult intently, imitate facial expressions, smile or coo, or laugh in response to what the adult does. She may turn away briefly to take a break, then come back for more. When she's had too much, she may curl her toes, arch her back, fuss, cry, or show other signs of stress, or she may simply shut down and go to sleep.

Every infant needs to have two or three very special people in her life who can recognize her unique characteristics and can read and respond to her cues. When an infant is placed in child care, one of those very special people must be you, her primary caregiver. As you respond consistently to the infant's needs, she learns to trust you just as she trusts her parent or other home caregivers. Over time, the two of you develop a relationship. Each learns how to engage the other, to get on the same wavelength, to share favorite games and routines. As you spend time in back-and-forth conversation, gazing into each others' eyes, talking and cooing, making and imitating faces, looking away briefly and coming back, you become attuned to one another. The infant reciprocates your special feelings for her, and her excitement or distress triggers pleasurable or sympathetic feelings in you as her caregiver.

In the video *Ten Things Every Child Needs* (WTTW Chicago, 1997), T. Berry Brazelton tells a story of how he connected with a 9-month-old child who had come for her well-baby visit. The baby blew a raspberry, and the mother remarked that this new skill was something that her daughter particularly enjoyed practicing. Dr. Brazelton continued his conversation with the mother, but he interspersed it with raspberries directed at the baby. Soon, the baby was blowing raspberries back at him. By the fifth exchange, she had come into his arms and was feeling his mouth. He was "on her wavelength," and they had become friends.

It takes many of these types of experiences for a momentary friendship to become an attachment. "Attachment," as described by Alice Honig (2002) in *Secure Relationships*, "is a strong emotional bond between a baby or young child and a caring adult who is part of the child's everyday life—the child's attachment figure" (p. 2). Attachment is not an ability that a child is born with. It develops over time as children experience the comfort of being held, spoken to, sung to, fed, carried around, and played with by a loving parent or substitute parent who is always there to read the child's cues and to recognize and respond to his needs.

Children who have developed a secure attachment to their primary caregiver are concerned or distressed when their caregiver leaves, and they greet their caregiver joyfully as soon as he or she returns. The caregiver provides a sense of security and helps the baby cope with the stress of new situations. A recent research study provides a dramatic illustration. Megan Gunnar, an infancy researcher at the University of Minnesota, measured babies' cortisol levels when they were getting their immunizations (Gunnar, 2001). Cortisol is a stress hormone, easily measured in saliva, that activates the fight or flight response. At high levels, it interferes with thinking and learning. When babies were seated on the examining table as they got their shots, their cortisol levels spiked. But when babies who were securely attached to a parent were held in the parent's

The attachment between this baby and her child-care provider is mutual. The provider has learned to read the baby's cues, and usually knows just what she needs.

arms, their cortisol levels did not go up. Both groups of babies cried, but those in their parent's arms were not physiologically stressed. Babies who had not developed a secure attachment to the parent (according to previous observations) did not receive this protective effect when they were held and given the shot.

Babies who are securely attached learn to self-regulate, which means that they can find ways to comfort themselves (such as sucking a thumb or clinging to a "blankie" when they are tired or upset) without the help of their caregiver. They learn to use their caregiver as a secure base for exploration, wandering farther and farther away and staying away for longer periods of time without feeling insecure.

Most important, children who develop a secure relationship with a parent or primary caregiver are predisposed to developing other close, meaningful relationships throughout their growing-up years and throughout their lives. Indeed, parents can help their babies feel the same sense of security with teachers and caregivers that they feel with their family members. As the parent, baby, and new person spend time together, the parent can show that she trusts the new person and can encourage the baby to interact with her. Some babies accept new people easily when their parents communicate this sense of trust; others need time to overcome their initial wariness. Obviously, age and temperament play a role. But, in general, a baby who has a strong relationship with one person will develop trusting relationships with others.

Unfortunately, all babies do not develop secure attachment relationships. Babies who are physically or genetically compromised, babies with depressed mothers, babies who live in violent or dysfunctional households, babies who experience inconsistent or intrusive parenting, and babies who have been abused or neglected may experience disruptions in their attachment systems. These compromised babies may fail to develop attachment behavior or may become insecurely attached. Young children who are insecurely attached may exhibit disturbing behaviors. They might become aggressive and defiant, or they might be impulsive, reckless, or even self-injurious.

HELPING CHILDREN DEVELOP SECURE ATTACHMENTS TO PRIMARY CAREGIVERS

In a family child-care home or child-care center, infants and toddlers do best when they have one primary caregiver to whom they become securely attached. This person can help them form relationships with other children in the program, and with other adults who may care for them during part of the day or who are involved with the care and teaching of the whole group.

Primary caregivers form attachments to babies, just as babies form attachments to them. When an infant is placed in your care, you become a special person in her life. As you respond consistently to the child's needs, she learns to trust you just as she trusts her parent or other home caregiver. Through the child's relationship with you, she can gain a sense of her own efficacy, a secure base for exploring and learning, and a sense of what is interesting and important to learn. Helping babies to develop secure relationships is fundamental to their subsequent adjustment and learning, a process that is outlined in the following progression.

- Babies who have already developed secure relationships with parents or with at-home caregivers are already primed to form secure attachment behaviors with their center-based caregivers.

- Even babies who are insecurely attached to their parents or home caregivers are able to form secure relationships with out-of-home caregivers given sufficient time with a consistent, loving caregiver who can read their cues and respond to their needs.

- The early relationships that infants develop with loving, nurturing, out-of-home caregivers provide the foundation for positive developmental outcomes such as reducing stress, building efficacy or self-esteem, and providing a bridge to other attachments.

- When caregivers and teachers talk and read frequently with children, show their delight in the children's questions, discoveries, and accomplishments, and share their own enjoyment of reading and investigation, then these positive outcomes include a love of words, books, and learning.

FORMING ATTACHMENTS

The following accounts are fictional, but they are based on real incidents. What does each vignette reveal about the importance of close relationships and the process of attachment?

Miss Carmen and Alfredo

Alfredo was placed in the We Care child-care center when he was 5 months old. His mother, Carlotta, was a teenager who was attending a nearby school. She was in a hurry on the first day in which she brought

(continued)

him to the center. She explained to the director that she could not stop and talk because she was already late for school. The director carried Alfredo into the infant suite and gave him to Miss Carmen, who would become his primary caregiver.

Miss Carmen was a seasoned caregiver who had been with the center for the past 14 years. At first, she was concerned about Alfredo's development. He appeared to be unusually listless. He would awaken from a long nap without crying and showed no reactions when she lifted him from his crib. When she changed his diaper and gave him a bottle, he seemed to look right through her, and when she gave him a rattle, he held it in his hand for a minute or two and then just let it drop. Miss Carmen decided that he needed more stimulation. She talked to him, sang lullabies, cradled him in her arms, massaged his arms and legs, and persisted in her efforts to interest him in a toy.

After 2 months, Miss Carmen felt that her efforts were paying off and that Alfredo was becoming more responsive. One morning, when his mother brought him into Miss Carmen's room, Alfredo lifted his arms and smiled when he saw Miss Carmen. She gave him a big hug and urged Carlotta to stop in after school one day so that they could talk together about his progress.

Daniel and Daisy

Daisy, like Carlotta, was a teenage mom with a 5-month-old boy. She decided to place her son, Daniel, in the Sunny Land Child-Care Center so that she could go back to school. Sunny Land was an attractive school with a nice playground and large classrooms, which were well stocked with toys. Daniel was assigned to one of the infant classrooms.

When Daisy brought Daniel into his assigned room, he and his mother were greeted by one of the classroom aides. The aide explained that she was in charge of diapering all the infants and would take good care of Daniel. When Daisy tried to pass him to the aide, he turned his head, started to whimper, and held tightly to his mother's shirt. Daisy apologized. "He is usually not like this," she explained to the aide. "He is a very outgoing child, full of laughs and not at all timid in new situations." Daisy continued to hold Daniel and looked around the large room.

Daisy counted 24 cribs, 24 babies, and 4 adults. Several infants were crying, and one young aide, who was apparently in charge of feeding, was moving frantically from crib to crib, giving each crying baby a bottle. Daisy decided on the spot that this was no place for Daniel. She excused herself politely and informed the director that she had changed her mind and was not placing Daniel in the school.

CREATING POSITIVE RELATIONSHIPS WITH INFANTS, TODDLERS, AND PRESCHOOL CHILDREN

Although the term *attachment behavior* is usually reserved for relationships that develop during infancy, developing positive relationships is a primary goal of children and adults throughout the life cycle. Caregivers and teachers of children ages birth to 5 years are responsible for developing positive relationships with every child in their care, regardless of developmental age. At the same time, they need to develop positive relationships with each child's family.

Developing Positive Relationships With Infants

Every infant entering child care needs to have a primary caregiver with whom she can build a trusting and lasting relationship. As you, the caregiver, respond consistently to an infant's needs, she learns to trust you just as she trusts her parent or other home caregivers. The following list highlights key points that you, as a primary caregiver, will want to remember:

- Relating to an infant implies attunement.

- When you are attuned to an infant, your special feeling for that infant is reciprocated, and the infant's excitement or distress triggers pleasurable or sympathetic feelings in you.

- When you develop a positive relationship with an infant, you become increasingly adept at reading the infant's cues, including facial expressions, changes in color or body positions, tensing of muscles, hiccups, spitting up, or different cries or babbles. An infant who is tossed in the air, tickled, or jiggled may begin by laughing out loud, but when he has had too much, he may show signs of stress, such as tensing his lips, turning white around the mouth, stiffening his body, hiccupping, spitting up, or grimacing.

His laughter may turn into crying. A baby who is under-stimulated may become floppy or flaccid, stare into space, bang his head repeatedly, pull at his hair, or bite his own hand.

- The better you know a baby and the more adept you become at reading his cues, the better you can adjust your responses to his signals. Some babies are comforted by hearing a lulla-by or listening to a music box. Others like to be patted gently or not so gently, swaddled, rocked, placed in a swing, or wheeled around in a carriage.

- Your success in reading a baby's cues strengthens the bonds between you and the baby in your care and provides a foundation for healthy social and emotional development.

Developing Positive Relationships With Toddlers

Whether a toddler is familiar with a child-care setting or whether he is experiencing out-of-home placement for the first time, the toddler's primary caregiver is the key to his successful adjustment. The following list highlights key points that you, as a primary caregiver, will want to remember:

- Some toddlers make an easy transition from home to child care, whereas for others, separation is traumatic. When a child has difficulty separating from his parents you, as his primary caregiver, are the one he turns to when his parents are out of sight.

- Whether a toddler goes off to play with his toys and his friends as soon as he arrives in the morning or whether he needs to be held and comforted before he is ready to leave your side, every toddler needs to know that he is special to you and that you are there for him.

- By spending special time with each toddler in your care and by demonstrating over and over again how important they are to you and how much you enjoy being with all of them, you build their self-confidence and make every day happy and productive.

Developing Positive Relationships With Preschool Children

Every child in your preschool class wants and needs to have a special bond with you. The following points are key to understanding this bond:

- As a teacher you become each child's base of security, surrogate parent, and encyclopedia.

- Very much as siblings do, children will vie for your attention.

- The way you feel about a child is likely to be reflected in the way the child feels about himself.

The bond between children and adults is based on communication. When teachers communicate to children their respect and concern, children feel safe and secure in their classroom, are ready to respond to their teacher's communications, and are emotionally ready to learn.

Fostering Children's Emotional Development

During the first 5 years of life, the emotional repertoires of children continue to expand, and children gain the capacity to experience and express a wider and more differentiated range of emotions. The caregiver is responsible for helping children recognize their own emotional state, for helping them cope with emotions that pose a threat to their well-being, and for helping them maintain or regain emotional equilibrium.

Erik Erikson (1963) describes three stages of psychosocial development during the first 6 years of life. At each stage, the child's task is to achieve a healthy balance between two opposing emotional states.

Trust Versus Mistrust. In the first stage of psychosocial development babies, (birth to 1 year) learn to trust—and also to mistrust. When infants have their needs met by a caring and responsive caregiver, they learn to trust others and to trust themselves. They also learn from their caregivers what is safe and what is dangerous or untrustworthy. Infants who are abused or neglected or who receive erratic care are likely to mistrust the world.

Autonomy Versus Shame and Doubt. "No" is a key word for toddlers (1–3 years), who are learning both to assert their independence and to avoid doing things that are dangerous or bad. Toddlers who are given opportunities to make their own decisions and to do things for themselves develop a sense of competence and become increasingly autonomous. When a child's attempts to be independent are repeatedly thwarted or when demands are frequently made of a child that are beyond his or her capacity to fulfill, then the child may doubt his ability to deal effectively with the world and may develop feelings of shame or worthlessness. Rather than correct his behavior or try harder, the child is likely to lash out angrily at anyone or any situation that makes him feel ashamed or humiliated.

Initiative Versus Guilt. In the third stage of psychosocial development, children learn to take initiative—within the bounds of acceptable behavior. (3 to 6 years). When children are developing initiative, they seek tasks that they can achieve on their own, they play happily with their peers, and they are delighted with the opportunity to assume the role of teacher's or mother's helper. When children fail to meet others' expectations and are constantly berated for doing things wrong, they are likely to feel guilty. Although a healthy sense of guilt over inevitable childhood misdeeds contributes to the development of a sense of morality, children who are paralyzed by guilt cannot take the initiative to form new relationships and master new challenges.

AGE-RELATED CHARACTERISTICS OF SOCIAL AND EMOTIONAL DEVELOPMENT

Although Erikson's conceptualization of psychosocial tasks provides a broad framework for understanding the development of emotions, recent scientific research provides new insights into the progression of social–emotional development in the infant, toddler, and preschool years and highlights the critical role played by the infant's primary caregivers. We now know, for example, that children's brains are affected by their early experiences. Babies who withdraw from the world develop smaller brains than those who actively explore and take in information. Babies who have learned to mistrust—who are constantly on edge and are not comforted—may develop brains that are likely to overreact to minor stress. As a result, they may have ongoing difficulty controlling their impulses.

In *From Neurons to Neighborhoods: The Science of Early Childhood Development* (National Research Council & Institute of Medicine, 2000), a panel of scientists review research from a variety of fields on the first 3 years of human life. They describe human development as "a dynamic and continuous interaction between biology and experience." They assert that "children are active participants in their own development reflecting the intrinsic human drive to explore and master one's own environment" and that human relationships—and the effects of relationships on relationships—are the building blocks of healthy development. They also assert that "the course of development can be altered by effective interventions that change the balance between risk and protection, thereby shifting the odds in favor of more adaptive outcomes" (pp. 3, 4).

Emotional Development During Infancy

Human infants come into this world primed for social interactions. They are completely dependent on adults for warmth, food, and comfort. As they begin to engage the world around them, they experience pleasure, distress, fear, anger, and surprise.

In the first 3 months of life, the infant's emotional status is closely related to his internal state. He is distressed when he is hungry or experiencing colic, he is enraged when his movements are restricted, he is fearful when an object looms close to his face, and he experiences pleasure when basic needs for food, rest, and comfort are satisfied. However, he also responds to his parents' and caregivers' attempts to comfort him or engage his attention but can also comfort himself by sucking his thumb or a pacifier or by adjusting his position. The infant's response to mother's voice, touch, and facial expressions rewards her efforts and gives her confidence in her ability to parent. If an infant is difficult to soothe or engage, his mother may feel inadequate or rejected.

Between the ages of 3 months and 6 months, the infant learns to shift his attention from internal to external events, reacting with a smile to the arrival of a familiar adult and cooing in response to the adult's overtures. The baby looks surprised if an object or a person reacts in a way that does not fit his expectations. By the age of 6 months, most infants also learn to smile and coo to elicit a response from an approaching adult.

Beginning at the age of 6 months, infants are likely to discriminate between familiar and unfamiliar people and reserve their biggest smiles for their consistent caregivers. Their faces light up with interest when a sibling comes into the room. The following characteristics are typical of an infant at this age:

- Babies love to watch other babies. In family- or center-based child care, they enjoy watching the other children in the group and may even show a preference for a particular child.

- In addition to differentiating between familiar and unfamiliar faces, the 6-month-old infant has developed a set of expectations about when an event should occur. If the baby's caregiver covers her face with a scarf and then emerges from under the scarf, the 6-month-old will register surprise and delight.

- At approximately 8 months of age, infants are likely to show anxiety around strangers and may cry or bury their heads when an unfamiliar person approaches them. They may also be fearful if a familiar adult has changed his appearance, and they will check with a trusted caregiver to make sure that the person is not dangerous. A baby will also show fear if the surface on which he is crawling appears to drop off, and he will look to a trusted adult for reassurance.

- As infants become more mobile, they are likely to show distress if their movements are restricted or if they cannot reach an object that they are attempting to retrieve.

By the end of the first year, infants transmit clear messages that indicate their emotional states. The 1-year-old expresses delight by smiling, chuckling, and squealing with excitement. When surprised, he spontaneously reacts, opening his eyes very wide, flinging his arms out, and spreading his fingers apart. When distressed, he screams, cries, moans, and may even throw a tantrum. When frightened, he creeps or runs to a favorite adult and demands to be picked up.

Although infants differ in the intensity of their emotional reactions, by their first birthday most infants are predictable in the kinds of stimuli or situations that evoke their anger, pleasure, fear, and distress.

Social and Emotional Development of Toddlers, Ages 1 to 2

During the second year, the toddler's emotional displays become more differentiated. Anger ranges from disappointment to rage, pleasure ranges from contentment to delight, fear ranges from wariness to panic, and sadness ranges from sorrow to grief.

At this age, toddlers are developing an awareness of personhood, or self. They learn to recognize themselves as individuals, separate from their parents or caregivers. They typically demonstrate this self-awareness when they perform some antic that makes adults laugh and then do it again to create more laughter. Another indicator of growing self-awareness is in more sophisticated mirror play—for example, a toddler looks in the mirror, recognizes that she has chocolate on her face, and touches her face rather than trying to rub the chocolate off the mirror.

At this age, toddlers are also becoming aware of the effect of their emotions on other people. They recognize that if they get mad when a child grabs a toy, then the child may give the toy back. If they cry when their ice cream falls on the floor, then their caregiver is likely to give them a new dish of ice cream. If they say "thank you," then their caregiver will respond with smiles and kisses.

Toddlers also develop social preferences. In family or group child care, they may gravitate to one or two other children who become their special playmates.

Social and Emotional Development of Toddlers, Ages 2 to 3

Adults find 2-year-olds both challenging and fascinating. At this age, toddlers develop a strong sense of self and want to do things by themselves and in their own way:

- By saying "no," a 2-year-old demonstrates that he is his own distinct person and has a right to make choices. At the same time, he is likely to say "no" in order to assert himself, even when he really means "yes." It is not unusual for a 2-year-old to say "no" when asked whether he wants a cookie and then get angry when the caregiver doesn't give it to him.

- Between the ages of 2 and 3, toddlers are also likely to say "me do it myself." Although a caregiver who is trying to take the class outside may get annoyed with a child who insists on putting on his own sweater with no help, this desire to be independent is an important toddler development.

Although toddlers want very much to be independent, at times they still want to be treated like babies. Caregivers need to remember that although toddlers struggle to be independent, they also need to know that an adult is nearby to take care of them and keep them safe.

Two-year olds have the capacity to empathize. If another child falls down and starts to cry, a 2-year-old may try to comfort him. Parents often describe an incident when they were hurt or upset and their toddler came to them and offered them his "blankie."

Playing "together" for a 2-year old means playing alongside one or two other children. Although 2-year-olds are not very good at sharing and may have trouble taking turns, they often select one or two special friends who become their preferred playmates. They also learn to avoid children who bite or who are otherwise aggressive.

Social and Emotional Development of Children in the Preschool Years

The preschool years bring dramatic advances in emotional development. These changes reflect the increased ability of the preschool child to self-regulate and show his increased awareness of other people's feelings. The following characteristics are typical:

- With increased ability to self-regulate, preschool children can modulate their emotional outbursts, and temper tantrums are usually infrequent. (Children who continue to have frequent temper tantrums may be having adjustment or emotional difficulties or developmental delays that could be ameliorated by early intervention services.)

- Preschool children can recognize that other people have feelings and preferences that are sometimes different from theirs.

- Preschoolers can empathize with storybook characters and can also recognize how a character's feelings change as a result of what happens in the story.

- Preschool children are beginning to internalize right from wrong and good from bad as they read adults' emotional responses.

By the time they are in preschool, most children have developed important social skills. They have learned to share and take turns and to participate in group activities. Although girls and boys enjoy playing together, we often see gender-related differences in their play behavior. Boys are likely to play in larger groups than girls and are more likely to engage in action-packed real or pretend play. Girls are likely to congregate in small groups, to engage in conversational play, and to play out pretend episodes that revolve around family life.

Individual differences are reflected in the social roles that children assume as they join with other children in play. Some children seem to be born leaders, initiating creative play ideas and attracting other children to join in their play. Other children are more likely to be followers, conforming to the requests of their chosen leader. Still other children are quite flexible, adept at leading but also content to play a supporting role. A few preschool children remain loners, playing by themselves or watching other children play without joining in.

ACTIVITIES TO SUPPORT ATTACHMENT AND EMOTIONAL DEVELOPMENT

This section includes activities and techniques that caregivers can provide to help infants, toddlers, and young children make healthy attachments and progress in emotional development. Activities are categorized according to the age groupings they best support.

Activities for Babies and Young Toddlers

Here are some things you can do with babies and young toddlers to help them develop secure attachments, efficacy, and a positive sense of self.

Tummy Time. Young babies sleep on their backs, eat cradled in someone's arms, travel while seated in strollers or car seats or while held upright in a front carrier or sling, and often play in bounce chairs or baby seats. They also need lots of tummy time. Lying on their stomachs forces them to lift their heads and develop their neck and trunk muscles. It gives them the opportunity to practice reaching, rolling, and eventually crawling. But tummy time is also an important time for connecting with others. Spend time on the floor with each baby each day. To encourage reaching, provide some toys for the baby, including balls that you can roll back and forth. Let the baby take the lead as you engage in cooing conversations or help her get to the toys that are just out of reach. You can also put babies on their tummies together so that they can watch one another.

Rock-a-Bye Baby. Rocking is a time-honored way of soothing a baby, but babies differ in the kind of motion they prefer. Some like slow, gentle rocking; others prefer more vigorous movements. Some like to be held upright on a shoulder; others prefer to be cradled in your arms or draped across your knees. Some are very sensitive to textures and may be agitated by contact with a wool sweater or soothed by a soft diaper or silky shirt. Because cultures differ in holding, carrying, and rocking techniques, different babies may be accustomed to different motions and positions. And of course, different techniques work best at different times, especially for babies who tend to get colicky or overexcited or who have fussy periods at particular times of the day. Spend time with each baby's parents, learning a child's preferences and patterns so you can use the techniques that the baby finds familiar and comforting. Remember, these techniques will change as the baby grows, so child-care providers should keep one another informed as these changes occur.

Mirror Play. A mirror over the changing table or mounted at floor level provides a wonderful way to introduce a baby to himself and to support his emerging self-concept. As the child studies the baby in the mirror, you can point out features, clothing, and actions. Once the child realizes that he is looking at a reflection of himself, you can use mirror play to enhance movement and dress-up activities. For example, you can have a child look in the mirror as you teach him a simple routine such as "How big is baby?" or give him a hat to put on when he is looking in the mirror.

Security Objects. A security object has the unique power of helping infants and young children cope with the temporary absence of a beloved caregiver. A baby blanket, "my blankie," is the preferred security object for most infants and toddlers. When young children are first placed in child care, it is important to give parents permission to bring the security object to school. Give the security object to the child when his parent leaves, when he is upset, or when he is napping. Otherwise, put the security object in the child's cubby or other safe place. Losing a security object can be a real calamity for a young child and his family.

Family Photos. Even young babies learn to recognize pictures of family members. Sometimes, the very first word you will hear a baby say is "Mama" or "Dada" when she sees a picture of a parent on the wall or in the crib. If you are careful to place the photo at "crawl level," you may even find an active crawler scooting across the floor to reach the photo.

Baby Journal. A great activity that parents and teachers can do together is to make a baby journal. Include pictures of baby's favorite things, a list of the baby's first babbles and first words, and family or class photos.

Soothing Sensations. Babies are comforted by different sensory experiences. They love the feel of silk or velvet, the sound of music or tinkling bells, the sight of bubbles blowing over their crib, and the pleasant scent of perfume that they associate with a favorite caregiver.

Monkey See, Monkey Do. Babies learn to imitate facial expressions, babbles or raspberries, as well as sounds and gestures such as clapping, banging, or waving their arms. Imitation is one way in which babies carry on a conversation.

Reading Time–Cuddle Time. One of the most wonderful ways to develop a close relationship with a baby is by holding her on your lap and reading a book to her. It does not matter that she cannot recognize the pictures, turn the pages, or understand the words. What does matter is that she delights at the sound of your voice and the feel of your arms wrapped around her.

Activities for 2- and 3-Year-Olds

Here are some fun and effective ways to build relationships with toddlers and help them deal with their sometimes stormy emotions.

Floor Time. Although 2- and 3-year-olds are quite capable of sitting at a table, they much prefer sitting on the floor. By sitting on the floor with children, you create an opportunity to join their play.

My Favorite Things. Establish a special day—for example, every Monday—when the children can bring a favorite thing from home and share it with the class. It may be a book, a photo of someone in the family, or a favorite toy.

A Place for Us. Create special places on the playground or indoors where two children can play together, read a book together, or listen to a book on tape.

Temper Tantrum Tricks. Demonstrate for children a special way to have a temper tantrum that always makes them feel good. "First you stamp your feet, next you swing your arms, then you make a really scary mad face, and last of all you make a loud 'ooooo' sound, that starts way down in the pit of your stomach and finally comes out of your mouth." Make sure that you choose an optimal time to teach temper "tantruming"—ideally, when everyone is having a good day. Then, when a child is about to tantrum, remind him of the best way to have a temper tantrum. If you have given the class some time to practice having these special temper tantrums, then the real tantrums will change into a laugh.

Read to Me. Find a time every day to sit each child on your lap and read her her own special story.

Books About Feelings. Choose some books for toddlers that deal with attachment and independence issues: a baby bird who cannot find his mother, a little animal torn between staying close and exploring the wider world, a child whose angry feelings get him in trouble and who needs to be reassured of a parent's love, a character who insists on doing things her way, a displaced older sibling, a picky eater.

Quick Changes. When children get too noisy, introduce a whisper time. Similarly, when children start running around the playground and you would like them to calm down, introduce a tiptoe game. When children walk on tiptoes, they will not be able to run.

Sweet Music. Rather than keep music on all day, use music purposefully—for example, to help children feel calm before meals and during naptime or to bring children together when you want to introduce a new activity.

Use Your Words. Help children learn words to use when they are bothered by another child's behavior, when they have upset another child, or when they are in conflict with another child: "Please don't draw on my picture." "Stop doing that. It hurts." "I'm sorry." "I won't do that again." "Let's not fight. Let's play." "Let's be friends."

Labeling Feelings. In circle time, show the children pictures of children who are smiling, crying, scowling, or looking scared. See whether the children can tell how each child feels. Make a feelings chart for your class, with a happy face, a sad face, an angry face, and a scared face, and nail an arrow in the middle of the chart. When a child does not seem happy, ask her to point the arrow to one of the faces to show you how she is feeling.

Activities for 4- and 5-Year-Olds

Here are some fun ways to help preschoolers make friends, express their feelings, and develop social skills.

Classroom Rituals. Classroom rituals serve many functions: to mark transitions, to celebrate special occasions, and to help children feel like they are a family. Classrooms may have special songs to signal a change of activities, clean-up time, playground time, lunchtime, or time to say good-bye. They may have certain traditions for celebrating special events—for example, a birthday child wears a special hat and becomes class leader for a day or the class may have monthly "silly days" when the children wear something silly, such as pajamas, a hat, or a bathing suit, to school.

Alone and Together. Create small, partially enclosed spaces in the classroom and on the playground where children can be by themselves or spend some private time with a special friend. Erect a small tent or structure on the playground that can serve as a hideaway. Create a reading nook in the classroom where children can read together or a quiet zone where a child can spend some "alone time."

Let's Pretend. Put together a set of prop boxes that encourage children to play out "helping" themes. For example, these boxes could include props to play doctor, firefighter, or veterinarian and props for a fix-it shop.

Puppet Friend. Select an appealing puppet to be the tenant of your classroom. Let the puppet greet the children during the morning circle time and talk about its feelings. "I am happy that it is such a nice sunny day so we can all go out on the playground. Oh, yes. Thank you so much for leaving my classroom all in order yesterday. Every one of our puzzles had all its pieces, and all our toys were put away in their right places."

Love Notes. Put a mailbox beside a table with notepaper and envelopes. Suggest to the children that they write love notes or make "I love you" pictures for their parents or their friends and put them in the mailbox.

Art Museum. Reserve a special wall in the classroom for displaying the children's artwork. Display collages and murals that were created by the whole class.

Our Very Own Room. Let the children choose a name for the classroom and create a list of rules that will keep their classroom a happy place in which to be (e.g., "We use our inside voices," "We use our words and not our hands when other children bother us," or "We help each other put the toys back on the shelf.").

We Love to Read. Let the children participate in selecting books for story time, and supply puppets or other props that allow them to act out their favorite stories.

Stone Soup. Initiate projects in which everyone in the class can participate—for example, make a patchwork quilt wall hanging or plant a garden on the playground.

Community Connections. Invite parents to your classroom to tell children about the jobs they do or to share artifacts, stories, and holiday traditions that represent their own culture.

Let's Make a Deal. With the help of your classroom puppet, teach children ways of resolving a conflict so that everyone is a winner.

CONCLUSION

I n the preface to *Heart-Start: The Emotional Foundations of School Readiness* (ZERO TO THREE, 1992), Berry Brazelton describes the characteristics of young children that are associated with success in school. These are "curiosity, confidence, the capacity to set a goal and work at it, and the ability to communicate with others and get along with them" (p. v). These are the very characteristics that are fostered in a good-quality early childhood program.

When children are in family child care or in a child-care center, their world revolves around their teacher. The responsibility of teacher is an awesome one that can also be a true pleasure. The teacher who develops an intimate relationship with a child helps him feel loved, worthy, and secure. The teacher is rewarded by that child's love, by the fun that they have together, and by the child's emotional progress. At the same time, this teacher knows that she is helping the child build a secure base from which to embark on new journeys of discovery. With such a strong foundation, the child is likely to enter school confident, eager to learn, and primed for success.

Reflection

What can you do to help each child in your care become a comfortable and confident explorer in your classroom or home?

Are there any children who might need special attention?

What can you do to help the children bond with you, with one another, and with the group as a whole?

REFERENCES

Brazelton, T. B., (1992). Preface. In ZERO TO THREE, *Heart start: The emotional foundations of school readiness* (p. v). Arlington, VA: ZERO TO THREE: National Center for Clinical Infant Programs.

Erikson, E. H. (1963). *Childhood and society* (2nd ed.). New York: W. W. Norton.

Gunnar, M. R. (2001). *Salivary cortisol measures in infant and child assessment.* In L. T. Singer & P. S. Zeskind (Eds.), *Biobehavioral assessment of the infant* (pp. 167–189). New York: Guilford.

Honig, A. S. (2002). *Secure relationships: Nurturing infant/toddler attachment in early care settings.* Washington, DC: National Association for the Education of Young Children.

National Research Council & Institute of Medicine. (2000). *From neurons to neighborhoods: The science of early childhood development.* Committee on Integrating the Science of Early Childhood Development and Social Sciences and Education. Washington, DC: National Academy Press.

WTTW Chicago. (Producer). (1997). *Ten things every child needs.* [Film]. (Available from the Robert R. McCormick Tribune Foundation, 435 North Michigan Avenue, Suite 770, Chicago, IL 60611).

ZERO TO THREE. (1992). *Heart start: The emotional foundations of school readiness.* Arlington, VA: Author.

CHAPTER 3

Engaging All Children

Inclusion

I was planting some seeds in my garden one day
When a seed from a weed came flying my way.
That seed from a weed had no way to know
That gardens aren't places where weeds ought to grow.
I went back to the garden to pluck out the bad seed
But, alas, I couldn't tell which was flower, which weed.

—MARILYN SEGAL, *unpublished poem*

I n the last chapter, we talked about the importance of building relationships with every child entrusted to our care. A young child who loves and trusts you is motivated to please, is delighted with the opportunity to communicate, and is ready and eager to learn. These early interactive relationships build the foundation for emergent literacy. As teachers come to know and appreciate the unique characteristics of a child, they can build on that child's strengths and meet that child's special needs. With a loving and caring teacher, every child—like the plants in our garden—can grow and flourish.

In this chapter, we focus on individual children. We recognize that each child is one of a kind, with a unique blend of strengths and needs. To meet the goal of helping every child be successful in school and in life, teachers need to be aware of the biological and environmental factors responsible for these differences. The first two sections of this chapter identify ways in which genetic and environmental factors interact to influence the course of a child's development. The third section focuses on how teachers can foster development by tuning in to each child's unique blend of environmental and genetic influences.

WAYS IN WHICH GENETIC FACTORS INFLUENCE THE COURSE OF DEVELOPMENT

M any people still imagine child development as being controlled by either nature or nurture. Those who think in terms of nature see development as something that merely unfolds according to its own timetable as long as the child is fed, protected, and cared for in some minimal way. In this view, being "ready to learn" is simply a matter of growing up. Some children are seen as naturally precocious, others as "late bloomers." Once a child is considered "ready" to learn, any failure to learn is seen as being the child's own fault—because he is lazy, stubborn, or just plain dumb.

Those who focus on nurture may go to the opposite extreme, giving the child neither credit nor responsibility. Failure is seen as being the fault of the parents or of the neighborhood or of the culture. Poor children, children who are from "dysfunctional families," and children who face other risks may be seen as doomed to failure. Alternatively, children may be seen as being infinitely malleable; thus, a good teacher should be able to teach anything to any child, regardless of what the child brings to the table.

Both of these frameworks are appealing in their simplicity, yet in some way, most of us realize that both are overly simplistic. Arnold Sameroff (1987) reminds us that both nature and nurture are necessary for any developmental process and that the contributions of both are not only active but also interactive. "Outcomes are the result of the interplay between child and context across time in which the state of one affects the next state of the other in a continuous dynamic process" (p. 168). Children have inborn temperaments and dispositions that are shaped by their experiences and that develop into habits, outlooks, approaches to learning, and abilities that influence what they gain from later experience.

Our folk wisdom tells us what science confirms: "As the twig is bent, so grows the tree." Early experiences have unique power because they can set the course powerfully, but not irrevocably. The shape of the tree can still be influenced by sunlight, rainfall, or pruning and by the weight of its own fruit or the density of its leaves.

Temperamental Variables

In any group of adults, one is likely to find differences in personality and demeanor. Some people will be intense; others will be "laid back." Some will be shy and introverted; others will be outgoing and talkative. When faced with a challenge or decision, some will be nervous, fretful, or hesitant; some will carefully weigh alternative courses of action; and some will eagerly, even impulsively, take a risk. These characteristics are, of course, influenced by the experiences people have had and the situations in which they find themselves. They also, however, reflect inborn characteristics, or temperaments. Temperamental characteristics can be seen most clearly when children are very young. These differences make responsive caregiving particularly important.

Ron Lally (Mangione, Lally, & Signer, 1990) has labeled young children as "flexible," "fearful," or "feisty" according to a cluster of temperamental characteristics that define their behavior:

- The flexible baby is happy, easy to comfort, predictable, and eager to engage in new experiences. These babies are easy to relate to and care for. It is important to give them their fair share of individual attention, even though they are not demanding.

- The fearful baby is slow to warm up, wary about new experiences and new people, and most comfortable in a familiar environment. Fearful babies do best with a gentle, patient, and consistent caregiver who gives them time to get used to new experiences and new environments.

- The feisty baby is active, outgoing, self-directed, and difficult to restrain. Feisty babies are likely to give battle when it is time to change their diaper and may resist falling asleep when they are overtired. A caregiver needs a healthy combination of energy, humor, patience, and firmness to keep the baby on an even keel.

- Although temperamental characteristics can be altered through experience, or may be manifested in different ways at different periods in the life cycle, the behavioral tendencies associated with temperament remain relatively stable throughout childhood and adulthood.

Temperamental differences manifest themselves in different ways and at different times during the life cycle. From the moment of birth, infants demonstrate their uniqueness:

- Differences in behavior in the first 3 months of life are related to the infant's internal state.

- Babies who are full term and who have no physiological problems are likely to be alert, active, and responsive as well as relatively predictable in terms of their sleep patterns, fussy periods, and demands for nursing.

- Babies who are premature, weigh less than 5 pounds, or both are less likely to be alert and are less regular in terms of when they are ready to nurse and how long they sleep.

- During the first 3 months of life, babies go through a period of physiological adjustment; some babies experience severe colic and are difficult to soothe. Although no one really understands the reason for this colic, it is likely to subside by the time the baby is 3 months old and has become attuned to her outside environment.

- By the end of the third month, parents see a real change in their baby as she becomes responsive to adults who approach her. She smiles, coos, and gurgles when adults talk to her, sleeps for longer periods, can go longer periods without being nursed, and is awake and alert for much more time during the day.

After the age of 3 months, babies are likely to demonstrate more stable temperamental differences:

- Some babies are generally happy and easy to comfort; others go through long fussy periods when they are difficult to comfort.

- Some babies have established a consistent schedule for sleeping and feeding; others are more erratic.

- Some babies respond to moderate stimulation, other babies shut down when they are exposed to moderate stimulation, and still others do not respond to stimulation unless it is vigorous.

- Some babies are easy to engage in playful interactions; others are more difficult to engage either because they are extremely active or because they tend to be lethargic.

- Some babies engage eagerly in new experiences; others are more timid and are slower to warm up.

Many of the temperamental variables that are manifested in the infancy period are reflected in toddler behavior:

Reading a favorite book with a parent or caregiver can calm a feisty toddler or help a fearful child warm up to a new situation.

- Infants who were seen as flexible are likely to continue being flexible in the toddler years. Flexible toddlers manifest many of the behaviors characteristic of the toddler period, but these manifestations are unlikely to be exaggerated. A flexible child, for instance, may go through a "no" stage or an "I-wanna-do-it-by-myself" stage and may have a temper tantrum when things do not go her way. Yet she remains easy to distract and will have no difficulty regaining her equilibrium.

- Infants who are fearful and slow to warm up will likely show these same characteristics during the toddler period and are likely to remain fearful of new experiences.

- Infants who are feisty are likely to become feisty toddlers. Challenging behaviors that are characteristic of toddlers are exaggerated when a toddler has a feisty temperament.

Like toddlers, preschool children are likely to manifest behavioral characteristics that could easily be predicted from their infant behavior.

Flexible infants and toddlers are likely to become flexible preschoolers. They are happy, friendly, and outgoing, and they will be able to assume the role of either leader or follower, depending on the situation.

Slow-to-warm-up infants and toddlers, on the other hand, are likely to become shy preschoolers who are among the last of their classmates to engage in a new adventure. At the same time, many of these watchful children develop strengths as thoughtful observers, empathetic friends, and critical thinkers. They tend to think before they act, attend carefully to what others are doing and feeling, and anticipate consequences. Some temperamentally shy preschoolers tend to be loners. Others find their niche in a small group with predictable behavior or take on roles as helpers and peacemakers.

Feisty infants are likely to become feisty toddlers who can be challenging because of their insistence on doing things their own way and because of their tendency to insist with loud voices and forceful actions. In the preschool period, this same feistiness can become an asset. Once they learn to "use their words," feisty toddlers often grow into creative leaders, initiating new play ideas and convincing other children to follow their example.

Caregivers and teachers who are tuned into temperamental differences are able to modify their own behavior in accordance with the temperamental characteristics of each child. In planning for a field trip to a nearby park, for example, they recognize that the slow-to-warm-up child might need extra reassurance, the feisty child may need some carefully articulated limits, and the flexible child might need the opportunity to serve in a leadership role.

Handicapping Conditions

Children with a diagnosed condition—for example, Down Syndrome, cerebral palsy, or a sensory deficit—face special challenges. Although some may require special schooling, most children with special needs function successfully when placed in a supportive early childhood setting with a teacher who is sensitive to their needs.

More important even than adapting the physical environment to accommodate children with special needs is helping parents recognize the benefits of an inclusive early childhood setting. Parents of children who have special needs may be concerned that teachers will not have the time or the training to meet the particular needs of their child. Parents of typically developing children may be afraid that the presence of children who have special needs will be threatening or damaging to their children. They may also worry that the teacher will spend a disproportionate amount of time with the children who have special needs.

Developing trusting relationships with parents and inviting parents to observe the interaction between typically developing children and children who have special needs is an effective way to assuage parental fears. A teacher who had recently been asked to accept children with special needs recounts the following incident:

A parent of a typically developing child named Everett was concerned about placing her son in a class with hearing impaired children who "talk funny." After a talk with Everett's teacher, the parent agreed to give it a try. The next day, the parent observed the children on the playground. At the end of the day, she reported back to the teacher. "You won't believe this," she told the teacher. "You know the first thing Everett said to me when he saw me on the playground? 'I played with this new kid Adam. His ears don't work so good but he's great at bouncing a ball!'"

An inclusive environment provides many benefits for both typically developing children and children with special needs. Typically developing children learn to appreciate children with different strengths and needs. They become more empathetic and enjoy taking on the role of teacher and helper. At the same time, children with special needs benefit from being with typically developing children who can serve as role models, enhancing their physical, language and social skills.

The teacher is the key to the success of an inclusive environment. An effective teacher creates a climate where every child feels welcome, worthy, and capable of learning. By developing an intimate relationship with each child, appreciating each child's differences, and supporting each child's strengths, the teacher is in a prime position to foster emotional development and to plant the seeds of emergent literacy.

Emotional Health of the Mother

Any factor that endangers the physical or emotional health of the mother can negatively effect the development of the unborn infant. Pregnant mothers who smoke or who abuse drugs or alcohol jeopardize the health and well-being of their unborn child. Babies whose mothers were ill, undernourished, traumatized, or exposed to toxic substances during pregnancy may also suffer. Those whose mothers suffer from chronic stress or depression are also at risk because hormones that are released when mothers are stressed affect the architecture of the baby's developing brain and reduce his ability to cope with environmental pressures. In addition, premature birth, similar to chronic stress and substance abuse, can place a child at risk for poor developmental outcomes.

Troublesome behavior that may be associated with prenatal insults include poor impulse control, attention deficit, poor self-regulation, and aggression. These behavior patterns can be changed through early intervention and positive experiences in a nurturing environment. When teachers recognize that these children are physiologically challenged and are not just being "bad," they are then in a better position to meet these children's needs and to reduce disruptive behavior. Maintaining a well-organized classroom and a consistent classroom schedule is likely to reduce children's disruptive behavior and foster positive interactions with their peers.

Although infants may be born with many strikes against them, the most remarkable characteristic of the human baby is adaptability. Our brains grow most rapidly before birth, but the connections between brain cells that enable us to think, feel, remember, and control our actions are established as a result of experience. These connections are formed most rapidly during the first 3 years of life, when the brain is most flexible. Thus, timely intervention can be amazingly effective, allowing children to make remarkable strides and moving infants who seemed doomed to failure out of the at-risk category. Later intervention can also be effective, but it may need to be more intensive and may take longer to show results.

WAYS IN WHICH ENVIRONMENTAL FACTORS INFLUENCE THE COURSE OF DEVELOPMENT

From *Neurons to Neighborhoods: The Science of Early Childhood Development* (National Research Council & Institute of Medicine, 2000) is an authoritative review of neurological, behavioral, and educational research by a National Academy of Sciences panel of experts. Drawing from this large body of research, its authors explain how "human development is shaped by a dynamic and continuous interaction between biology and experience" (p. 23). The science is clear: The course of a child's development can be affected by genetic factors, by prenatal experience, by the various environmental influences that the child encounters throughout life, and by the child's own behavior and learning. All of these factors interact in complex ways. Risk factors that compromise development can be offset by factors that protect or enhance development.

Unfortunately, risk factors compound. In one study, children with two risk factors had four times the chance of a negative outcome as those with one or none; those with three or more risk factors had a tenfold risk. Fortunately, however, protective factors such as an easy temperament, positive parenting, early intervention, and a strong ongoing relationship with a teacher or other trusted adult can also have a multiplier effect.

Looking beneath the statistics, we can see how particular environmental factors or experiences can be especially damaging to young children. Experiencing violence either as a victim or as a witness in the first 2 years of life can affect the physiology of the brain, compromise the child's ability to develop impulse control or manage stress, and interfere with healthy social and emotional development as well as learning. The stress hormones released when the child is hurt or frightened damage brain cells and connections. Repeated trauma teaches the child's nervous system to remain on high alert, diverting energy from learning and growth. A child who is chronically on edge may overreact to slight provocation or be overwhelmed and shut down. When the child's parent is traumatized by violence, the parent may be unresponsive to the child just when the child most needs help in restoring and maintaining equilibrium.

Inadequate parenting related to maternal depression, unpredictable family behavior patterns, or parenting styles that either are overly permissive or are restrictive and punitive can interfere with the child's ability to form trusting relationships and can reduce his motivation to learn. Similarly, attending inferior child-care programs that provide little guidance, stimulation, or appropriate activities can deprive a child of the kind of experiences associated with success in school.

Protective Factors

Just as risk factors in the early years can compromise healthy development, protective factors can increase a child's resilience. A resilient child can cope with challenges and "bounce back" from setbacks rather than be derailed by them. A child who is strong, healthy, and well nourished is in a better position to withstand stress than one who is sickly. A child who is physically attractive and has a flexible temperament usually has an easy time getting help from adults who can buffer negative experiences. A confident child who has an optimistic outlook can overcome problems that would frustrate or derail a child with weaker self-esteem. Parents, grandparents, siblings, and caregivers all contribute to a child's developing sense of confidence. Furthermore, because the child looks to these key people to interpret experience, their calming explanations and reassurance reduce the child's stress and increase his repertoire of coping strategies.

A quality preschool experience in and of itself can be a protective factor that buffers the effects of many negative factors, including inadequate parenting. In high-quality group care, the child learns to cope with a moderate level of stress or challenge. She develops physical, social, and problem-solving skills. She learns to express her feelings and desires and to get a positive response from others. As she masters language, she learns to ask questions, make predictions, imagine alternatives, and use humor to defuse tension.

Learning to read will open further avenues of support, information, and imagination that will help the child overcome the challenges that she will inevitably encounter.

Differences Associated With Culture

Culture is defined as the intergenerational transmission of beliefs, values, rituals, and practices. Everyone has a culture. For each one of us, culture is the lens through which we view our world. It is reflected in our worldview and in the way we bring up our children. In *From Neurons to Neighborhoods* (National Research Council & Institute of Medicine, 2000), the authors describe ways in which culture shapes a child's behavior and development—through parents' expectations, goals, and aspirations for their children; through the values that govern differential approaches to discipline; through gender roles; through religious or spiritual values; and through ideas and beliefs about health, illness, and disability. The better we understand the culture of the family, the more successful we will be in partnering with the families and supporting their children's development.

Families from every culture want the best for their children, and what they define as "best" determines how they socialize their children. Each culture has a set of core beliefs about how children should behave and what they need to learn to become successful adults. Many European cultures, for example, value individualism and stress the importance of individual achievement and independence. American myths amplify these values, honoring "rugged individualism," "the self-made man," and the United States as the "land of opportunity." In contrast, many Asian, African, and Latin American cultures (and some European ones as well) value interdependence and stress the importance of cooperation and caring for one another. The following vignette provides some insight into why these differences in culture need to be considered carefully.

M s. Helen, the caregiver of a toddler group, had a mixed class of children, half Latino and half African American. She was a firm believer in self-help and encouraged children to pour their own milk and feed themselves. Mrs. Cortez, Pedro's mother, was visiting during lunch. She put a bib on her son, poured his milk in a cup, and fed him lunch. Ms. Helen felt that Mrs. Cortez was spoiling her son Pedro, trying to keep him a baby. She was about to say something to her, but then she decided she should talk to her director before she said anything. Her director explained that feeding their toddlers was the way that many Hispanic families show their children the importance of taking care of other people.

One difference in child-rearing beliefs is the importance placed on keeping clean versus the importance of encouraging children to explore, even if they get dirty. Cultures that value individualism tend to encourage exploration. Caregivers make a point of inviting children to carry on their own explorations such as digging in the dirt, dipping their fingers in paste, spattering finger paint, and picking up food with their fingers. In cultures where cleanliness is a top priority and where exploration is less of a priority, getting one's hands or clothes dirty is considered inappropriate. Consider the following example:

When Mrs. Chang arrived at the family child-care home with her daughter Sun Lei, she handed the child-care provider, Mrs. Brown, a smock and a hairnet. Mrs. Brown thanked her profusely and put the two items in the dress-up corner. She then invited Sun Lei to come out into the backyard where the children were having fun playing in the mud. After Mrs. Brown admired an earthworm that one of the children had dug up, she asked the children to come inside and wash their hands. When all hands were washed she called the children into the kitchen to help her prepare the lunch. Sun Lei enthusiastically mixed the spaghetti with the tomato sauce, splattering sauce in her hair and onto her T-shirt. When Mrs. Chang picked up her daughter at the end of the day, she scolded her for getting dirty. As she said goodbye, she asked the provider politely to make sure that Sun Lei always puts on her smock and her hairnet if she plays with something messy.

Another difference among cultures is found in the attitudes that cultures have toward individualism. In some cultures where individualism is valued, children are encouraged to do their best and are praised for being a winner. In other cultures where interdependence and group solidarity are the predominant values, children are taught to put the group's interests above their own. For example, a Japanese proverb teaches, "The nail that sticks out is hammered down." The following vignette provides an example of how these differences are played out in a child-care setting:

A group of Seminole children were attending a Head Start class at which the majority of the children were Caucasian. During circle time, the teacher showed the children some photos of different kinds of animals. She asked each child to tell her the name of one of the animals. When she showed Timmy a photo of a camel, he looked down and did not answer. She then showed the same photo to Sunshine and asked her what the animal was called. Sunshine also looked down without answering the question. The teacher was confused. She was sure that Sunshine knew the answer. After class, the assistant teacher, who was familiar with Seminole culture, explained. "Sunshine did know the answer, but she didn't want to look smarter than her friend."

For children, culture is a holding environment that provides a sense of security and a feeling of belonging. It influences the way that they feel, the things that they fear, and the way that they behave. It is largely responsible for their choice of friends, their attitude toward their teacher, their motivation to learn, their likes and dislikes, and even the food they choose to eat. For teachers and caregivers, understanding and appreciating the culture of each child provides the opportunity to partner with parents, supporting their goals and aspirations for their child and making every child feel worthy and welcome.

Differences Associated With Home Language

Recognizing that children for whom English is a second language are often placed in child-care programs where English is the only language spoken, educators are concerned that these children may be at a disadvantage. How will teachers communicate with children who do not speak English? How will the other children react to a child who cannot speak English? How will the child know what the other children are saying to her? How will the child communicate with the other children? How will the teacher communicate with the child's parents? In most cases, the teacher's fears turn out to be groundless. Children have an amazing capacity to learn a new language. They not only can learn a language faster than an adult or even an older child but also can become bilingual or even multilingual, speaking each language without a trace of an accent.

As a matter of fact, despite teachers' concerns about non-English-speaking children, being able to speak more than one language has many advantages. Multilingual children can interact with children and adults from different linguistic communities. They can become their parents' best interpreters if their parents do not know English. Even more important, children who master more than one language are sensitized to different perspectives and different points of view. They become flexible thinkers, capable of recognizing the perspectives of other people. They are likely to excel at tests of cognitive flexibility that require labeling the same item in more than one way.

Although being bilingual brings many advantages, some research suggests that, in the development of emergent literacy skills, children who do not know English may lag behind children from homes where English is spoken. To be successful in learning to read when they enter kindergarten, children need to have acquired a speaking vocabulary of at least 6,000–7,000 words. Learning that many new words, even for children who learn very quickly, can take 2 to 3 years. Similarly, children who have less experience with English may not be as tuned in to its sound patterns as those who have been babbling English sounds and hearing English nursery rhymes since babyhood. They therefore may have more difficulty than their peers in learning letter–sound correspondences—unless they learn to make these connections in their home language. Even then, they may continue to struggle with English phonics and spelling. The following vignettes involve children from non-English-speaking families.

Hernandez was brought to Sunny Acres by his mother in the middle of the school year. The director had told the teacher of the 4-year-olds that Hernandez was joining her class. Miss Frazzled was upset. She was a new teacher, she did not know any Spanish, and she was already having trouble managing her rather rambunctious class. When Hernandez came into the classroom a week later, Miss Frazzled took him over to the block corner where three boys were building a fort. Hernandez watched the boys for several minutes, then picked up a block and put it on top of the fort. "That's not where it goes," one boy insisted, and snatched the block off of the fort. Hernandez walked over to the housekeeping area where some girls were dressing up their dolls. "No boys allowed," one girl shouted in a very cross voice. Hernandez walked away and sat in a corner by himself. When his mother came in a few minutes later to see how he was doing, Hernandez burst into tears. His mother took him back to her car and they never returned to the center.

Antonio was brought to Kid's Place by his mother in the middle of the school year. The director asked the teacher of the 4-year-olds whether she would like to have a new boy from Venezuela come to her classroom. Miss Kid-Lover was delighted. "We have been reading books about children from different parts of the world. It would be great to have a child from South America join the class. Does he speak any English?" "Not a word," the director admitted. "All the better," Miss Kid-Lover responded. "We'll teach him English, and he'll teach us Spanish."

The next week when Antonio came into the classroom, the children smiled and welcomed him. During morning circle time, the children introduced themselves to Antonio. Jonathan began the introductions. "*Me llamo* Jonathan. My name is Jonathan." Nina was next. "*Me llamo* Nina. My name is Nina." Antonio was the last to introduce himself. "*Me llamo* Antonio," he said in a strong voice. Then he added more tentatively, "My name is Antonio." All the children clapped.

Reflection

Compare the vignettes about Hernandez and Antonio. How is the attitude of each teacher reflected in the behavior of the children?

Differences Associated With Community

The community in which a child grows up can have a profound effect on how easily she learns to read and how well she does in school. Some communities are rich in resources that support literacy, providing lots of planned activities for children and safe spaces where they can play freely. Parents and teachers can easily obtain high quality children's books; libraries or mobile vans, bookstores and toy stores, and sometimes even grocery stores or drug stores offer a broad selection. Reading is important to the adults in the community; children often see grown-ups reading newspapers and magazines, using hymnals and song sheets, working with computers, making lists, following written directions, sending mail, posting notices, and seeking written information. Families support one another and are supported by an array of institutions such as child-care programs, drop-in centers, home visiting programs, places of worship, health clinics, and community-based organizations. In some of these communities, children have the opportunity to learn a second or third language from their playmates or classmates.

Other communities are characterized by pervasive poverty, neglect, and family isolation. These communities may suffer from high levels of street crime and violence—and, consequently, even higher levels of fear. Basic amenities such as safe parks and playgrounds as well as good sources of children's books are in short supply. Housing may be substandard, exposing children to lead and other toxins that can harm their growing brains and to indoor allergens that have contributed to a dramatic rise in asthma. Overcrowded conditions can make it difficult for young children to relax, play, or get enough sleep.

In 1994, Felton Earls, a psychiatrist at Harvard School of Public Health, launched a 10-year study of 11,000 children in 343 Chicago neighborhoods. The study explored children's lives in great detail, through direct observations, interviews with parents, and discussions with older children. Earls wanted to learn what factors distinguished neighborhoods in which children were thriving from those in which children tended to experience difficulty. An important factor emerged, one that is not usually considered: the availability of adults to children in the streets, courtyards, and playgrounds. In some neighborhoods, adults always seemed to be around; children of different ages could play freely with adult oversight, though not necessarily close supervision. In other neighborhoods, few adults were available to children. Earls and his colleagues found that "collective efficacy," which they defined as "mutual trust and a willingness to intervene in the supervision of children and the maintenance of public order," was a strong predictor of lower rates of violent crime and an important contributor to children's overall healthy development (Sampson, Raudenbush, & Earls, 1997).

Of all of the factors that differentiate communities, the factor that has been most closely associated with lack of success in school is poverty. In the National Research Council study *Preventing Reading Difficulties in Young Children* (Snow, Burns, & Griffin, 1998), a distinguished panel of scientists examined the relationship between poverty and reading achievement. They note that children who are poor are more likely to have parents who (a) are poor readers; (b) speak a nonstandard dialect different from what the children will be expected to speak, read, and write in school; and (c) do not spend enough time talking to or reading to their children. At the same time, public schools and early education programs in high-poverty neighborhoods often lack well-trained teachers and adequate resources. Reviewing a number of studies, the scientists concluded that

> [F]amilies rated low in SES [socioeconomic status] are not only less affluent and less educated than other families but also tend to live in communities in which the average family SES is low and [tend] to receive less adequate nutrition and health services, including prenatal and pediatric care. In other ways, too, low SES often encompasses a broad array of conditions that may be detrimental to the health, safety, and development of young children, which on their own may serve as risk factors that are linked to poverty. (Snow, Burns, & Griffin, 1998, p. 125)

This research puts extra responsibilities on teachers who work in child-care centers or family child-care homes located in poor communities. Beyond providing the child with a rich program in emergent literacy, the teacher is also responsible for encouraging parents to talk with and to read to children and advocating for better schools within low-income communities.

ACCOMMODATING THE INDIVIDUAL NEEDS OF ALL CHILDREN

Early childhood teachers who are committed to meeting the needs of each child in their care discover all too soon that this task is can be a challenging one. How do we plan activities when the group with whom we are working is a mixed-age group or a group with a range of abilities? How do we support the individual needs of children who need special attention? How do we help children respect and appreciate differences? How do we accommodate children who are easily overwhelmed by too much stimulation? How do we respond to the needs of children who experience difficulty joining a group? How do we make sure that children who are flexible and compliant are not overlooked? Although none of these questions have a specific correct answer, we can offer some suggestions that help teachers meet the needs of all children in the classroom, including children with special needs.

Planning Activities for a Mixed-Age Group or a Group With a Wide Range of Abilities

When planning activities for groups of children in which ages are mixed or abilities vary widely, child-care providers should seek activities that are fun for children regardless of their age or functional level. Here are some examples:

- Give each child an opportunity to plant seeds in a classroom garden.

- Provide a group activity such as making a mural where each child produces an individual picture that is then incorporated into the mural.

- Give each child play dough and plastic alphabet letters. Children who are learning the alphabet can roll out the play dough and use the letters to stamp their names or initials or to make simple words. Children who have less dexterity or who are not aware of what letters are will still have fun manipulating the play dough and sticking in the letters.

- Play library, and let each child select a book that she would like to read. Pair the children so that children who have good language skills partner with children who are just learning language. After the children have looked at the books for a few minutes, give each pair an opportunity to share their book with the group. The older or more adept child can tell the story of the book or talk about the pictures while his partner holds up the book and shows it to the other children.

- In family child care where there is a baby in the group, play out a theme like a doctor's office or a family picnic. The older children will be delighted to include the baby in their play, as most preschool children do not like to play the role of baby. The baby is bound to enjoy being the center of attention.

- Music and dance activities can engage children with a wide range of abilities and developmental levels. Some children can use rattles and shakers; others can use more complex instruments. A baby can be given a scarf to wave. Children can make their own instruments using plastic jars or bottles, sand, beans, rice, rubber bands, aluminum pie plates, wooden spoons, cardboard oatmeal containers, and other recycled materials.

Supporting Individual Children Who Have Special Needs

Children who have special needs benefit from special times during which they can work with the caregiver on an individual basis. "Free choice" time, when all the other children have selected a favorite activity, enables the caregiver to focus on individual children who need special help. The subsections that follow present specific ways to support developing self-awareness, language and literacy, and thinking skills in children who are hearing impaired, visually impaired, or physically challenged.

Children Who Are Hearing Impaired. Children who can hear but cannot hear well need a two-pronged strategy: 1) Help them to use the hearing they have, and 2) Engage their other senses.

▼ **Developing self-awareness**

- Call the child by name during his teacher-time session.

- Before you engage in an activity with a child, be sure to establish eye contact.

- Let the child feel your lips as you begin to talk.

▼ **Developing language and literacy**

- When you speak to a child with a hearing impairment, try to limit background noise and speak in a normal tone. Shouting can make it harder rather than easier for the child to hear you, especially if the child is wearing a hearing aid.

- As you sing a song to a child, let her feel your lips and your throat muscles.

- Describe what you are doing in a short sentence. "I am playing with a truck." When the child picks up the truck, say, "You are playing with the truck," emphasizing the word *truck*.

- Keep a hand mirror in a convenient place. Let the child watch her own lips when she plays with sounds.

- Have the child listen to songs and to books on tape, using a headset at a comfortable volume. Join the child in this activity and engage her in acting out the songs or in pointing out pictures in a paper copy of the same book that is being played on tape.

▼ **Promoting thinking skills**

- Help the child tune in to sounds by playing hide-and-seek. Hide a music box or radio under a blanket or mat while the child is not looking. See if she can find the music box or radio by listening.

Children Who Are Visually Impaired. Children who have limited vision or none at all can use other senses to explore and learn about the world—including the world of books.

▼ **Developing self-awareness**

- Guide the baby through a tasting experience. Place her hand in the cereal and then in her mouth. After a while she will feed herself.

▼ **Developing language, literacy, and writing**

- Begin to build the toddler's vocabulary by introducing words that he can experience. Say "up" every time you lift the baby from the crib, or urge the toddler to stand up.

- Play speech and gesture games such as "Patty-Cake," "This Little Piggy," and "So Big." Help the child imitate the gestures by moving his hands until he learns the pattern.

- Call the child's name before you walk over to him. Start softly and gradually increase your volume until he responds.

- Read touchable books with toddlers and preschoolers who are visually impaired, and encourage them to handle the books on their own. Look for books with raised designs, cutouts, textures, scratch-and-sniff pictures, and sturdy moving parts. You can also make books with simple pictures that the child can feel. For example, you might use a stencil or cookie cutter to draw animals on felt, cut out the pieces, and glue them onto sturdy paper pages.

- Use a computer to enlarge print and to make it easier for the child to see the pictures and words that correspond with a story.

- Give the child experience feeling and looking at letters. You can use large plastic letters stuck in play dough and letters cut from sandpaper or felt. You can also encourage the child to write in finger paint or shaving cream.

▼ **Promoting thinking skills**

- Give the child extra opportunity to handle objects of different shapes, widths, and textures. Challenge the child to find two objects that are alike. This pairing technique gives the child practice in identifying similarities and differences in objects on the basis of feel.

Children Who Are Physically Challenged. Children with motor impairments or delays need special opportunities to exercise their muscles and develop efficacy.

▼ Developing self-awareness

- Play a special version of the push–pull game. Sit the baby or toddler on a mat and push the mat away saying "bye-bye." Greet the baby with a special "hi" as you pull the mat back.

- Invent your own modification of "Trot, Trot to Boston" and "Pop Goes the Weasel." If the child cannot sit up, move her legs up and down as you recite "Pop Goes the Weasel." When you reach the "Pop," release the child's legs for a second and then catch them.

- Avoid quick movements in all the games you play so that the child will not be startled.

▼ Promoting language, literature, and writing

- Help the child strengthen his oral muscles and improve his voice volume by playing blowing games such as blowing soap bubbles with a straw, blowing out candles, or blowing a feather across a table. To keep the child from sucking in the soap bubbles, pinch the straw about halfway down and cut out a small diamond shape by making two diagonal slits.

- Put cream cheese or frosting on the child's lips and encourage her to lick it off.

- If the child is having trouble with finger–thumb grasp, let him practice a grasping activity with a built-in reward. Make gelatin thicker than usual, and cut it into cubes. Let the child finger-feed himself, first with one hand and then with the other.

- Encourage the child to write and draw with finger paint or with shaving cream that is spread on a smooth, washable surface.

▼ **Promoting thinking skills**

- A baby with motor impairments may be slowed in learning cause and effect if she does not have much opportunity to make things happen and see the results. Help her use the movements that she can produce and control to make interesting things happen. For example, you might take a ribbon that has a bell or mobile attached to it and tie the ribbon to the child's wrist, so she can shake her arm and cause the bell to ring or the mobile to dance.

Helping Children Respect and Appreciate Differences

Although most young children are quite accepting of differences and are especially tolerant of children with a sensory impairment, there are occasional exceptions. For example, one child might call a child who is overweight a "fatty," might refer to a child who wears glasses as "four-eyes," or might label a child who learns slowly a "dummy." Rather than ignore the child's name-calling, speak to the name-caller in a calm voice. You might say, "Tommy likes it better when you call him by his name, which is Tommy, than when you call him 'Fatty,'" "Tammy wears glasses so she can see better," and "Ask Alisha if she would like you to help her put the puzzle together."

Here are just a few strategies that can help children understand and appreciate differences.

- Read books to children about children who have different disabilities. After you read the book, talk to the group about the importance of respecting every child's feelings.

- Use the class puppet to help children develop the ability to empathize with a child who feels left out or picked on. Show the children, through your puppet play, that the puppet feels left out, and encourage the class to brainstorm about ways that they can help the puppet feel more accepted.

- Encourage children to recognize differences and to talk about these differences in a way that encourages understanding and avoids hard feelings.

- Provide children with opportunities to serve in a helper role with children who have special needs. Teach them to ask if help is wanted and to be patient when a classmate wants to try to do something himself.

Accommodating Children Who Have Difficulty Joining a Group

Some children who are fearful, nonsocial, or hyperactive may have difficulty joining a group activity. Here are some ideas for fostering participation:

- Rather than insist that they join you in circle time, give them permission to engage in a different activity while you are conducting circle time.

- Ask a child who resists circle time to be your helper, distributing instruments for rhythm band play or passing out colorful silk scarves to each child during dance time.

- Begin by including the reluctant child in an activity with one or two other children. Keep the activity short. Once the child feels comfortable with a small group, gradually increase the number of children in the group. You can also start with a short activity and gradually introduce activities that take a longer time.

Accommodating the Needs of Children Who Are Flexible and Compliant

Parents of the so-called "good kids" are likely to be concerned that their child will not get his share of teacher attention, but this concern does not have to become an issue. An experienced teacher is poised to meet the needs of the flexible and compliant child while still meeting the needs of children who are challenged. The trick, of course, is to build on each child's strengths while offering an appropriate level of challenge.

- Children who are flexible and compliant are most likely to enjoy being in the helper role. Pair the flexible child with a child who has special needs. Be sure to praise the flexible child for being such a good teacher and helper.

- Plan activities that all children can enjoy whether or not they have a handicapping condition.

- Introduce turn-taking games, which are often helpful in building social interaction. Nonverbal turn taking can be especially useful as a starting point (e.g., building a block tower together). Verbal games include passing the beanbag during a song.

CONCLUSION

Just as all children can benefit from an inclusive classroom or home setting, so can all teachers. It is especially rewarding to watch typically developing children and children who have special needs play joyfully together. The typically developing children increase their ability to empathize, satisfy their need to be helpful, and feel good about being wanted and needed by other children. They also learn that every child has strengths regardless of the challenges that they face. The child who is faced with developmental challenges also benefits from being with typically developing children. He learns new skills while playing with children who are happy to be his teacher, and he learns to appreciate his own strengths as he makes and keeps good friends. The child with developmental challenges develops language skills as he is included in activities and shares in conversations.

The teacher benefits from watching the almost daily progress of the children with whom she is working and hones her own skills as she develops supportive relationships with each child. She also learns to recognize those children who should be referred for in-depth evaluation and who might benefit from specialized therapy. The teacher who recognizes and appreciates individual differences and who creates strong bonds with every child in the group has taken the first and most critical step in fostering emergent literacy and in preparing children for success in school and in life.

References

Mangione, P. L., Lally, J. R., & Signer, S. (1990). *Flexible, fearful, or fiesty: The different temperaments of infants and toddlers.* [Video magazine]. Sacramento, CA: CDE Press.

National Research Council & Institute of Medicine. (2000). *From neurons to neighborhoods: The science of early childhood development.* Committee on Integrating the Science of Early Childhood Development. J. P. Shonkoff & D. A. Phillips (Eds.). Board on Children, Youth, and Families, Commission on Behavioral and Social Sciences and Education. Washington, DC: National Academy Press.

Sameroff, A. J. (1987). The social context of development. In N. Eisenberg (Ed.), *Contemporary topics in developmental psychology* (pp. 169–187). New York: Wiley.

Sampson, R. J., Raudenbush, S. W., & Earls, F. (1997). Neighborhoods and violent crime: A multilevel study of collective efficacy. *Science, 277* (Aug. 15), 918.

Snow, C. E., Burns, M. S., & Griffin, P. (Eds.). (1998). *Preventing reading difficulties in young children.* Report of the Committee of the Prevention of Reading Difficulties in Young Children, convened by the National Research Council. Washington, DC: National Academy Press.

CHAPTER

4

Building the Language Foundation

Happy talk, keep talking happy talk.
Talk about things you like to do!
You gotta have a dream—
If you don't have a dream—
How you gonna have a dream come true?

—Rodgers & Hammerstein (1949/1998)

Humans are social animals, and their children come into the world ready to communicate. Language and symbolic thought, the hallmarks of humanity, develop very early. The first 5 years of life, and especially the years between 1 and 4, are prime time for language learning. The brain is growing and developing rapidly, forming new connections as it learns. These connections, in turn, enable rapid information processing and new learning.

Virtually every child who can physically speak and hear (and many who cannot) masters at least one language by age 5. Their learning is so rapid that some scientists have postulated a "language instinct" that is hardwired into the brain and activated by hearing, practice, and conversation. But being able to speak a language fluently is not the whole story. Research shows that the qualitative differences in the way language is used are what matter—and these, like language learning in general, are rooted in early experience.

In Chapters 2 and 3, we saw how the early relationships that children develop with caregivers and parents provide the basis for later learning. We also saw how these relationships contribute to children's understanding and use of language and how "using their words" helps children regulate their own behavior, make friends, resolve conflicts, solve problems, and ask questions that further their learning. These social and emotional skills and approaches to learning play a major role in children's adaptation to kindergarten and in their later school success. Thus, a strong early language foundation builds what Daniel Goleman (1995) calls "emotional intelligence" and prepares children to do well in school.

How well young children learn to use language also has direct effects on how easily they will learn to read. As they grow, reading will become increasingly critical to their school success. According to a panel of experts convened by the National Academy of Sciences, "A person who is not at least a modestly skilled reader by the end of third grade is quite unlikely to graduate from high school" (Snow, Burns, & Griffin, 1998, p. 21). Children who come to the school setting with stronger prereading and language skills are, not surprisingly, more likely to become proficient readers in the primary grades.

The elements of language mastery that make the most difference in how well children will do in school and how easily they will learn to read fall into three categories:

1. Use of language (language pragmatics)

2. Vocabulary

3. Awareness of word parts and sounds

Teachers, caregivers, and parents should intentionally support all of these categories during the toddler and preschool years.

THE ROLE OF LANGUAGE IN FOSTERING LEARNING

C hildren learn through all of their senses, and language is only one mode of asking questions and learning new ideas. But even when children are learning by watching and imitating or by trying out their own ideas and solutions, language is likely to play a key role. Naming, categorizing, mentally ordering and reviewing events, and drawing conclusions are all highly language-dependent activities.

Think about something you have learned—for example, how to ride a bike or bake a cake, the multiplication tables, or how planets travel around the sun. Now think of all the different ways that language came into play during your learning. Language is obviously important for giving directions, sharing information, labeling objects, and describing their relationship. But language is also used for myriad other teaching and learning purposes, including asking questions, making requests, offering explanations, reciting poems or lists, debating ideas, making up stories, sharing feelings, providing comfort or encouragement, and making people laugh. Furthermore, inner language provides the basis of thinking. Thought processes such as recollection, hypothesizing, evaluating, reaching decisions, and planning ahead depend on inner language.

Children learn about the different uses of language from listening to spoken language. If adults use language almost solely to tell children what to do and how to do it, then children will use language in a restricted way. If children hear language spoken to accomplish many purposes, then they will recognize the power of language and will use language in many different ways.

In oral language, the words alone do not carry the full meaning; gestures, facial expressions, tone of voice, and shared context are also important. Gestures, facial expressions, and tone of voice reflect the different functions that language is serving. For example, depending on how it is said, "No" can be a negative answer to a question or it can mean "I can't believe it!" We vary the volume, pitch, speed, rhythm, and cadence of our voices to express different meanings and to elicit different responses from our listeners.

Written language is language out of context. Although the pictures in storybooks may support (or occasionally humorously contradict) the words on the page, the reader has to supply the intonations and inflections and must infer much of the context. Listening to lots of stories read aloud prepares children to understand the decontextualized language that they will encounter in their textbooks where the meaning is communicated only by the words. Equally important is participating in lots and lots of conversations that go beyond the here and now to include the past and the future, the imaginary and the hypothetical, feelings and abstractions, ideas and opinions, and wishes and dreams.

Researchers have found that young children who hear mainly directives and reprimands, however gently phrased, do not learn language as well as children who also hear lots of open-ended questions, descriptions, jokes, speculations, and explanations. Children who hear only directives and reprimands tend to lag both in vocabulary and in language pragmatics, or functional use. They are slower to develop inner speech and, thus, are less facile with problem solving. As they get older, their original writing is likely to be less expressive and their questions less probing.

The emotional tenor of the conversation also matters. Children can tell when adults are truly interested in what they are saying and when they are just giving perfunctory replies. Children need to hear words that affirm their capabilities, and they need to receive responses that show that their ideas, opinions, and feelings are being taken seriously. Children's belief in themselves as learners and their eagerness to learn new things is grounded in their early conversations with the people who are important in their lives.

THE ROLE OF LANGUAGE IN FOSTERING LITERACY

Language plays multiple roles in fostering literacy. For beginning readers who are working on "breaking the code" (i.e., identifying the words on the page), reading is a process of educated guesswork. The more they know about language, the more clues they have as to what the words may be saying and what they mean. And the more clues they have, the more quickly they are likely to figure out the words and sentences.

Books for beginning readers provide many clues. Pictures tell part of the story, and children who can name and describe the pictures have words at the tips of their tongues that are likely to be used in the story. The letters in the words provide phonemic or sound clues, and children who can name the letters or who know their associated sounds can often guess likely candidates with the right beginning sound even before they "sound out" the whole word. Beginning texts are filled with regularly spelled and common words; children unconsciously use their familiarity with the sound patterns of their language to help them figure out how the letters go together and what word they make.

Without realizing it, children also use syntactic or grammar clues to identify words and interpret sentences. Because of their familiarity with language patterns, they know what sort of word is likely to come next in a sentence and can tell when a guess does not fit with the rules of their language. Children also use their knowledge of how sentences are constructed to interpret what they are reading and to distinguish between words with the same spelling (e.g., I *read* the book yesterday versus I can *read* the book myself).

Finally, many books for beginners use repetition, alliteration, and rhyme to give children additional clues. Children who have had lots of practice with nursery rhymes, ABC books, word games, and similarly predictable children's books are likely to pick up these clues quickly. Having learned to tune in to parts of words, they can separate the pieces and blend them back together when they learn what sounds the various letters and letter combinations stand for.

Being able to interpret and combine the clues quickly is what reading is all about. Skilled readers look at every letter and every word, but only very briefly. Their interpretation of the marks on the page is automatic, enabling them to concentrate on the meaning of the text as a whole. Struggling readers often spend so much time analyzing an individual word that they forget what the sentence or story means, and they also tend to miss some of the clues that could help them figure out the word.

Once children have passed the initial code-breaking or decoding stage, vocabulary assumes greater importance. Now, the book authors use longer and less common words with greater frequency and embed them in more complex sentences. Students with good vocabularies already know some of the rare words, and that knowledge helps them figure out the meaning of the unfamiliar words from the context. Their knowledge of syntax (grammar) is also helpful. Again, much of this vocabulary development occurs so rapidly that children do not even know that they are learning new words.

As children spend less time learning to read and more time reading to learn, their vocabularies expand. Those children who started out knowing more words are likely to learn new ones at a faster pace as they read "harder" books. These new words, in turn, make it easier for them to read and enjoy more sophisticated writing, thus further increasing their vocabularies. Thus children who start grade school with the advantage of a strong vocabulary tend to increase their edge, while those whose vocabularies are weak may need special help.

BUILDING THE FOUNDATION: KEY RESEARCH FINDINGS

In 1965, Betty Hart and Todd Risley were working with a half-day preschool program designed to boost the cognitive functioning and school readiness of low-income children. They zeroed in on language and developed methods to measure the growth in children's vocabularies, as evidenced in the children's daily conversations in the classroom and on the playground. This method involved tape-recording the children, transcribing their words, and keeping track of words that were new or that were used in new ways.

Using vocabulary growth as an outcome measure, Hart and Risley tracked the effect of various educational strategies. They also compared the children in the preschool, all of whom came from poor families, with counterparts in a university-based preschool, all of whom came from professional families.

Their most successful intervention to increase vocabulary involved a theme-based curriculum that was centered around field trips. Teachers would use books, puzzles, and other educational materials as well as lots of formal and informal discussion to prepare children for a trip to the bank or fire station, introducing specialized vocabulary that would be reinforced during the trip and then practiced in pretend play.

The children eagerly lapped up the new words, concepts, and experiences, and used their new vocabulary as they played "bank," "store," "fire station," and "farm" in the house corner and block area and on the playground. Yet, when the researchers studied the rates at which the children's overall vocabularies were growing, they discovered that these rates still fell short of those of the wealthier children in the university-based preschool. This ever-widening gap did not bode well for the educational futures of the low-income children.

Concluding that they were providing too little too late, Hart and Risley decided to look at what children in different income strata were learning in their everyday home interactions in their first 3 years. The two researchers observed 42 children and their families for 1 hour per month for 2½ years, beginning when the children were 10 months old. The researchers carefully tracked the children's emerging "in-use" vocabularies, as they had in their preschool observations. In addition, they recorded and analyzed everything that was said to the child during their observations.

After years of intensive analysis, Hart and Risley (1995) were able to substantiate some remarkable conclusions:

- Wide differences existed among the families in the amount of language used—especially in the amount of language addressed to the child. These differences, which were strongly associated with social class, are reflected in the size and growth rate of children's vocabularies.

- Children who heard more words developed larger vocabularies by 3 years of age.

- The children whose parents were on welfare heard an average of about 9 million words spoken to them in ordinary conversation by the time they were 3, those from working class families heard about 18 million, and those from professional families heard nearly 33 million! (These estimates were arrived at by multiplying the average number of words the researchers recorded per hour by the number of hours that the typical child would be awake. The hidden assumption, of course, is that children are spending most of their waking hours with their parents, or with people who talk to them about as much as their parents do.)

- Not only the number of words addressed to the child but also key features of parents' communication styles (described in the next two bullets) contributed to children's vocabularies and IQ scores at age 3 as well as to their vocabulary and general language scores in third grade.

- Not surprisingly, children who heard more "yeses" and received more encouragement—including repetition or expansion of their language, answers to their questions, praise, and approval—and who heard proportionally fewer "nos" did significantly better.

- Other communication style features that made a difference included (a) *language diversity* (measured by the number of different nouns and descriptive words used per hour by parents), (b) *symbolic emphasis* (a measure of *information richness* derived by counting nouns, modifiers, and past-tense verbs and then dividing by the number of utterances), (c) *guidance style* (giving children choices, measured by looking at the proportion of questions in relation to commands), and (d) *responsiveness* (listening and letting the child take the lead.)

The features of parents' communication styles that Hart and Risley identified as making a difference in the language development of the children in their study are similar to what experts identify as "good" quality in child-care and early education programs. The following highlight language-related items from the ITERS and ECERS scales, as summarized by Helburn and Bergmann (2002). Key words have been italicized to emphasize similarities with Hart and Rigby's findings. For infants and toddlers, these quality features include the following:

- Staff members *do a lot of talking* to babies and toddlers. They engage in verbal play; *name and talk about objects, pictures, and actions;* read books to children and say nursery rhymes; *respond* to children's crying, gestures, sounds, and words; and maintain eye contact while talking to the child.

- Caregivers are patient with a crying baby or upset toddler.

- Staff members are *warm and affectionate,* initiate verbal and physical play, and *show delight in children's activity* (pp. 70–71).

For preschoolers, quality features include the following:

- *Frequent adult–child conversations* occur.

- *Language is used primarily to exchange information* with children and to participate in social interactions.

- Staff members *add information* to *expand on children's ideas.*

- Staff members *encourage communication* between children.

- Staff members use *nonpunitive discipline methods,* model social skills, and help children develop appropriate social behavior (pp. 66–67).

The Home-School Study of Language and Literacy Development echoed and deepened these findings. In this extensive observational study of low-income toddlers and preschoolers (reported in Dickinson & Tabors, 2001), Catherine Snow, David Dickinson, Patton Tabors, and their colleagues recorded children's conversations at home and at their child-care programs. They continued to collect data until the children were in grade school and then analyzed their learning outcomes. The clearest and most striking finding was that children who as preschoolers engaged with adults in more "decontextualized" or "nonimmediate" talk (i.e., in conversation that goes beyond the here and now to include references to past, future, and imagined events and to abstract ideas) fare better on reading comprehension tests through the sixth grade. They also found, as did Hart and Risley, that a large vocabulary at school entry is a strong indicator of later success. Finally, the study identified particular techniques used by parents and especially by teachers that tended to foster language and literacy development.

LEARNING IN TWO LANGUAGES

B eing bilingual is such a distinct advantage that some forward-thinking preschool programs are teaching all children to speak and eventually read in two languages. Children who have been exposed to two or even three languages in the early years are likely to speak each of these languages fluently and without an accent when they are older, as long as they have opportunities to practice and to continue learning. Thus, parents who speak a language other than English should be encouraged to continue to speak with their child in their home language, even when the child is placed in a child-care setting where all or most of the staff members speak English. The firmer the foundation that young children have in their home language, the easier it is for them to learn a second language.

Children who will be taught to read in English ideally should have 2 years of English practice in which to grow accustomed to English sound patterns and build a critical mass of English vocabulary words. This recommendation does not, however, mean that they should stop learning their first language. In fact, parents should be encouraged to use their home language to tell and read stories to their children. They should also sing songs and discuss new ideas and experiences so that the children move toward literacy in both languages.

If none of the staff members in a child-care setting speak the child's home language, then it is a good idea for one or more of the staff members to learn a few phrases in the child's home language. Children adjust to a new setting more easily if they hear their home language spoken. The initial fears of a child who comes into a setting and hears everyone speaking a foreign language are eased when she hears a familiar phrase. Speaking a few phrases in her language helps bridge the gap between home and child care and at the same time sends an important message. It lets the child know that the teacher respects and would like to learn the language that the child's family speaks.

STAGES OF LANGUAGE DEVELOPMENT AND WAYS TO SUPPORT THEM

To understand how to best support language learning, it helps to have a map of its developmental stages. In the following discussion, remember that the ages are approximate. All children go through similar stages, but they traverse the milestones at different rates. For example, a child who is a slow talker may or may not be delayed in language development. Many children show typical or even advanced understanding of language (receptive language) but lag behind in speech (expressive language).

From Cooing to Babbling: Birth to 8 Months

Ms. Chatterbox appeared to be having a conversation with 2-month old Tyler, who she was holding in her arms, but her words were also meant for Ms. All-Ears, her new assistant. "Yes, Tyler . . . You like to be talked to, don't you? . . . You want to hold my finger? . . . Hold tight . . .You're holding my finger very tight . . . Um, hmm . . . Yes you are . . . And you're looking right at my face . . . And you can say ooh . . . ooh . . .You say ooh very nicely. Ms. All Ears can see that you like talking. And you're learning so much, aren't you?"

Children's language development begins very early. During their first month, babies recognize and turn toward the voices of their most frequent caregivers. They make eye contact, watch eyes and mouths, imitate facial expressions, and begin to learn the turn-taking "dance" of communication exchange.

Although babies' first communications may not be intentional, attentive parents and other caregivers are able to interpret their meanings. For example, they can distinguish the rhythmic, intense cry that means "I'm hungry," the sharp cry that means "I'm in pain," and the whiny cry that means "I'm uncomfortable." Often without realizing which signals they are noticing, caregivers recognize that when a baby hiccups, tenses or stiffens her body, tightens her lips, screws up her face, or curls her toes, the baby is saying, "I am over-stimulated or overwhelmed and I need to be soothed." Most impor-tant, they tune in to the baby's rhythm of interaction. They follow the baby's lead as she makes eye contact, engages in back-and-forth play, signals that she needs a break by briefly turning away, and then resumes the play when ready.

These "conversations," begun with glances, stares, and grimaces, soon take on a verbal quality. As they gaze into each other's eyes, the adult talks gently to the baby, and the baby coos back. Soon, the baby learns to "take turns"—listen, coo, listen, coo. Before long, most babies learn how to take over the lead, cooing to elicit a smile from the parent or caregiver, then smiling and cooing back.

Adults all over the world speak to babies in a language that psy-chologists refer to as "parentese." They use low, smooth murmurs for soothing; rising intonation to elicit or direct attention; a rising and falling pattern to indicate approval; and sharp, quick sounds to mean "Stop!" or "Don't!" Indeed, parents of young babies often discover that it does not matter what they say, as long as they say it in par-entese. Often, a baby who fusses when his mother talks on the phone or carries on a conversation with another adult will be perfectly con-tent if his mother continues the conversation while looking at him and adopting the high pitch and sing-song inflections of parentese.

Along with its recognizable melodies, parentese has features that grab the baby's attention and foster language learning. Its high pitch and accompanying eye contact mark it as language and, specifically, as language directed to the baby. Words are enunciated more clearly than in typical speech, usually with elongated vowels, making it easier to hear where one word ends and a new one begins. Key words, especially nouns and verbs, are often given exaggerated emphasis, making it easier to associate a word with a thing or action. The speaker often repeats the same sentences over and over with slight variations, giving the baby more opportunities to focus on the key words.

By the time they are 6 months old, most babies have begun to babble, or to play with speech sounds, by repeating consonants. *Ba-ba-ba-ba* is a common first babble. Between 6 and 8 months, babbling increases in frequency and new babbles are added, such as *na-na-na-na, da-da-da-da,* and *la-la-la-la.* Cooing conversations are now replaced by babbling conversations as caregiver and baby take turns repeating a particular babble sound. Infants have also learned to use babbling as a way of initiating a conversation and maintaining contact with their caregiver.

Shared Communication: 8 Months to 1 Year

At first, babies throughout the world babble the same sounds, but gradually, babies drop those sounds not used in their languages. At the same time, the baby begins to imitate the inflections she hears, and her babbling, though still only gibberish, comes to sound more and more like meaningful sentences. The babbling segments echo the rhythm, intonation, and sound patterns of the language (or languages) of the baby's caregivers. This form of vocalizing is often called "expressive jargon." It sounds as if the baby is carrying on a conversation, but the utterances have no meaning. Nevertheless, these sounds hold a conversation partner's attention and strengthen the bonds of attachment as baby and grown-up enjoy the game together.

Although the baby's utterances may still be meaningless, she is nevertheless coming to understand that words have meaning and even to recognize the events and actions for which some of the words stand. As babies practice playing games such as Peekaboo and Pop Goes the Weasel, they learn to anticipate the Boo or Pop and to associate it with the action that follows. As they hear the emphasized words of parentese, they begin to associate these words with actions and objects. "Oh," says the caregiver. "You want your *bottle*," and suddenly the caregiver senses that the baby seems to understand that food is on its way.

By the time they are 10 or 12 months old, most babies have tuned in to the meaning of language, and some can show off their knowledge when prompted to complete well-practiced routines. When their caregiver says, "Wave bye-bye," they respond by waving their arms; they may attempt to clap when their caregiver says "patty cake." They may touch Daddy's nose on command, point to the pig in a favorite book, or respond with an appropriate grunt when asked, "What does the pig say?" Some babies will also respond to the word *no*. When the caregiver says "No," the baby will stop, at least for a second, before going back to what she was doing.

During this period, babies will also learn to communicate through purposeful nonverbal signs. The baby will lift his arms to signal "Pick me up," will point with one finger to tell you to look at something, and will push away your hands or turn or shake his head to signal "I don't want that." As caregivers interpret and respond to a baby's signs, the baby learns the value of conversational exchanges.

The importance of talking with babies before they can talk themselves cannot be overestimated. The more that researchers study infants, the more astounded they are at the extent of infants' capabilities and at the rapidity of their learning.

LANGUAGE ACTIVITIES FOR INFANTS

Lullabies. Babies love lullabies. Choose one or two to use when a baby needs help falling asleep. Over time, the baby will learn to associate these lullabies with naptime. You can use lullabies at other times, too—to soothe a crying baby, when feeding or burping, when a child has gotten overexcited and needs help calming down, and when *you* are feeling stressed and need a break. Share favorites from your own childhood. Have parents make tapes of their children's favorite lullabies and of lullabies in their home languages.

All Smiles. At about 5 or 6 weeks old, babies learn to smile when someone talks and smiles at them. Some babies smile easily; others are coy and need lots of prodding. See how many ways you can find to make each baby smile. If you work with a mixed-age group, have the older children help you find new ways to make the babies smile. Post a large chart of "How to Make Our Babies Smile."

Babbling Fun. Play back-and-forth babbling games with babies who are in the babbling stage. Repeat their babbles and see whether they will repeat yours. Tape-record babies' babbles and see how they react when you play the tape back for them. Encourage babbling babies to add their voices to the chorus when older children are singing upbeat songs or playing with rhythm instruments by including them in the circle and giving them rattles to shake.

(continued)

LANGUAGE ACTIVITIES FOR INFANTS (*continued*)

Changing Table Chatter. Diaper changing time is a great time for language activities! As you change a baby's diaper, you can name body parts, have the baby point to your nose and mouth, show her her hands in the mirror, or play tickle games like Tummy Kisses and This Little Piggy Went to Market. You might take an extra minute or two to exercise the baby's arms and legs, accompanying your actions with rhymes such as:

> Spread out baby's arms,
> Now touch her nose.
> Spread out baby's legs,
> And now find her toes.

> Up and down my baby's legs go.
> First we go fast,
> And then we go slow!

Making Friends. Babies love to watch other babies, as well as older children. Position two babies who are not yet crawling face to face so they can "talk" to each other. Give them identical or similar toys, and see whether they will imitate each other. Try giving them each one end of a scarf. Or place them side by side as they play with a cradle gym.

Peekaboo, Chase, and Hide-and-Seek. With its many variations, Peekaboo is a sure way to get most babies to smile, laugh, and engage in a turn-taking game. When babies learn to crawl away, they enjoy being chased or hiding and being found. The words that go with the games— "Peekaboo, I see you; I'm going to get you!" and "Here I come, ready or not!"—are an important part of the fun.

Bouncing Games. Games such as Trot, Trot to Boston, and Pop Goes the Weasel help babies listen to individual words as they learn when to expect the surprise drop or bounce.

How Big Is Baby? "How big is baby? (Lift baby's arms.) So big!" This classic game is a first show-off routine for many babies. You can teach it one-on-one or try it in a group where children can watch and imitate one another's actions.

Hand Clapping Rhymes "Pat-a-Cake" is an old favorite, but every culture has its own collection of hand-clapping rhymes. Here is one from Cuba that is fun to do in Spanish and in English: *Hola Mis Amigos,*

(**continued**)

Language Activities for Infants *(continued)*

sí, sí, sí. (Hello everybody, yes indeed.) You can teach routines like these by letting the baby watch you or by clapping the baby's hands for her. Once she has learned a game, you can play it together in quiet moments, at diaper-changing time, while waiting for lunch, or to help settle in after she has waved bye-bye to Dad.

Playing Together. As you play with babies, give them words to label their actions and words to describe the consequences of their actions: "You're chewing the rattle. You turned it upside down! Uh-oh. Are you going to throw it on the floor? Boom! You dropped it. What a big noise!"

Reflection

What are your favorite baby language games? Which ones do particular children in your care prefer? What differences do you see among babies in their responses to language games?

Discovering Words: 12 to 18 Months

A child's first steps and first words are exciting milestones, often chronicled in baby books and celebrated by the whole family. For some children, walking and talking are simultaneous achievements, but most babies concentrate on one first and then move on to the other. The following vignette shows how wide the differences can be among children who are developmentally on track.

Kenneth and Brenan are cousins, ages 14 and 15 months. As they enter the park near his home, Kenneth runs ahead. His mother helps him climb onto the horse swing, and Kenneth immediately begins riding at top speed, in total silence. Meanwhile, Brenan toddles over, holding tightly to both of his mother's hands. His mother places him on the horse next to the one his cousin is riding, where, remaining stock still, Brenan proudly exclaims, "I'm going fast. I'm going very, very fast!" Kenneth's mother asks, "Is my baby OK? Brenan is talking so well, yet my son Kenneth isn't even talking yet." Brenan's mother follows with the opposite concern, "Is my baby OK?

Kenneth is running, yet Brenan is just starting to learn to walk." "They're both fine!" the boys' grandmother insists. "They're just putting their energies into different places right now."

Although some babies have 50-word vocabularies by their first birthday and others will not say their first word until close to their second birthday, most toddlers are likely to develop a meaningful vocabulary of two or three words between 12 and 14 months of age. Favorite first words are *da-da, bow-wow,* and *ba-ba* (meaning bottle, ball, baby, or banana). These words represent objects or people who are important to a 1-year-old. They are also easy to say.

For many toddlers, the desire to talk outpaces the ability to pronounce the words. Their tendency to shorten words and leave out letters accounts for nicknames like "bubba" for *brother* and "Geggy" for *Gregory.* Indeed, toddlers commonly drop one part of a consonant blend, turning *spoon* to "poon," *truck* to "tuck," and *blanket* to "bankie." Another common strategy that toddlers use is substitution. Consonants that are difficult to pronounce, for example, *k* or *t,* are replaced by easier-to-pronounce consonants such as *b* or *d. Truck* might become "guck" and *kitty* may become "diddy."

One- to 2-year-olds expand their receptive vocabulary faster than their expressive vocabulary. They can point to familiar objects on request, identify photos of familiar people or objects, and follow simple commands such as "Show me your shoes," "Find your belly button," or "Give Mommy a kiss." Some toddlers learn to repeat phrases that they have heard many times—"Happy birthday", "Go bye-bye," "All done," and "No more."

LANGUAGE ACTIVITIES FOR YOUNG TODDLERS

Name Walk. Take a toddler for a walk around the classroom or playground. Name and touch things as you go, encouraging the toddler to repeat the words or to take the initiative in naming. Ask the child what he wants to visit next.

Photo Album. Ask parents (or older children if you have a mixed-age group) to help you make photo albums for toddlers with clear and

(continued)

LANGUAGE ACTIVITIES FOR YOUNG TODDLERS *(continued)*

simple pictures of family members, pets, the toddler herself engaged in familiar activities such as eating, sleeping, reading a book, or playing with a favorite toy. The albums can also include pictures (either photos or pictures cut from magazines) of familiar objects. Help each toddler name the pictures in her book and in her friends' books. (Assume that the albums will be chewed, dragged, crinkled, and pulled on. Use small albums with plastic slots for pictures or else laminate the photos, punch holes in the edges, and tie them together with yarn.)

Pictures to Name. Toddlers like to point out pictures in books and may also be able to name some. But all the pictures do not have to be in books. Put some on the walls at toddler eye level. Use family photos, pictures cut from magazines and calendars, stickers, and older children's drawings.

Animal Sounds. Using picture books or toy animals, teach young toddlers the names of animals and the sounds they make. They will probably be able to point to an animal that you name long before they can say its name themselves. However, many young toddlers are surprisingly good at learning animal sounds, even before they can say words.

Circle Rhymes. Circle-time activities are fun for young toddlers, as long as the toddlers are free to leave when they wish. Movement rhymes are especially fun to learn and perform in a group. Toddler favorites include "The Wheels on the Bus" and "Hokey Pokey."

Words, Words, Words. The more words you use with young toddlers, the more they will have an opportunity to learn. Talk about what you are doing when a toddler is watching you: "Oh, some milk spilled. It made a big, white puddle. I better get my sponge. Do you want to help me wipe the table?" Give the child words for what she is doing: "Vrrm, vrrm. You're making your car go fast. Can you make it go under the tunnel?" Point out the things you see or notice: "I hear an airplane. It makes a loud noise. Look. See the plane high up in the sky?" Be sure to use descriptive words and phrases as well as nouns and verbs.

Go Fetch. Toddlers love to be helpful. Take advantage of their new ability to move around and to follow a simple direction by asking them to get an item for you—for example, a diaper, toy, or sponge. At first, make sure that the item is within sight. As their receptive language improves, they will be able to get things from familiar places even when they cannot see them, and they will develop the ability to pick out particular items such as "Johnny's shoes", "the red block", "or the elephant book" in your cubby.

(continued)

LANGUAGE ACTIVITIES FOR YOUNG TODDLERS *(continued)*

Words of Warning. Exploring is an important part of toddlerhood. You have probably already set up the environment to encourage exploration while at the same time minimizing dangers and your need to say "no." But no matter how thorough you are at toddler proofing, situations will always occur when toddlers do things that need to be stopped right away. Use playtime to teach words of warning such as *hot, stop*, and *careful* in addition to *no*. For example, you might play a stop-and-go game when children are using their riding toys on the playground, even holding up a stop sign. You can teach *careful* when you show children the safe way to get on to a swing or chair or when you supervise their handling of a fragile object. A good time to teach *hot* is when toddlers are pretending to cook.

Texture Fun. Give toddlers lots of opportunities to feel different textures, such as fur, cotton, corduroy, sandpaper, silk, Silly Putty, stone, denim, and dough. Teach words like *soft, hard, rough, smooth, sticky, damp, wet, dry, squishy,* and *bumpy* as the child strokes the materials.

Bubbles. Toddlers love to watch, chase, catch, and pop soap bubbles. Some toddlers can even learn to blow! Bubble play gives you lots of opportunities to introduce words such as *big, pop, float, land, blow, away, catch, fly, wind,* and *wet*.

Talking in Sentences: 18 Months to 3 Years

"Sawyer's really starting to talk," his mother reported. "When I say something to him, he likes to repeat some of the words. Like yesterday—he wanted to go see the frog statue on our neighbor's lawn and was pulling on my hand. 'He wants to see the frog down the street,' I explained to his father. 'Frog. Street. Go,' Sawyer insisted. Then he looked up at his Dad, who'd been away on a business trip for 4 days, and said, 'Daddy work. Miss.' The other day, he put a blanket over his head, peeked out with one eye, and announced, 'Hiding.'" Sawyer is just 19 months old, but already he is beginning to use his words to make his wishes and feelings known, to tell us what he is doing or seeing, and to get what he wants.

Sometime between the beginning of the second year and the middle of the third, language development heats up considerably. The toddler begins to put words together into short sentences such as "More juice," "Baby crying," and "Daddy bye-bye car." This new ability to combine words allows the toddler to say things that she has never heard. As she discovers the power of words to communicate, she uses language for many different purposes: to make requests, call out greetings, direct attention to something she finds interesting, ask questions, describe what she sees or hears or what she is doing, entertain herself and others, protest, and invite interaction. To the child's parents, it seems as if a minor miracle is occurring.

Some children move from single words to conversation in a rapid burst; others gradually increase the length and complexity of their communications. By the time they are 3, most toddlers can string three or four words together, and their meaning is easier to fathom: "That Daddy car." "See car. Daddy come home." Some 2-year-olds will utter even longer sentences: "I got new red shoes." "I hided in the closet." "Molly cried cause she hurt her knee."

As the child relies increasingly on language to communicate, vocabulary development skyrockets. According to Stephen Pinker, author of *The Language Instinct* (1995), "Vocabulary growth jumps to the new-word-every-two-hours minimum rate that the child will maintain through adolescence" (pp. 267–268). The typical 2-year-old knows between 50 and 100 words. Three-year-olds who are developmentally on target understand about 2,000 words and use nearly 1,000 different words in their everyday speech!

Toddlers' development of language goes hand-in-hand with the emergence of their personalities. A favorite word of most 2-year-olds is a very forceful *no*. When a 2-year-old says "no," he is declaring to the world that he is a person with the right to make a choice. Two-year-olds are both endearing and frustrating because they want so badly to do things themselves, in their own way, and because they try so hard to make themselves understood.

Articulation difficulties are quite common at this stage, making the child sound as if he is mumbling even when he is speaking slowly. Similarly, many 2-year-olds still substitute sounds they can say for those that give them difficulty, so *cookie* may be "tootie," *rabbit* may be "wabbit," *park* could become "poke," and *yellow* could become "wewow." Their frustration is minimized when a parent, primary caregiver, older sibling, or older friend can translate for them with new people. Familiar people, both adults and children, are especially important at this age when children have a lot to say but are not yet good at making themselves understood.

By the end of their third year, toddlers have expanded their receptive and expressive vocabulary. They are able to follow a simple two-part command such as "Go to daddy and give him a kiss" or "Put the puzzle back on the shelf." They are also beginning to ask questions, usually ones that begin with *what* or *where*: "Where Mommy go?" "What dat baby eating?"

At about the same time that this toddler begins putting words together, she starts to pretend. At first, the pretending looks like deferred imitation: she will put a hat on her head or "drink" from an empty cup. In effect, she is labeling the objects with her actions, showing that she knows their purpose. Soon, however, she will use one object to represent another. She may "drink" from a block and then hold it out to an adult for a refill, perhaps using words such as "cup" or "more milk" to make her intention clear. By their third birthday, most preschoolers are adept pretenders, acting out a variety of scenarios alone, with friends, with adults, and in their play with toys and small objects. Familiar themes such as eating, sleeping, cooking, and going places, or favorite stories from books and videos, are reenacted in skeletal form and gradually elaborated into complicated stories that are played out over and over again with endless variations.

When child development experts speak of the preschool period as "the magic years" or say that "play is the work of children," they are talking about this endlessly compelling work of pretending.

LANGUAGE ACTIVITIES FOR OLDER TODDLERS

Nature Walk. New walkers like to go places, but they also like to stop and look at things on the way. When a child stops to look at something, supply words for his discovery. A simple walk around the playground can be not only a chance to visit the slide and the sand box, to see the green grass and a pretty yellow flower, to find a big rock, and to discover a wiggly worm in patch of dirt but also an opportunity to learn and practice all of those new words.

(continued)

LANGUAGE ACTIVITIES FOR OLDER TODDLERS *(continued)*

Name Games.   Help toddlers learn the names of the other children in the group by using the names in daily songs and routines. For example, "Hello Jae Lin, yes indeed, yes indeed my darling" or, in another activity, "I roll the ball to Kayla . . . she rolls it back to me."

What's Coming Up.   Use words to prepare toddlers for transitions. "Play time is almost over. Then we have to clean up so we can have lunch." "Let's get our jackets on so we can go outside." "Daddy will come after snack time."

Problem Solving.   Give toddlers simple problems to solve—for example, opening a shoebox, fitting shapes into a shape sorter, putting nesting blocks in order, or getting a clothes pin out of a soda bottle. Use words to cue them when they get stuck. "Let's see what's in the box. Can you take the lid off?" "I think the red one goes next." Encourage them to use words, too, by asking them simple questions: "Which one should we try next?" "Which part is stuck?"

Sentence Expansions.   Expand toddlers' sentences for them by filling in the missing words. For example, if a child says, "Juice all gone," you can say, "Your juice is all gone. Do you want some more?"

Which One Do You Want?   Give toddlers choices whenever you can. It helps them feel powerful and in control. It is also a great way to teach new words, especially colors, shapes, and other adjectives. "Should we put your boots on first or your jacket?" "Do you want the red truck or the blue one?"

Shopping Cart.   An imaginary shopping trip can be great fun for 2-year-olds, who enjoy collecting and transporting lots of stuff. Use a play shopping cart, a small stroller, or a riding toy with a basket, or give children tote bags to fill. As you go around the classroom, encourage the children to ask for the things that they want to "buy." At clean-up time, you can play the game in reverse, with children acting as storekeepers who need to put items on their shelves. Place things in the cart or tote bag and then encourage the children to name the items as you help the children put them back where they belong.

Telephone.   Use toy telephones to encourage toddlers to talk to friends or to you. When you participate, you might ask about events in the immediate past (e.g., "What did you have for lunch?") or the near future (e.g., "Are you going over to Michael's house?").

(continued)

Loud and Soft. Two-year-olds are just learning how to modulate their voices, and they enjoy experimenting with loud and soft. Play simple games in which you give the group a word or phrase to say. Have them say it loud, then even louder, and then really, really loud. Then, have them say it soft, then softer, and finally, whispering. Often, it is easier for 2-year-olds to use their "inside voices" after they have had a chance to make some noise and have practiced the difference between loud and soft.

Collections. Group small toys into collections such as cars and trucks, farm animals, sand toys, dollhouse people and furniture, or tea sets. Name the items as you and the child play with them. Encourage the child to ask you for the items he needs for his play and to find you the items that you need for yours. "Oh, where did the baby pig go?"

Memory Lane. Talk with older toddlers about events in the recent past. Ask questions that encourage them to talk about what they remember. You can also use pictures to spark their recollections.

Carrying on Conversations: 3 to 4 Years

Although the spurt in language development occurs at different times during the third year, by the age of 3, most children have mastered enough language to take part in a real conversation. The following conversation took place between a mother and her not-yet 3-year-old son, as they played together on the big train at the park.

Jack: 'Tand here. I drive train.

Mother: Where are we going today, Jack?

Jack: To Tontord.

Mother: Oh, you want to go to Concord? Should we buy some cookies at the bakery in Concord?

Jack: *(handing his mother an imaginary cookie)* Here tootie.

Mother: Thank you, Jack. Umm. This is a delicious chocolate chip cookie.

Jack: *(driving the train again)* Choo, choo. Goo, goo. I drive train.

Mother: Jack, what kind of engine does this train have?

Jack: 'Team engine. See 'moke 'tack?

Mother: Does it have a tender?

Jack: (*pointing to the small platform behind the engine*) Here tender.

Mother: Do we need some more coal for the fire?

Jack: (*jumping off the train and pulling up pieces of grass*) I get toal. Need lotta toal for fire.

Mother: That will make a hot fire.

Jack: (*throwing "toal" into the "fire"*) Fire hot. Train go fast. (*He turns the steering wheel rapidly back and forth.*) I drive fast. Go Botton.

Three-year-olds are likely to use language for several different purposes: to make requests, to ask questions, to play with words, to join in singing songs, to give directions, to talk about their feelings, and to share information.

Talking with individual children about topics that interest them is a great way to build their vocabularies!

As children use longer and longer sentences in their conversations, they begin to master the syntax of language. By 3½, most children can differentiate past, present, and future; can use adjectives, verbs, and pronouns appropriately; and can differentiate singular and plural nouns.

Although 3-year-olds are making huge strides in their mastery of syntax, they do make grammatical errors. The errors they make most frequently actually reveal their understanding of the rules of grammar. Having learned a rule—for example, adding s to indicate more than one—they generalize it to all situations, whether or not it applies. If you show a child a picture and say "I see a mouse," then show him a picture with two mice, he will probably say, "I see two mouses." However, even if he knows the word *men*, he is quite likely to apply the plural rule to *man* in conversation: "The mans are fixing the street." Sentences such as "I hitted my brother" and "The sheeps eated all the grass" are typical of children who have just learned the rules. In fact, learning the exceptions can be more difficult than learning the rules!

Children who are learning two languages simultaneously are likely to make overgeneralization errors (such as those described above) in both languages, but they are not likely to mix the grammatical rules. For example, they will put adjectives before nouns in English (the red book) but after nouns in Spanish (*el libro rojo*). Older children and adults who are learning a second language for the first time are much more likely to misapply their grammatical knowledge of their first language to their second.

Whether a child makes a grammatical mistake because he has not learned a rule, because he overgeneralizes a rule, or because he is learning a nonstandard dialect with slightly different rules, telling the child that he is wrong or teaching him to say the word correctly is unlikely to work. Moreover, corrections interrupt the child's communication by taking the focus off of the meaning of his message. A far more effective technique is to continue the conversation, using the correct form in a way that shows you understood what the child said and are taking his comment seriously. For example, when a child proudly announces, "I eated all my lunch," a teacher can respond, "I see you ate all your lunch! You were really hungry today."

As children participate in conversations, their receptive language continues to outpace their spoken words. Most 3-year-olds can follow two-step requests (e.g., "Go get the napkins and put them on the table"), although their own sentences are likely to be shorter.

But the gap between receptive and expressive language, in both vocabulary and syntax, is beginning to close. Three-year-olds can repeat most of what they can understand, and practicing new words in a variety of situations helps them to remember those new words.

As the conversation stage progresses, the child is more and more able to hold up her end. She may come to school full of excitement and tell you about her new shoes or her birthday party or the mess her baby brother made. She can talk about things beyond the here and now, and she expects adults to be interested in what she has to say. She no longer needs prompts to tell the whole story; she can now string together several sentences at a time.

Being able to sustain the conversation enables 3-year-old conversationalists to engage a wide variety of partners. Most 3-year-olds will carry on conversations with their toys as well as with their friends and can animate little figures or puppets and make them talk to one another. Indeed, most 3-year-olds will spend many hours in this kind of play, especially if adults have modeled it for them. "Hey, farmer. I want some food." "Here's your food, pig." "I need some more." "Here." "Oink, oink. Thank you."

Another notable advance in the beginning conversation stage is a new facility with questions. As the child learns the rules for forming questions, his question "Where Daddy?" becomes "Where did Daddy go?" and "Mommy home?" becomes "When will Mommy come home?" More important, though, is a new ability to string questions together to find out what he really wants to know. Each answer that you give generates a new question for the child. At first, the questions focus largely on the here and now or on the child's immediate feelings and perceptions. "What is that lady doing? Where is she going? What's she going to do then? Why don't you know?" Soon, however, the child begins asking more probing questions, including the classic, "How did the baby get in that lady's tummy?"

LANGUAGE ACTIVITIES FOR 3-YEAR-OLDS

Show-and-Tell. Show-and-tell is a traditional preschool and primary grade favorite that even 3-year-olds can enjoy, as long as you keep it brief.

Pearls of Wisdom. With their inquisitive minds and limited vocabularies, 3-year-olds often say astounding things. They may unintentionally

(continued)

coin a word that is just right for a situation, for example, by calling a sea turtle a "turtlebird" or mashed potatoes "mushed potatoes." Sometimes, they sound like wise philosophers or poets, as when Xavier rejected a hot dog because "the mustard bites my mouth" or when Shandra described the pile of toys in the middle of the classroom floor as "a traffic jam" or when Sam explained that his hair was red "because that's the way the artist made me." Collect these pearls of wisdom to share with parents and to keep in children's portfolios along with their artwork and your notes on their accomplishments. Some teachers make a habit of posting children's words in the classroom so children can see that their words are valued and that they can be captured in print. Be sure to acknowledge the speaker.

This Is a Picture of . . . .   Artwork created by 3-year-olds is not always recognizable. In fact, for many children, a drawing is more about process than product. For example, they may draw a series of dots as they make their felt-tipped marker bunny hop across the page or scribble over the girl they just drew to show that it is raining harder and harder. Talk with children as they draw or paint. Encourage them to tell the story of what they are making. After they have finished, write some of their words as a caption (with their permission, of course). Or ask them to tell about the picture and write down exactly what they say. As you encourage their expressive language, you are also communicating the value of their words and helping them make the connection between written and spoken language.

Puppet Show.   Puppets are a great way to encourage language, for both children who like to perform and those who tend to be shy. A simple way to begin is for the teacher to animate a puppet (or doll or stuffed animal) and begin a conversation with it. Give the puppet a strong character and an appropriate voice. For example, your puppet might be a baby, a bossy child or adult, a grouch, or a clown. Once you have modeled talking to the puppet, you can have the puppet talk with the children. Another approach is for the teacher to talk to a puppet (or doll, stuffed animal, or miniature figure) that a child is playing with, encouraging the child to speak for the puppet.

Song Variations.   Classic preschool songs such as "The Wheels on the Bus" and "Old MacDonald Had a Farm" lend themselves to endless variations and are a great way to reinforce vocabulary. The bus can transport all sorts of people, toys, and animals; the farm can include not only animals but also tractors, lawn mowers, and other equipment. Or the wheels in the song can become those on a train, fire engine, or plane; similarly, Old MacDonald could have a zoo, a birthday party, or a pond instead of a farm.

(continued)

LANGUAGE ACTIVITIES FOR 3-YEAR-OLDS *(continued)*

Sand and Water. Sand and water play are staples of early childhood education. They can also provide wonderful opportunities for language learning—if the teacher gets involved in setting up experiences, engaging children in conversation, and making suggestions to extend the play. The water table can be a bathtub for baby dolls. It can become a laboratory for exploring soap bubble properties, learning about floating and sinking, or mixing colors; or it can become a place for making "rain," waterfalls, whirlpools, and waves. Likewise, the sand box allows for pretend play with cooking and restaurant themes; for experimenting with emptying, filling, molding, and sculpting with different consistencies of sand; and for all kinds of individual and cooperative construction of holes, castles, cities, rivers, dams, roads, tunnels, wedding cakes, and even volcanoes. As children work together, request help or materials, describe their constructions and discoveries, and make plans and predictions, they can learn and practice verbs such as *sift, pour, dump, dig, splatter, splash, sprinkle, drip, dribble, poke, collapse, flow, pat, slosh*, and *leak* as well as adjectives such as *damp, soapy, slippery, slick, rough, sticky, full, squishy, muddy, powdery, bubbly, heavy, deep, upside-down*, and *clean*.

Big Words. Many 3-year-olds fall in love with words, especially big ones. They may learn the names of dinosaurs, planets, different kinds of work trucks, or exotic sea animals. They may repeat impressive-sounding phrases from favorite stories—for example, "chamomile tea" and "Mr. McGregor's garden." In their imaginative play, they may enjoy coming up with crazy new foods like spaghetti sandwiches, watermelon casserole, or spinach ice cream. Encourage this interest by playing along. Sprinkle your conversation with exotic words. Give children the proper names of animals, vehicles, flowers, tools and gadgets, and articles of clothing. As you join children in mini or maxi pretend play, add creative elements that will stretch their vocabularies. "What a great sand castle! I think I'll make mine with some turrets on top. Are you going to build a moat around yours?" "Oh, thank you for the delicious spaghetti. Now I'd like some nice sticky baklava for dessert. Do you make it with honey and cinnamon?"

Make a Scene. Three-year-olds can collaborate on a simple mural if you set the stage. Create a backdrop, which can be as simple as sky and grass. Cut pictures from magazines, or let children use photographs or their own drawings to represent items in the scene. Help the children place the items appropriately and glue or tape them to the mural. Children will enjoy naming the things in their scene and pointing them out for visitors.

(continued)

LANGUAGE ACTIVITIES FOR 3-YEAR-OLDS *(continued)*

Buildarama.   Set aside a low table or a protected area of the classroom where children can build a city, farm, or fantasy world that they do not need to take down. In addition to blocks, give them miniature figures and vehicles, small cardboard boxes, aluminum pie plates, and other unusual materials to work with. As they build, play in, and change their imaginary world, you are likely to hear lots of conversation and have many opportunities to ask open-ended questions and introduce new words.

Ask for Help.   Three-year-olds like to be independent, so most teachers make sure that the things 3-year-olds want to play with are easily accessible. But putting some desirable objects out of reach or in sealed containers can also be a good way to get reluctant talkers to practice using their words. To get what they want, they need to ask for help.

Curiouser and Curiouser.   An obvious way to stimulate children's language and questioning skills is to give them an intriguing object or puzzle. Here are some examples:

- Make "oobleck" by mixing cornstarch and water, adding a little food color if you wish. Encourage children to vary the texture by adding more water or more cornstarch and to talk about what happens. What does the mixture feel like? What happens when you pull, poke, stretch, knead, squish, or mold it?

- Plant a sweet potato or yam in a jar of water, using toothpicks to keep about half of the tuber above the water. After a few days, roots will begin to sprout. Encourage children to talk about the changes they notice and to guess what will happen in the future.

- Put small items in a bag. See whether children can identify them by feel alone. Model the problem-solving process for the children by describing the size, shape, sound, and texture of an item before you guess its name.

- Using a digital camera, take pictures of some common objects. Print out the pictures. Then use the computer to zoom in on part of the picture. See whether the children can match the parts with the wholes. Encourage them to talk together about the details that give them clues.

- Ask parents to help you find mystery objects for the children to explore, describe, identify, and use in building projects and collages. These might be natural objects such as pinecones, seed pods, and shells, unusual tools or kitchen gadgets, magnets and compasses, or parts of defunct machines.

Fluency: 4 Years Through Adulthood

Although 4-year-olds continue to make grammatical and pronunciation errors, most have mastered the basics of their first language and are considered fluent. Their vocabularies, of course, will continue to grow, along with the range of uses to which they can put their language and the facility with which they can interpret as well as use complex constructions and stylistic devices. They are just at the beginning of the fluency stage, but they have learned the language well enough to use it with gusto for their own purposes.

Parents of 4-year-olds are likely to joke that they should not have worked so hard teaching their children to speak because now they cannot "shut them up." With the exception of a few children who are temperamentally shy, 4-year-olds generally enjoy being center stage and will use their facility with words to hold the floor.

Four-year-olds are maturing intellectually as well as linguistically, and their conversation goes well beyond the here and now. They can make up stories, recount events, negotiate roles with their peers, and play out complex scenarios such as the celebration of a birthday party—complete with games, presents, and cake—or a trip to Mars to help an astronaut colony fight off alien invaders. With steadily improving memories, they can learn to recite simple rhymes and may even memorize the words of a favorite book—at least well enough to correct anyone who dares to skip a word or line.

Four-year-olds are unquestionably in the "why" stage. They use their favorite word *why* both to challenge a parent's "no" (e.g., "Why can't I?") and to find out how the world works (e.g., "Why does it get dark at night?" "Why do people have to die?"). They also ask who, what, where, and when questions (e.g., "Where was I before I was born?" "What makes the rain fall out of the sky?" "When is it going to be tomorrow?" and "Who is the boss of the weather?"). By the age of 5, children also tend to have lots of how questions (e.g., "How does a car work? What happens to the gas?" "How do they make candles?" "How do you shoot a layup?" and "How did you do that card trick?") and a lot of questions that show that they have been pondering how the information they have gleaned from various sources fits together (e.g., "What will happen if the Earth gets sucked into a black hole?" "Why does the Moon sometimes look like a ball and sometimes look like a half circle or a crescent?" "Where did dinosaurs choose to lay their eggs?" and "If snow is frozen water, why is it white?").

Although they often miss the point of a joke, 4-year-olds love to join in the laughter. The jokes they like best involve ridiculous names and obvious impossibilities. For example, Caroline, whose big brother had a habit of bringing home stray kittens, thought it was hysterical when her father named them "Corn Flakes," "Pancake," and "Maple Syrup." She loved to repeat her father's joke: "We're having kittens for breakfast."

Some 4-year-olds are beginning to appreciate word play and enjoy repeating simple knock-knock jokes, such as:

Knock, knock.
Who's there?
Banana.
Banana who?
Knock, Knock.
Who's there?
Banana.
Banana who?
Knock, knock.
Who's there?
Orange.
Orange who?
Orange you glad I didn't say banana?

A few children can even create jokes of their own. "See that broken traffic light?" asked one precocious 4-year-old. "Someone went through it." But by far the most typical 4-year-old humor is bathroom humor. Four-year-olds know that just saying a word like "pee-pee" or "poopy caca" is enough to set off a chain of laughter among their classmates.

Given a multistep task such as tying a shoelace (some 4-year-olds can manage this feat but most cannot) or making a bead necklace with a repeating pattern, 4-year-olds can use language to help them remember the steps. By the age of 5, they will learn to use inner language to make plans, to reflect on what they have done, and to solve simple problems. They will also count in their heads (often, with the help of their fingers) rather than count out loud.

The ability to silently talk oneself through a problem is an important development. Children who have had lots of practice thinking out loud develop habits of thought that prepare them to be good problem solvers and critical thinkers.

LANGUAGE ACTIVITIES FOR 4- AND 5-YEAR-OLDS

Language Games. Four-year-olds can hold their own in language-based circle games, as long as the group is not too large. Start with games such as Bear Hunt, where everyone participates together. Then move on to the listening games before attempting those that require creative input.

- *Bear Hunt*—Lead the group on a "bear hunt" by having them repeat each line you say, with appropriate gestures: We're going on a bear hunt, get your camera, ready? Let's go. I see a bridge, can't go under it, can't go around it, gotta go over it, tromp-tromp. I see some tall grass . . . I see a fallen tree . . . I see a cave . . . I see a bear! Run! (Repeat the lines in reverse order, at double speed.) Phew! We made it.

- *Who Stole the Cookies From the Cookie Jar?*—Have the group clap or tap their knees in rhythm as you chant: "Who stole the cookies from the cookie jar?" Without breaking the rhythm, name a child: "Alice stole the cookies from the cookie jar." Alice responds, still in rhythm, "Who me?" You answer, "Yes you." Alice: "Couldn't be." You: "Then who?" Alice chooses another child: "Jason stole the cookies from the cookie jar." And the game continues.

- *Telephone*—Children sit or stand in a circle. The first child whispers a word or short message into the ear of her neighbor. That child then passes on the word or message by whispering to her neighbor, and so on. The last child says the message aloud, and then the first child tells the original message.

- *Categories*—With children seated in a circle, start a rhythm of two knee slaps followed by two claps. When the children are comfortable with the rhythm, begin the chant, speaking only on the claps: "Categories *(knee slap, knee slap)* Names of *(knee slap, knee slap)* animals *(knee slap, knee slap)* such as *(knee slap, knee slap)* Kitten *(knee slap, knee slap)*." The next child in the circle names an animal. If he cannot think of an animal fast enough, he can skip a cycle. If he still cannot think of one, he can say "new category" and name another category.

(continued)

LANGUAGE ACTIVITIES FOR 4- AND 5-YEAR-OLDS *(continued)*

- *I Packed My Bag and in It I Put*—Start a story: "I packed my bag and in it I put some socks." The next person in the circle repeats, "I packed my bag and in it I put," and adds a new item. Children take turns suggesting items. When they have mastered this basic version, turn it into a memory game. Now, each child has to repeat all of the items that have been previously mentioned before adding a new one.

- *Fortunately/Unfortunately*—Start a story such as the following: "Yesterday, I went for a walk to the store. Unfortunately, a *Tyrannosaurus rex* jumped out of the bushes and blocked my path. Fortunately...." The next person in the circle adds a sentence or two, and then says "unfortunately....." Continue alternating *fortunately* and *unfortunately* until everyone has had a chance to contribute.

Books on Tape. Buy or make tapes of children's favorite books so they can listen and "read" along. Be sure that the tapes signal when to turn the pages.

Act Out a Story. In their pretend play, 4-year-olds often replay stories they have heard or have seen on TV or in movies. But acting out a story with several characters can be a challenge. One way to make it easier is for the teacher to act as narrator and then cue the children when to act out their roles or say their lines. A simple folk story such as "The Three Billy Goats Gruff" or "The Three Little Pigs" works well because the lines are few and easy to remember.

Act Out My Story. Four-year-olds can dictate simple stories. One way to make this activity even more rewarding is to start a Playwriting Club. After dictating a story to an adult, each author in the club selects classmates to act it out. The teacher acts as narrator, reading the story and cuing the actors.

Same and Different. A common preschool learning activity is to ask children to find two things that are the same or to identify the item in a group that is different. This activity takes many forms, including lotto games, matching games, card games such as Go Fish or Old Maid, opposite puzzles, worksheets, and sorting tasks. Usually, these games involve shapes, colors, and simple pictures. Using pictures from real life can make these games much more interesting and elicit much richer language. The child has to look carefully at the pictures and find something that is the same or something that is different. For example, two pictures might each show three people eating; however, in one picture,

(continued)

LANGUAGE ACTIVITIES FOR 4- AND 5-YEAR-OLDS *(continued)*

they are eating with their fingers, and in the other, they are using chopsticks. You can cut interesting pictures from magazines or calendars or download them from the Internet and paste them onto index cards to make simple games.

Sequence Puzzles. Take pictures of the children as they work on building, cooking, or art projects. Be sure to get photos of the beginning preparation, the execution of key steps, and the enjoyment of the final result. Have children work in pairs to put the pictures in order.

Collective Journal. After an exciting experience such as a field trip, group project, or visit from someone in the community, have the class write a collective journal entry. You might use large chart paper to record their words, or you can capture them on a computer. Let each child voluntarily contribute a memory or impression, and put her name next to the contribution. Post the journal in a public place, along with photographs, drawings, or souvenirs.

Working Together. Preschoolers are natural collaborators in their pretend play, but they also enjoy collaborative problem solving. Activities such as the following give children practice with using language to solve problems:

- Engage a group of three or four children in putting together a large puzzle such as a floor puzzle or a 30-piece table puzzle. Give each child some of the pieces.

- Give each of three or four children blocks of a different shape. Challenge the group to use all of the blocks to build a bridge or to make the tallest building they can that will stay up.

- Ask a group of children to sort out some game pieces or miniature toys that have gotten mixed up.

- Give each of two children a different paint color. Have them share an easel and paint a picture together.

- Put several items in a grab bag—for example, miniature plastic foods, vehicles, people, or animals. Ask each child to pull two items out of the bag. With two or three children in a group, let the children either tell or act out a story using some or all of the items that they have selected.

Learning to Listen. Four-year-olds can be such eager talkers that sometimes you also need to help them listen or wait their turns in a group. Here are some techniques that experienced teachers have found effective:

(continued)

LANGUAGE ACTIVITIES FOR 4- AND 5-YEAR-OLDS (*continued*)

- *Magic Dust*—Before beginning a lesson or reading a story, tell the children that you have some imaginary "magic dust" that will help them listen closely and remember what they hear. Offer the "dust" to each child individually and sprinkle those who want it. Be sure to make eye contact with each child when you are "sprinkling" and again as you begin the lesson or reading.

- *Circle Seating*—To keep children from all crowding in to see the book you are reading or the intriguing object you are holding, have them sit in a circle on pillows or carpet squares. If they get too excited, you can remind them that you will show the pictures or pass around the object when everyone is on their seats so they can all see.

- *Raising Hands*—Most elementary school teachers ask children to raise their hands and wait to be called on before speaking in a large group. When working with the class as a whole, you can ask the children whether they would like to try this technique so everyone can get a turn to speak. If you involve children in establishing the hand-raising rule, you are less likely to quash their spontaneity.

- *Listening Corner*—Set aside a corner of the room for quiet, private conversations. If a child has a lot to say and the group is losing interest, tell the child you would like to hear the rest of the story later and that you'll meet him in the "listening corner." The child may want to dictate the story to you, tell it into a tape recorder, or just continue the conversation.

Class Books. Capitalize on the children's love of riddles, jokes, and little-known facts by making some class books of their favorites. Let children illustrate the riddles, jokes, and facts that they and their friends contribute. You can add these books to your permanent collection and share them at reading time. Or you can have copies printed for the whole class so each child can take one home.

LEARNING TOGETHER

E very conversation that you have with a baby or young child is a learning opportunity—for both of you. You learn something about what the child wants, enjoys, cares about, thinks, remembers, imagines, or wants to know and how she is making sense of her world. At the same time, you have the opportunity to provide her with the communication practice, interesting vocabulary, and word and sound play that build the foundation for literacy.

Reflection

Think about a conversation you had with a child that was especially memorable.

How did the conversation get started?

What did you learn about the child through the conversation?

What was remarkable about the conversation?

REFERENCES

Dickinson, D. K., & Tabors, P. O. (2001). *Beginning literacy with language.* Baltimore: Paul H. Brookes.

Goleman, D. (1995). *Emotional intelligence: Why it can matter more than IQ.* New York: Bantam Books.

Helburn, S. W., & Bergmann, B. R. (2002). *America's child care problem: The way out.* New York: Palgrave Macmillan.

Hart, B., & Risley, T. R. (1995). *Meaningful differences in the everyday experiences of young American children.* Baltimore: Paul H. Brookes.

Pinker, S. (1995). *The language instinct: How the mind creates language.* New York: Perennial.

Rodgers, R., & Hammerstein, O. (1949/1998). Happy talk [music by Richard Rodgers, lyrics by Oscar Hammerstein II, recorded by Muriel Smith]. On *South Pacific—Original Broadway Cast* [CD]. Culver City, CA: Sony. (Original release date: 1949).

Snow, C. E., Burns, M. S., & Griffin, P. (Eds.). (1998). *Preventing reading difficulties in young children.* Report of the Committee on the Prevention of Reading Difficulties in Young Children, convened by the National Research Council. Washington, DC: National Academy Press.

CHAPTER 5

Classroom Conversations

Questions

How can I go to sleep at night?
How can I go to bed?
When oh so many puzzling things
Keep churning in my head.
Today turns into yesterday
And here turns into there;
Tomorrow never comes at all;
I do not think it's fair.

—MARILYN SEGAL (2000)

L anguage can be amazing, yet it is so pervasive that we tend to take it for granted. When we tell jokes, write poetry, or mediate a conflict, we choose our words carefully. Most of the time, though, our focus is on the content of the message—not on how it is phrased. For children, too, the point of language is not to learn it, but to use it. And the very best way to learn or teach language is to use it in meaningful contexts.

Classrooms and family child-care homes where children thrive are filled with genuine conversations. Teachers talk with children frequently because they are curious about what the children are thinking. Children talk frequently with adults because they have ideas and experiences that they want to share and questions that need answers. Children talk constantly with one another because that is how they play. Everybody's minds are churning, and everyone is having fun.

CONNECTING WITH CHILDREN

M s. Newby was worried. She had worked hard on her curriculum, and her classroom of 3-year-olds was very busy. The children started coming at 8:00, and by the time she got them all settled in for circle time, it was nearly 9:00. At 9:30, they went outside, and then, before she knew it, it was time for hand-washing and snack. By the time she got through reading time, music, lunch, nap time, art activities, and cleanup, the day was gone. "How will I ever get to know these children?" Mrs. Newby wondered. "I never get a chance to talk with them!"

Even in the busiest toddler and preschool classrooms, a well-organized teacher can find time to engage with each child, not just for a few minutes, but many times each day. The key is to balance activities involving the whole group (including moving from one place to another) with lots of time for children to choose their own activities and play together in small groups. Teachers engage individual children in conversation when they greet them in the morning; change their diapers; help them with dressing and hand-washing tasks; solicit their help with meal preparation, serving, and clean-up; help them select and complete activities; read the stories they request; accompany them on walks; answer their questions; and respond to their bids for attention, comfort, or assistance. But the best time for conversations is playtime!

The following example is taken from the Home-School Study of Language and Literacy Development, as reported in *Beginning Literacy With Language* (Dickinson & Tabors, 2001, p. 239). This book presents the results of a longitudinal study of low-income children's home and school language experiences and identify the teaching strategies that proved to most effectively foster robust vocabulary development in the preschool years and literacy success in the early elementary grades. In this excerpt, we see how a teacher, Ann, introduces words such as *daring* and *oxygen tanks* into two 4-year-olds' pretend game, expanding the children's vocabulary and, at the same time, making their play more interesting:

Ann: You must be very brave and daring men to go down there and take all these sharks back to the special place.

Casey: We're protecting them.

Ann: Do you have to wear special suits? What kind do you wear in the water?

Bryan: I wear climbing.

Ann: A climbing suit?

Casey: Yeah.

Ann: What do you wear?

Casey: A shark suit.

Ann: Those things on your back. Are those oxygen tanks? To help you breathe underwater?

Bryan: They can breathe underwater.

Ann: Wow, that's a special trick to learn to do. (Dickinson, 2001)

In this example, Ann entered the play as an observer who was trying to make sense of the scene. Teachers can also enter as participants by taking on a role. Children especially enjoy having adults as "customers," and this role enables teachers to make all kinds of requests that expand both the children's play scenario and their language. For example, as a customer at the gas station, the teacher might need her tires inflated, her windshield wipers replaced, the hole in her noisy muffler repaired, and her oil changed so her engine will run smoothly.

When a young child is busy at play, an adult's participation is almost always welcome. Because the conversation centers on what the child is doing, it holds his interest and furthers his purposes. In the beginning, a child's contribution to the conversation may be nonverbal. For example, a 2-year-old is quietly feeding a baby doll a bottle. "Oh," says her teacher, "Your baby loves the way you are giving her the bottle." The child then picks up the doll and burps it. "You were right," the teacher responds. "Your baby doll needed to burp."

As the child becomes more verbal, his contribution to the conversation may come to include words as well as actions:

David: (*sitting on a riding toy*) Vroom, vroom.

Teacher: You're driving fast today, David.

David: (*turning wheel back and forth*) Vroom. Vroom-vroom.

Teacher: Where are you going?

David: I go McDonald's.

Teacher: You're going to McDonald's? Are you going to get French fries?

David: (*riding over to the play kitchen*) I get French fries.

Teacher: Can you get some for me, too?

David: (*handing his teacher some play food*) Here French fries.

Teacher: Do you have any salt?

David: (*handing her an imaginary salt shaker*) Here salt.

Teacher: (*sprinkling "salt" on the fries and taking an imaginary bite*) Thank you. These are delicious.

David: Want more?

The first and most important step in engaging a young child in conversation is to stoop down to her level and make eye contact.

Once she has acknowledged your presence by looking or speaking, the conversation can begin. The child may initiate the conversation by telling you something, asking you a question, or making a gesture—such as offering you a toy—that invites a response.

Often, a child will acknowledge your presence with a brief glance, then go back to her solitary play. Then it is up to you to initiate the conversation. Your opening line is most likely to be successful if it acknowledges his play world. You can begin by asking a question (e.g., "Is something wrong with Teddy, doctor?") or by making a comment (e.g., "I see you are examining Teddy's ears. I hope he doesn't have an ear infection.").

As you join the child at play, your role will shift from observer and commentator to prop getter and playmate. As you bring new props, play out a role, ask questions, and make suggestions, you will have opportunities to get to know the child and to expand both his language and his imaginative play.

Circles of Communication

Stanley Greenspan is a child and adolescent psychiatrist who has made a career of working with young children, particularly children who have had difficulties with communication. He and his colleagues describe interchanges similar to the one between David and his teacher in terms of circles of communication (Greenspan, Wieder, & Simmons, 1998). Noticing David's play, his teacher initiated an interchange or "opened a circle." David responded nonverbally by turning the wheel and making sound effects in a way that showed he had understood what his teacher said. His response "closed" the circle. His teacher then opened another circle by asking a question. David's response closed that circle in a way that kept the conversation going. His teacher picked up on his idea, closing his circle and opening a new one. The conversation continued as a chain of circles, each linked to the one before.

Conversations that "go somewhere" involve chains of opened and closed circles. Children need to have these kinds of conversations many times each day. With practice, children learn to sustain longer and longer chains, holding up their end with responses that close one circle and open another.

Asking Questions

Maisha, who had just turned 1, was looking at a catalog with her teacher. When they came to the page with a watch on it, Maisha pointed to the picture. "That's a watch," said her teacher. Maisha repeated "watch" and looked at her teacher for approval. "Look," said her teacher, extending her hand. "I have a watch, too." Then she held the watch to Maisha's ear. Maisha listened intently to the ticking, then put her ear to the book. Her question was obvious. "Does this one tick, too?"[1]

Children's questions are gifts. They provide windows into their growing minds and open communication circles that become teaching opportunities. Our answers to these questions can keep curiosity alive. In addition to supplying the requested knowledge, our responses can fuel the child's eagerness to learn and affirm the child's sense of himself as a person with important ideas.

Of course, as in the example above, children's questions do not always begin with who, what, when, where, why, what if, or how come. They may also be gestures (such as a point, quizzical look, or shrug), experiments (such as dropping a toy from a highchair or pulling on a cord to see what happens), tentative statements (such as, "Trees make the wind blow, right?"), or hypotheses (such as, "I think the penny will sink 'cuz it's heavy").

As teachers, we not only *give* answers but also help children to *find* answers. When children discover the results of their experiments and explorations, we can give them words to describe what happened and provide opportunities for further exploration.

Teachers can also extend children's knowledge and language facility by asking *them* questions:

- What did your Daddy say when you showed him the picture you drew in school?

- What sorts of things does your family like to save?

- Why do you think our play dough got sticky?

---

[1]This story comes from Reggio Emilia, Italy, and is told through photographs as part of the Reggio Emilia *The Hundred Languages of Children* exhibit. The sequence of photos is also shown in *ReChild*, Number 5, October 2001, pp. 2–12. Retrieved from http://zerosei.comune.re.it/pdfs/rechild05.pdf on July 30, 2004.

- How can we fix your tower so it is not so tippy?

- How can we help Amanda feel better?

- What else do we need for our grocery store?

- How do you think the story will end?

Open-ended questions such as these invite conversation. We ask them because we really want to know the answers.

In contrast, some of the questions that adults ask children are focused on compliance. We want to find out whether or not a child did something she was supposed to do (or not supposed to do). "Did you remember to wash your hands?" "Did you give my note to your mother?" This type of question is usually answered with one or two words or, at most, a brief phrase: "Yes," "Not yet," "She wasn't home."

Other questions are more like quizzes. "What color is this block?" "Where is the puppy hiding?" "What does the cow say?" Although children may sound enthusiastic when they shout out the answer, they seldom expand on their answers or engage in a conversation. However, when teachers ask open-ended questions, they are inviting a response that could be the starting point of a real conversation—and a real learning opportunity.

The following two conversations start at the same place, with a child's excited announcement that her family got a new puppy. One conversation is full of questions with short answers that eventually lose the child's interest. The teacher seems to be working quite hard to keep the conversation going. In the second, the teacher responds to the child's excitement and asks open-ended questions to help her tell her story. The child uses much more language, and both teacher and child are engaged.

Conversation 1: Short Answer Questions

    Child: We got a new puppy yesterday.

Teacher: What's your puppy's name?

    Child: Snoopy.

Teacher: Is Snoopy a boy puppy or a girl puppy?

    Child: A girl puppy.

Teacher: What color is Snoopy?

Child: Black and white.

Teacher: What kind of dog is she?

Child: I dunno.

Conversation 2: Open-Ended Questions

Child: We got a new puppy yesterday.

Teacher: Wow. I know you've been wanting a pet for a long time. How did you get the puppy?

Child: Daddy took me to that place, where they have pets that get lost and they can't find their owners.

Teacher: Yeah. The pound, they have lots of pets there. How did you decide which one to get?

Child: There were lots of dogs and cats. Snoopy was the cutest. And she liked me!

Teacher: I bet she liked you. How did you know? What did she do?

Child: She kept wagging her tail and running around her cage. When they let her out, she climbed in my lap and licked my face!

Reflection

What is the most interesting conversation you had with a child lately? What did you learn? What do you think the child learned? How can you follow up the conversation and extend the learning?

TALKING ABOUT FEELINGS, EXPECTATIONS, AND TIME

Small children have intense feelings, but they often lack the words to describe them. Teachers can help by giving them the words. "I can see you are very angry now." "That's a beautiful picture. I bet you feel really proud." "I know you wanted to go out on the playground today, but it's raining much too hard. I'm sorry that you are disappointed." Showing children photos of people with different expressions can also help them to recognize and name emotional states, as can reading stories and talking about how the characters feel. Once children learn to talk about their feelings, they can more easily communicate bad or hurt feelings with other children without getting physical. "I don't like it when you snatch my toy. It makes me mad and sad."

Puppet play can be especially useful for dealing with emotional issues. A helpless or cranky baby doll can elicit comforting and nurturing. A greedy puppet who hogs all the toys can encourage children to talk about the importance of sharing. A friendly puppet can draw out a child who is feeling shy, a silly puppet can make a sad child laugh, and a sad puppet can help children understand what it feels like to be teased.

One of the hardest feelings for young children to handle is frustration. When something does not work the way it is supposed to, when they just cannot make that puzzle piece fit, or when the building they worked so hard on collapses, they are apt to dissolve into tears. Fortunately, young children are also very creative and suggestible. A toddler who is about to cry can be prompted to "use your words" to ask for help instead. The collapsed building can become a mountain for the trucks to drive on, and the child will be all smiles.

Waiting is another challenge—and another place where words can help. Knowing that the field trip will be "tomorrow," that Daddy will pick them up "after lunch," and that they can go out to the playground "as soon as we finish cleaning up" helps children to feel in control, anticipate exciting events, and tolerate the wait. However, because young children do not have a good sense of time, their judgment about how long it takes for something to happen is determined by how much they like what they are doing rather than by how much clock time has passed. On the one hand, if mother tells a child that his friend will be over in 10 minutes, he might ask his mother every 2 minutes where his friend is. On the other hand, if his mother tells him that he has only 10 more minutes to play before bedtime, the child will protest vehemently when his mother announces 15 minutes later that it is bedtime. "But, Mommy, you promised me I still had 10 minutes to play."

THINKING THINGS THROUGH

F our-year-old Darryl listened closely as his teacher explained about plants and animals. Suddenly, his eyes grew wide, and he blurted out with excitement: "I'm alive. I eat. I breathe. I move. I must be an animal!" Darryl's reasoning showed that he had really understood the lesson. He knew that animals were living things that could eat, move, and breathe, and could apply the concept to himself, though he did not usually think of himself as an "animal." Darryl beamed with pride as his delighted teacher praised his "good thinking."

At 4, Darryl had mastered the rudiments of logical thinking: He understood that items in a category share common characteristics, and he could reason that something that shared the defining characteristics of a category belonged in that group. Younger children are apt to have a logic of their own, which can lead to amusing conclusions. The following vignette provides an example:

T hree-year-old Jennifer had heard enough talk about the impending hurricane. "They say the eye might come right over us." "Maybe, or it could change course and go out to sea." "We'd better get prepared, anyway. Have you stocked up?" "Cheese is good for hurricanes." "Stop!," Jennifer cried. "Make the hurricane go away!" "Do you know what a hurricane is?" her mother asked gently. "Yes," stated Jennifer emphatically. "It's a one-eyed monster that eats cheese and doesn't know where it's going!"

Parents and teachers are often amazed at how much children grasp. At the same time, we are constantly reminded how new things are for young children and how much needs explaining. At our best, we go beyond giving children words and, instead, help them to really understand. In an interview for a television special, the physicist Richard Feynman explained how his father had taught him to think when he was a very young child:

Even when I was a small boy [my father] used to sit me on his lap and read to me from the *Encyclopedia Britannica*, and we would read, say, about dinosaurs, and maybe it would be talking about . . . the *Tyrannosaurus rex,* and it would say something like, "This thing is 25 feet high and the head is 6 feet across," . . . he'd stop and say, "Let's see what that means. That would mean that if he stood in our front yard he would be high enough to put his head through the window but not quite because the head is a little bit too wide and it would break the window." . . . Everything we'd read would be translated as best we could into some reality and so I learned to do that—everything that I read I try to figure out what it really means. (Feynman & Robbins, 2000, p. 3)

Although we often "think aloud," much of the language that we use as adults remains inside our heads. We use inner language to reason and explain, to recall past events and experiences, to solve problems, and to make plans. Young children use inner language to guide their behavior and also, like us, to remember, review, reason, and plan.

Most children begin to use inner language at about age 2. For a long time, they are not aware of the fact that they use inner language. They often speak it aloud. For example, it is quite common for a 2-year-old to tell herself "No," "Hot," or "Don't touch" when faced with a tempting object. Three- and 4-year olds can talk themselves through problem-solving situations such as putting together a puzzle or stringing beads in a pattern. "Turn it around. The fat part goes on top." "Red, red, blue. Red, red, blue."

Using language to reason, as Darryl did when he figured out that he was an animal, takes lots of practice. Children who get good at talking through problems become adept at thinking through problems. And children who hear adults talk through problems learn to talk through problems themselves.

Challenging children to think about how to solve a problem, recall a past event, or make a plan for the future helps them to develop inner language and to become aware of its power. Hearing how other children recall or explain past events, think through problems, and formulate plans helps children realize that people can think differently and approach problems in different ways. They learn that, just as they, themselves, use language to formulate their thoughts, so do other people. For example, consider the following vignette:

> E duardo and his father were walking to the park. Eduardo's friend, Pedro, who had his new puppy on a leash, was going with them. Eduardo was mad because Pedro would not let him have a turn to hold the puppy's leash. "You're a meany," he shouted at his friend. "You got to give me a turn!" Eduardo's father intervened. "You feel angry," he said to his son. "You would really like to have a turn walking the puppy." "Yeah, I want my turn!" Pedro responded. "Yes, I know you want a turn. Why do you suppose Pedro won't let you walk his dog?" "Because he is a meany and he doesn't want to share." "Can you think of another reason?" "Cause he's scared that his puppy'll run away." "You are probably right," his father agreed. "Why don't you ask Pedro if you could both hold the leash?"

Using Rare Words and Decontextualized Dialogue

T he Home-School Study of Language and Literacy Development (as reported in Dickinson & Tabors, 2001) demonstrated the importance of asking young children open-ended, intellectually challenging questions and of seizing opportunities to elaborate their play. The study also underlined the importance of using rare and interesting words with children. When working with young children, we tend to simplify our speech so they will understand us. Often, we limit our vocabularies to words that they already know. This approach turns out to be a mistake. Young children who hear a variety of words in meaningful conversation learn many new words each day. They readily learn the names of their classmates and of the dolls, action figures, animals, vehicles, and storybook characters that become their "friends." Many 3- and 4-year-olds become fascinated with words, especially with those that are long and hard to say. Indeed, part of the reason why dinosaurs are so appealing to so many children may be that they have such long and interesting names.

Teachers who use rich, descriptive language in their ordinary conversations with children find that children pick up descriptive words and names when the context makes their meanings clear. And researchers find that children who know a wide range of words as preschoolers become better readers and writers than those with more limited early vocabularies (Hart & Risley, 1995; Snow, Burns, & Griffin, 1998).

Another feature of language that makes a difference in children's literacy development is whether it goes beyond the here and now to talk about the past or future, about imaginary situations or possibilities, or about abstract ideas. Dickinson and Tabors (2001) refer to this as "decontextualized language" if it goes beyond the immediate situation or context that its speaker and listener are sharing. They find that children who get more experience with decontextualized language in preschool become more adept learners in elementary school. Not only have they learned the forms of words that indicate past, future, "may be," and "might have been," but they have also practiced using language to recall events, conjure up imaginary worlds, ask and answer open-ended questions, make predictions, and think through problems.

Reflection

Choose a simple activity that you enjoy doing with children—for example, making play dough or cookies, building a sand castle or block city, or taking a walk around the block. List 10–20 interesting words that you might use to describe what you are doing; what you see, hear, feel, taste, and smell; or what you created.

HELPING CHILDREN CONNECT WITH ONE ANOTHER

The conversations that occur among children can be as significant a source of learning as conversations between children and adults. Children learn new words, phrases, and verbal routines from one another, and their shared play gives them an opportunity to practice the language they know. Most important, though, peer play provides an arena for communication, negotiation, problem solving, imagination, and decontextualized conversation that can rarely be equaled by teacher-directed activity.

Young children seem drawn to one another. Babies carry on "conversations" with each other by imitating each other's actions, expressions, and outbursts. Toddlers may connect by showing each other their belly buttons, saying each other's names, engaging in impromptu games of chase or follow the leader, or exchanging a few words as they play side by side.

Preschoolers can use words to initiate and maintain relationships. They can exchange ideas and information, issue orders and invitations, negotiate sharing and turn taking, and plan and act out imaginative play scenarios.

Creating Settings for Conversation and Play

Most preschool classrooms and many family child-care homes contain a "house corner," with a play kitchen, cooking utensils, play food, dolls, and perhaps a cradle, shopping cart, riding toy, play keys, and cash register. Children readily engage in the cooking, eating, shopping, and care-taking play that this kind of corner suggests. Simple additions can encourage more varied play and can induce children to practice a wider vocabulary. Menus, writing pads, and trays can suggest a restaurant theme. A length of hose and some hats can turn the restaurant into a fire station; a doctor's kit or even some bandages and empty bottles can suggest a hospital, doctor's office, or veterinary clinic; pictures, artifacts, and ethnic foods can build connections to children's home cultures or spark a trip to an exotic locale. Combining two themes—for example, setting up a home and a fire station or a store and a spaceship—can lead to exciting, language-rich interactions when the homebodies report a fire in the kitchen or the astronauts shop for supplies for their journey.

Another common classroom feature is the "block area," where children can construct their own mini-play worlds from an array of small props and building materials. Working alone or in groups of two or three, children will build racetracks, zoos, sports stadiums, dinosaur museums, and even whole fairy lands. Each project carries with it the opportunity to practice specialized vocabulary and the opportunity for a tuned-in teacher to comment on the construction, suggest new elements, and contribute new words. The sandbox and art area provide similar opportunities for children to represent their ideas and for teachers to introduce new words as they help the children explain and elaborate their representations.

Researchers have found that children converse more when they are engaged in a collaborative project than when they are just playing side by side. Furthermore, some settings are especially conducive to collaboration and conversation:

- A sandbox tends to elicit more conversation than a water table because children are more likely to engage in joint building projects or to connect their individual constructions.

- Computers can elicit a surprising amount of conversation, more than any other area in some studies—depending, of course, on the software. Open-ended games, with lots of visual surprises and decision points, encourage children to make predictions, share discoveries, and discuss courses of action.

- Forts, playhouses, lofts, and other quiet, sheltered spaces encourage private conversations and small-group interaction.

- A writing center where children can make cards, books, labels, lists, signs (such as "Leave Up," "Don't Touch," or "Hammy the Hamster"), and props for pretend play (such as treasure maps, play tickets, restaurant menus, and road signs) encourages conversation as well as reading, letter naming, and writing.

- A simple stage (any raised area will do) or puppet stage (cut from a cardboard box) encourages children to put on shows. Most of the conversation will occur in the planning and rehearsal stages.

- Bulletin-board displays of various sorts can encourage children to talk with one another about the pictures. By far the most generative are pictures of the children themselves.

- Pictures taken at a field trip or special event will elicit lots of storytelling and "decontextualized talk" as children recall the experience.

- A block city or miniworld that can be kept up for a week or so elicits more conversation than does a building area that has to be cleaned up each day. If you can set aside a low table or platform, children can combine blocks, recycled materials, miniature animals, vehicles, and figures, as well as other odds and ends to create an interesting fantasy world. This activity will elicit not only lots of ongoing fantasy play but also discussions about what needs to be added and joint problem solving around how to build the desired additions.

Infusing play areas and displays with content related to what children are learning—or better yet, letting the children participate in the process—enhances the likelihood that children will use rare words in their conversations. For example, you might help the children transform the house corner into a gas station and automotive repair shop, build a farm in the block corner or at the sand table, or turn a loft into a space station with views of stars and planets.

Helping Children Get Started

When children are playing together in a pretend play center, the teacher can jumpstart a conversation by suggesting a common goal that requires communication. For example, if two children are playing with play food, the teacher could encourage them to plan a picnic. "Today looks like a fun day to go to the beach. Why don't you two decide what kinds of supplies you will need to pack up for your picnic?" After a while, children who have gotten to know one another will learn to engage in conversations during play without any prompting from the teacher.

Teachers can also help children "use their words" when they are upset by another child's words or actions. A child may come to the teacher complaining that one of his friends will not share a toy. Instead of stepping in, the teacher can suggest a way for the child to handle the problem. "Maybe you could ask him, 'Can I have that toy when you finish your turn?'"

Facilitating Group Conversations

When the whole class is together, it is difficult for everyone to participate in the conversation. Some children have a lot to say and want to monopolize the discussion. Others patiently wait their turns but may forget what they wanted to say before they can get a chance to say it. Still others lose interest or change the subject. Small groups of three to five people make conversations much easier, especially when children are engaged in a joint project or game.

Even in small groups, it is often a challenge to get reluctant talkers to participate and to help children accept taking turns when they like to monopolize the conversation. Children may also need to learn how to stick to the point. A conversation does not occur if one child says, "I am making a birthday cake," and the child beside her says, "Our puppy chewed up Daddy's slipper." Ideally, teachers should eavesdrop for a while to get a sense of how children themselves are handling these challenges. Then, if intervention seems warranted, the teacher can gently slow down the talkative child, redirect the off-topic child, or make a space for a shy child who seems to want to say something. "Let's hear what Brian thinks about that." Sometimes, the best thing a teacher can do is to leave; when children are not vying for the teacher's attention, they are more likely to talk with one another.

However, when children are busy pretending together, the teacher can often extend the play by providing a helping hand. "Hey, fishermen, do you need some more bait? We have some minnows at our shop that the big fish really go for." A teacher can often help a shy child join the play by setting up a role for him that complements what other children are doing.

Understanding Conversational Styles

Children's conversational styles are determined in part by temperamental characteristics. Some children are temperamentally shy and passive. Some children are fearful and engage slowly in new experiences. Some children are flexible and enjoy social interactions. Some children are feisty and like to be the boss.

- Children who are flexible enjoy social interactions. They will not only initiate conversations but also respond positively when another child initiates the conversation.

- Children who are shy or passive will respond to an initiation but are unlikely to initiate the conversation.

- Children who are fearful or "slow to warm up" may take a long time to get comfortable with potential playmates. They are unlikely to initiate the conversation and may be slow in responding to initiation.

- Children who are feisty tend to take charge and insist on directing the play. They are quite likely to initiate the conversation but less likely to wait for a response.

Age, gender, culture, familiarity, prior experience, and group composition also make a difference:

- Older children tend to use more words and are less dependent on props or shared context. They are also more aware of the listener's perspective and tend to be more tuned in to the listener's response.

- Girls are often more verbal than same-age boys and may be better at using words to express feelings, maintain relationships, and play out elaborate, detailed scenarios. Boys often include more action in their play and may happily construct stories with their friends that jump wildly from one brief, exciting episode to another.

- Children's styles of conversation and play reflect their culture's unspoken rules about who initiates interaction with whom under what circumstances; what behaviors and interactions are acceptable for boys or for girls; appropriate topics for conversation and pretending; acceptable voice volume and body language; proper greetings and leave-takings; and use of slang, stock phrases, and nicknames. Children whose home cultures are different from the prevailing school culture may learn to use different approaches with different people or in different settings.

- Children who play together often may develop their own routines, codes, and rhythms of conversation. They are likely to engage in pretend play activities that stretch across several days.

- Children who spend a lot of time watching television may fixate on cartoon show actions, sound effects, and stock phrases and storylines. They may need adult help to diversify their play and encourage their creativity.

- Children who have had lots of practice with adults and other children, who have been coached in including their play-partner's ideas and taking account of his wishes, or who have learned lots of stories tend to be better at coming up with fun play ideas and at keeping the conversation going.

TEACHING TECHNIQUES: WORKING WITH CHILDREN IN GROUPS

Child-initiated play is a rich source of language development, especially when teachers are actively involved in creating the setting, helping children get started, facilitating group conversations, adding ideas to extend the play, and attending to individual conversational styles. But teacher-initiated conversation and instruction are also important. The classrooms and family child-care homes that are most effective in promoting language development include a well-planned curriculum and intentional teaching. In addition to setting up interesting environments and challenges and encouraging children's efforts, effective teachers also model, demonstrate, question, explain, and instruct. The whole group is brought together for "lessons" or "circle time," and small groups are engaged in learning tasks and teacher-led conversations that are filled with open-ended questions.

Elaine Weitzman and Janice Greenberg, in *Learning Language and Loving It* (2002), describe the SSCAN technique for interacting with children in groups (p. 152):

- Small groups work best.

- Set up an appropriate activity.

- Carefully observe each child's level of participation and interaction.

- Adapt your response to each child's needs.

- Now keep it going!

Effective Teaching Techniques

After reviewing an extensive body of research on preschool curriculum and teaching methods, the authors of *Eager to Learn: Educating Our Preschoolers* (Bowman, Donovan, & Burns, 2000) concluded that a variety of effective methods could be used for teaching young children in groups. Although no one approach was best for every child or every teacher, a planned curriculum and intentional instruction were essential.

Getting Attention. Effective teachers know how to get and hold children's attention. Recognizing that most young children are not very good at paying attention while an adult is talking to a group, teachers attract children's attention rather than demand it. The late Mr. Rogers was a master at this technique: He made every child feel as if he were talking only to her and as if he really cared about what she had to say. He looked directly at the camera, making eye contact with his television audience. He "took his time," but also kept the pace varied and the "lessons" short. He engaged children with high interest content and with people, pictures, books, objects, and puppets. He explained things carefully, without talking down to children. Still, some children found his pace too slow and preferred a more upbeat approach.

Call and Response. Although open-ended questions should predominate, games in which the teacher asks a question and the class shouts the answer in chorus can be useful for helping children master specific information and vocabulary. "What animal is this?" "A panda." "And what do pandas eat?" "Bamboo!" This fast-paced back-and-forth drill echoes the "call-and-response" techniques used by traditional storytellers and inspirational speakers in many cultures and religious groups. Children who are familiar with these practices may find this style of learning more comfortable than being asked questions individually in a group setting.

Repetition. Children learn through repetition. Going over the same material in different ways helps to make it stick. Young children also

A skilled teacher monitors each child's interest and uses a variety of techniques to hold their attention.

enjoy going over the same material in the same way. They often memorize favorite books and delight in being able to join in the "reading."

Music and Movement. Music and movement games can be effective ways of introducing or reviewing information and vocabulary. For example, after a field trip to a local fire station, the children might help make up a song about "The Wheels on the Fire Engine," complete with appropriate motions and sound effects.

Reflection. The High/Scope approach (High/Scope Educational Research Foundation, 2004), a well-researched set of techniques and activities that have proven effective in infant, toddler, preschool, and primary grade programs, includes a formula that is played out several times each day: Plan, Work, Reflect. Children plan what they want to do, do it, and then talk about what they learned and what they are going to do next. Reflection is a critical part of the process. Children think aloud about what happened, what worked, what surprised them, what they would want to do differently. As they reflect, they are using decontextualized language, reviewing what they have learned, thinking through problems, and often using rare words. But to the child and his classmates, reflection is just a time to share discoveries!

Learning Through Play. Play is the way that young children learn. Adults can add ideas, challenges, rare words, toys and materials, storylines, and exciting things to discover. They can give instructions or suggestions and can model behavior. But ultimately, the words and concepts and activities that interest the children—those that are fun to say, do, and share and that become part of the children's own projects and adventures—are the ones that will stick.

Suggested Activities and Approaches for Children With Special Needs

Learning to speak and to exchange meaningful communications is a critical task for young children. It is not always easy. Because language and communication are so fundamental to both academic and social–emotional learning, problems need be caught and addressed early. Language–communication delay is the most common condition for which children receive early intervention referrals. In most cases, early intervention is successful, especially when teachers and parents also understand the problem and use effective intervention techniques. Some of the communication challenges listed below are characteristic of children with handicapping conditions such as hearing impairment, attention deficit disorder, cerebral palsy, or autism spectrum disorder. Other challenges are more likely to be considered temporary conditions. In either case, teachers, caregivers, and parents can make a difference by incorporating therapeutic techniques into everyday routines, games, and conversations.

Child Who Does Not Make Eye Contact or Who Speaks Nonstop Without Waiting for a Response

Most children acquire the "rules of conversation" naturally, by engaging in cooing, babbling, and peekaboo games as infants; playing hiding, chasing, pointing, and labeling games as toddlers; and moving on to question-and-answer exchanges and cooperative games as preschoolers. A few children, however, need to be taught these basics:

- A conversation requires that one person initiates the conversation and the second person responds.

- Conversations require joint attention. Both parties must establish eye contact before a conversation can begin.

- A conversation requires turn taking and the recognition of the appropriate time to take a turn.

Child Who Is Nonverbal

Children who are nonverbal can carry on a conversation through gestures, body language, and facial expressions. A good way to carry on a conversation with a nonverbal child is to watch for and respond to her cues. If a child startles when she hears a loud noise, you might say, "That is a loud noise. Let's cover our ears." If a child pushes his dish away before finishing his meal, you might say, "You don't want to eat any more. Would you like to play?" If the child then responds by looking at the toys, bring him over to the toys, saying, "Let's find a toy." Nonverbal children are likely to understand what you say before they develop expressive language.

By responding to their nonverbal cues, you are teaching children that conversations involve an exchange, or turn taking. If a child responds by making some sounds that are word approximations, he might be attempting to use words. Repeat what you guess the child is saying. "You want the truck?" Another way to encourage early language is to give children communication temptations. "We have your favorite snacks. Would you like a cracker or a banana?" You can also encourage a child to verbalize by giving her a toy in a jar that she cannot open without asking for help.

If most of the other children in the group are verbal, find things that the nonverbal child can do well, such as building with blocks or putting a puzzle together. Let the other children see what the nonverbal child can do. When they recognize her strengths, they will accept the nonverbal child as a worthy playmate and will likely invite her to join their play, thus giving her new opportunities to hear and practice language.

Child Who Is Shy

Children who are shy may be reluctant to initiate conversations and may feel uncomfortable in a situation in which they feel that they are supposed to answer a question or tell you what they want. Instead of asking a shy child whether he wants something, ask him to show you what he wants. If he shows you a toy car, say, "You want to play with the car." When a shy child does not feel pressured to talk, he is more likely to join in the play. As the child learns to trust you and have fun with you, he is likely to get over being shy and will begin to engage in a conversation.

A shy child will tend to be more comfortable and talkative with just one playmate at a time, so try to provide opportunities for the child to play with a favored peer in a quiet, somewhat secluded space. In a larger group, invite the child to participate but leave the choice up to her. For example, you might let her "pass" in a turn-taking game but then ask again at the end if she would like to have a turn. Letting the child be your helper can also be effective, especially if the "help" can be given nonverbally at first (e.g., helping you hold up a book) but then also includes a simple verbal component (e.g., helping you say the title of the book). Puppets may also be useful. A child who hesitates to speak for herself might be perfectly willing to make a puppet talk or to tell a silly puppet what he is doing wrong (e.g., "A shoe does not belong on your head!").

Bring the child's interests to school—for example, by inviting the child to bring a photograph of a new pet. The caregiver can ask questions and give opportunities for the child to talk and share his interests. This activity not only can help the child participate but also can help build a sense of belonging.

Child Who Stutters or Who Has Word-Finding Problems

The child who stutters or who has difficulty finding or articulating a word becomes anxious when he is under pressure. Select times to engage him in a conversation when you are able to give him your full attention. When a child starts to speak to you, show him by your facial expression and by your body language that you are not in a hurry and are interested in what he is saying. Suggesting a word or finishing the sentence for him can be counterproductive—sending the wrong message and at the same time depriving the child of an opportunity to practice his conversational skills.

Child Whose Speech Is Difficult to Understand

If a child uses speech that is difficult to understand, ask the child to speak slowly and, if you still have difficulty understanding her, ask her to say it one more time. Repeat what you thought she said. If you have misunderstood her, then she likely will be able to repeat the word or words you got wrong or else show you what she wants. Do not lose the opportunity to carry on a productive conversation with a child by pretending you understood when you did not.

Child Who Has a Mild Hearing Impairment

If a child has a minor hearing impairment, speak to her in a normal tone rather than trying to shout. Speak directly to the child at eye level so that she can focus on your face. Although she will not actually be reading your lips (unless she has been trained to do so), she will get clues from your lip movements and facial expressions that confirm what she thinks she is hearing, which makes it easier for her to follow the conversation. Speak clearly but naturally, without exaggerating your mouth movements or artificially emphasizing words. Choose a quiet place and a quiet time to carry on a conversation. Avoid standing in front of a window or other light source, or speaking to the child in a darkened room.

Note that children who have middle ear infections may have a temporary hearing loss. Most, though not all, will regain full hearing when the pressure subsides.

Conversation Starters and Play Propositions

Reggio Emilia, Italy, is a town with a unique distinction: Its preschools are a tourist attraction. Most children in the town are in public preschool by the time they are 2 or 3, and by age 5 they are producing such extraordinary artwork and showing such sophisticated understanding that people travel from around the world to see firsthand what their teachers are doing.

Reggio teachers observe children carefully and document both their learning and their questions. The teachers plan carefully together, constructing units and activities that will build on children's interests and spark new questions. In their planning, teachers identify their own questions about what the children are thinking, what they will do with particular materials, or how they make sense of complicated concepts. The activities they create reflect these questions and are called "play propositions." In setting them up, the teachers are asking: "Would you like to play around with this? What will you learn? What will you teach me?"

Such experiences might also be called "conversation starters." The following paragraphs describe a few examples that have become favorites with toddler, preschool, and family child-care teachers.

Experiment With Sounds.   Give children a variety of containers such as coffee cans, plastic pails, cardboard oatmeal boxes, pie plates, and pans. Supply them with shakable materials such as macaroni, small toys, plastic chips, sand, rice, and wooden clothespins. Show them how to make different sounds by dropping, pouring, and shaking. Encourage children to talk about all the different sounds they can make and how they are the same and different.

Play "What's Wrong With This Picture?"   Choose a book with mixed-up pictures—for example, *Wacky Wednesday*, by Theo LeSieg (1974), or cut pictures from magazines and make changes such as cutting a leg off of a chair, turning a vase of flowers upside down, drawing a clock face with letters instead of numbers, or putting a shark under the table. Determine whether the children can find all of the things that are wrong with the pictures.

Take a Rain Walk.   Have parents bring in raincoats, boots, and umbrellas so you can take children for a walk in the rain. Depending on the age of the children, you might catch the rain in a cup, listen to rain sounds on different surfaces, make muddy footprints and watch them wash away, float a stick in a gutter and follow its path downstream, or try to catch raindrops on your tongues. In addition, you might measure the depth and width of a puddle, study your reflections, watch the ripples that the raindrops make, and make more ripples by jumping or tossing a pebble. Talk with children about the experience and help them make drawings or collages to tell their stories. Go out again after the rain has stopped and then a day later. Are the puddles and streams still there? Where did they go?

Read About What's Under the Ground. Read children a picture book about what's under the ground—for example, Ruth Krauss's *The Carrot Seed* (1989) or Lynn Cherry's *How Groundhog's Garden Grew* (2003). Ask them to draw pictures of what they think is under the ground at their school or near their homes. Go out together and look under rocks and leaves. Look down holes, or dig one yourself. Pull up weeds or root vegetables and examine their roots. Talk with children about their discoveries. What do they think will happen to the plants and animals as the seasons change? What questions do they have? If children show an interest, you can follow up by planting beans or radishes, forcing some bulbs indoors and planting others in the garden, purchasing an ant farm, getting nature guides and picture books from the library, or constructing a terrarium in a large glass jar.

Make a Mystery Bag or Mystery Box. Place a small toy inside a bag. Let children take turns reaching into the bag and guessing what the toy is. Let everyone take a turn to say their guess and why they think their guess is right before you take out the toy. Help children talk through their thinking. When children get good at the game, you can make it more challenging. Choose a toy with a distinctive shape or sound, place it in a shoebox, and close the lid. You might use a long block, a hard rubber ball, some marbles, or a maraca. Now the children will have to guess the toy's shape and size by the sounds they hear when they tip or shake the box in different directions.

Mix Colors. Learning colors is especially fun when children can make them themselves. Given paints or dyes of different colors, young children often mix them all together and end up with brown, which may or may not be the color they wanted. However, teachers can set up the activity in a way that encourages experimentation and discussion:

- Add food coloring to shaving cream. Put a different color shaving cream (pink, yellow, blue, and plain white) on each side of a small table. Encourage children to finger paint with the shaving cream and to talk about the different colors that they make as they paint separately and together.

- A variation on the shaving foam and food coloring activity is to add colored ice cubes to shaving foam. The ice slowly melts and colors the foam.

- Give three or four children each a different color of tempera paint. What colors can each pair of children make by putting their paints together? What happens when the whole group combines colors? What happens when you use a little of one color and a lot of another?

- Get crayons and paints in a range of skin and hair colors, or mix the colors yourself. Encourage children to find colors that match their own skin and hair. Create a class portrait by having each child color a stick puppet, hand puppet, or paper cutout. You can also trace children's bodies on large brown paper, sketch in the clothes, and let children work together to paint themselves. Encourage children to talk about all of the beautiful colors that people come in.

- Fill a long, shallow container with water. Have children help to put several drops of one color of food coloring at one end and several drops of a different color at the other. Then add several drops of liquid soap and watch the colors mix!

- Make homemade play dough with the children, using different food coloring colors. Let the children mix different colors of play dough to see what new colors they can make.

- Make a paint set in an egg carton by filling each cup with a mixture of half water and half school glue. Help children add a few drops of food coloring to each cup, in different combinations, until they get colors they like. Using cotton swabs as paintbrushes, let children use their custom colors to paint on wood or rocks or to make collages.

Build a Box House.   Help the children turn a large box into a playhouse, spaceship, phone booth, taco stand, or whatever suits their fancy. Involve the children in all phases of the project: choosing what to make; deciding where the windows and doors go; selecting colors and decorations for the various parts; painting the box and gluing on decorations; bringing in pillows, toys, and other props; and, of course, playing together in the finished environment. Even toddlers will enjoy participating and will have lots of chances to learn and use new words.

Set Up a Store.   Create a class store, using play foods; real food packaging such as empty boxes, yogurt containers, and juice cartons; and magazine cutouts pasted on cardboard, along with play money, paper bags, and a play cash register or homemade money box. Encourage children to take on different roles as shoppers, shelf stockers, customer service representatives (who help customers find the things on their shopping lists), and checkout clerks. With older children, you may want to price items and add a calculator for totaling orders.

Construct an Obstacle Course.   Have children help you create an obstacle course that includes things to climb *on, over, under, around, along,* and *through.*

Set Aside a Sharing Time.   Set aside times for sharing or show and tell. Children can bring a book or toy from home, or they can choose a favorite from the class. Each child gets a turn to tell the group about his special toy or book. Most important, the other children should ask the child questions about the toy or book. Be sure to keep the groups small enough or the opportunities frequent enough so that every child gets a turn to share and to ask at least one question.

Trace Shadows.   Encourage children to explore the shadows of objects and the shadows they can make with their bodies. You can use sidewalk chalk to trace shadows. If children get interested, they might trace their shadows or the shadows of fixed objects at different times of the day. Do the shadows always point in the same direction? Where is the sun when the shadows are long and when they are short? What shadows can children make on the ceiling or walls of the classroom by using flashlights? What kinds of "shadows" can they make with colored gels, glasses of water, or other transparent or translucent objects?

Adopt a Class Puppet. Introduce a special puppet or large doll to your class. Give the puppet a name and a character, and have the puppet introduce herself to the children. The puppet can ask the children questions and can encourage the children to ask her questions. Children can also help the puppet feel at home by reading her stories, showing her around the classroom, or making her a valentine. Make the puppet a permanent class member who joins you at circle time to introduce new units or who makes requests of the children and of you. You can also use the puppet to engage individual children and small groups in conversation.

Mush Mud. In the sandbox, water table, or a corner of the garden, create a place where children can mix water with sand or dirt to create different consistencies of mud. Give them lots of different diggers, pourers, and containers as well as rocks, shells, seedpods and other objects that can be used to create dams and decorations. Use words like *dry, moist, gooey, sift, squeeze, drip, splash, squishy, lumpy, sticky*, and *firm* as you talk with children about what they are doing and making.

Building Relationships

All children need guidance and practice in carrying on a conversation, just as all children need guidance and practice in turn taking. Conversations are the building blocks of meaningful relationships. As adults engage in conversations with children, they build a strong rapport. As children carry on conversations with one another, they establish and maintain friendships.

Reflection

What changes can you make in your room arrangement, teaching methods, and class schedule to enhance classroom conversations?

> What steps can you take to make sure that all children are included in frequent, authentic conversations that build relationships and advance their learning?

REFERENCES

Bowman, B. T., Donovan, M. S., & Burns, M. S. (Eds.). (2000). *Eager to learn: Educating our preschoolers.* Washington, DC: National Academy Press.

Cherry, L. (2003). *How groundhog's garden grew.* New York: The Blue Sky Press.

Dickinson, D. K. (2001). Large group and free-play times: Conversational settings supporting language and literacy development. In D. K. Dickinson & P. O. Tabors (Eds.), *Beginning literacy with language,* (p. 239). Baltimore: Paul H. Brookes.

Dickinson, D. K., & Tabors, P. O. (Eds.). (2001). *Beginning literacy with language.* Baltimore: Paul H. Brookes.

Feynman, R., & Robbins, J. R. (Eds.). (2000). *The pleasure of finding things out: The best short works of Richard Feynman.* New York: Perseus.

Greenspan, S. I., Wieder, S., & Simmons, R. (1998). *The child with special needs: Encouraging intellectual and emotional growth.* Boulder, CO: Perseus.

Hart, B., & Risley, T. (1995). *Meaningful differences in the everyday experience of young American children.* Baltimore: Paul H. Brookes.

High/Scope Educational Research Foundation. (2004). "High/Scope Early Childhood Assessment." Retrieved from www.highscope.org/Assessment/homepage.htm on September 3, 2004.

Krauss, R. (1989). *The carrot seed* (Rev. ed.). New York: Harper Trophy.

LeSieg, T. (1974). *Wacky Wednesday.* New York: Random House.

Segal, M. (2000). Questions. In B. Bardige & M. Segal, *Your child at play: Five to eight.* New York: Newmarket Press.

Snow, C. E., Burns, M. S., & Griffin, P. (1998). *Preventing reading difficulties in young children.* Report of the Committee on the Prevention of Reading Difficulties in Young Children, convened by the National Research Council. C. E. Snow, M. S. Burns, & P. Griffin, (Eds.). Washington, DC: National Academy Press.

Snow, C. E., Dickinson, D. K., & Tabors, P. O. (Ongoing research). The Home-School Study of Language and Literacy Development (description and summary of findings). Retrieved from http://www.gse.harvard.edu/~pild/homeschoolstudy.htm on July 20, 2004.

Snow, C. E., Tabors, P. O., & Dickinson, D. K. (2001). Language development in the preschool years. In D. K. Dickinson & P. O. Tabors (Eds.), *Beginning literacy with language* (pp. 1–30). Baltimore: Paul H. Brookes.

Weitzman, E., & Greenberg, J. (2002). *Learning language and loving it: A guide to promoting children's social, language, and literacy development in early childhood settings* (2nd ed.). Toronto, Ontario, Canada: The Hanen Centre.

CHAPTER 6

Using Books to Support Language

I Like This Book

I like this book.
I like it a lot,
And I am going to pass it down
To my great great great great
Great great great great
Grandchild.

—KORI BARDIGE (age 6), *unpublished poem*

K ori wrote this poem on her sixth birthday. Her mother, Betty, had given her a special present—a blank book half filled with poems that Betty had written as a child. The book had been given to Betty on *her* sixth birthday, by her grandmother—Kori's much-loved great-grandmother, Gigi. "I Like This Book" was Kori's first contribution.

Long before young children can read or write, books can have special meaning for them. A favorite book may be a link to home, a reminder of the special time they spend with a parent each day before going off to child care or on the way to bed. It may be a source of laughter and play, of discovery or fantasy, even of some of her first words. A book character or illustration can become an imaginary friend. A beautifully or humorously illustrated book may prompt a child to tell his own story. A book with textured pages, peep holes, or hidden pictures can become a favorite game or discovery activity. A homemade book, with a child's own words or drawings or with photographs of family, friends, and special events, can be a treasured keepsake.

What makes a book special to a young child is usually not just what it contains, but what the people who read it with him bring to the reading. Speaking in different voices, exaggerating sound effects, making a game of naming pictures or chanting the chorus together, repeating funny words and tongue twisters, reminiscing about shared adventures, letting the child tell parts of the story, and drawing parallels to the child's own experience are just a few of the techniques that make reading a book special.

A collection of carefully selected, age-appropriate books is essential for every infant, toddler, preschool, and multiage classroom. A skilled teacher infuses books throughout the space and throughout the day. That teacher uses books to start and sustain conversations with individual children and small groups and to spark conversations among the children themselves. At times, she chooses a book especially for a child who needs comfort, reassurance, or redirection. She reads aloud from books that provide the comfort of familiar language and that stretch children's linguistic repertoires with rare words, literary language, and word play. The teacher encourages children to incorporate books into their pretend play, both as props in games like "office" and "library" and as inspiration for their own dramatic performances.

In classrooms and homes that promote literacy, books also serve as an important teaching tool. Adults use books to pique children's curiosity, to convey knowledge and concepts, and to develop thinking and learning skills. They also, of course, teach children how books work and how to learn from them.

Even babies can fall in love with books. Photographs of babies, familiar people, objects, and animals; books of nursery rhymes; books with hidden pictures; touch-and-feel books with different textures, scents or both; and books with alliterations, rhythm, and rhyme (and the soothing cadence of a familiar voice reading the literary language) all have special appeal.

Reflection

What books do you remember from your childhood? Did you have favorites? What made them special? What are your favorite books to share with the children in your care? Do you and the children do anything special when you read or talk about these books?

THE BENEFITS OF BOOKS

I n 1998, the International Reading Association and the National Association for the Education of Young Children issued a joint position statement, *Overview of Learning to Read and Write: Developmentally Appropriate Practices for Young Children*. Drawing on research, the authors of this joint statement asserted,

> Excellent instruction builds on what children already know, and can do, and provides knowledge, skills, and dispositions for lifelong learning. Children need to learn not only the technical skills of reading and writing but also how to use these tools to better their thinking and reasoning (Neuman, 1998, p. 8). The single most important activity for building these understandings and skills essential for reading success appears to be *reading aloud to children* (Bus, van Ijzendoorn, & Pellegrini, 1995, emphasis added).

Why is reading aloud to young children so important? Part of the answer may lie in the books themselves. Books for young children are filled with pictures that present information and expand children's worlds. They are also filled with language, and that language is often special. For example, here are some of the special features of literary language that are used in *Goodnight Moon* (Brown, 1947), a classic toddler favorite:

- It often uses literary devices such as alliteration and rhyme that call attention to the sounds of words: "In the great green room there was a telephone . . . . There were three little bears, sitting on chairs."

- It contains rare words that expand children's vocabularies or spark questions such as, What does "a bowl full of mush" taste like?

- Its sentences tend to be complex, using structures such as embedded phrases and clauses: "a picture of a cow jumping over the moon," "a quiet old lady who was whispering 'hush.'"

- It has a special rhythm and cadence.

Literary language is also distinctive because:

- It is likely to be more descriptive than spoken language, containing more adjectives and adverbs;

- It tends to substitute less common synonyms for familiar words (a character who is feeling sad may be described as "tearful," "gloomy," "moping," or even "inconsolable"); and

- It may use story conventions such as "Once upon a time."

Thus, children who have lots of experience with books are likely to develop richer vocabularies and deeper understanding of the meanings, sounds, and uses of words than those with less literary experience. They are also likely to be familiar with the conventions of language and story form that they will encounter when they begin to read for themselves.

Much of the power of books, however, comes not from the books themselves but from the play, conversation, relationships, and thinking that they support:

- Six-month-old Keisha falls asleep each night listening to her father read *Goodnight Moon* (Brown, 1947). She is too young to understand the words, but their sounds are soothing, and her father's familiar chant gives her a sense of safety.

- One-year-old Sophie can oink like a pig, hoot like an owl, and quack like a duck. She practices these sounds while looking at a book of animal babies with her big sister.

- Two-year-old Jack's favorite book is Richard Scarry's *Cars and Trucks and Things That Go* (1998), an earlier edition of which had belonged to his father. Jack loves to point to the different kinds of vehicles and to try to say their names.

- Three-year-old Sameer likes to look through family albums with his grandmother. He especially likes the pictures of his grandmother as a girl in India. As they look at the pictures together, Sameer peppers his grandmother with questions.

- Four-year-old Iselina speaks mostly Spanish, though she is learning English rapidly in her mostly English-speaking classroom. Her teacher has been careful to include some Spanish-language and Spanish–English books in the classroom and to teach the class some Spanish songs, words, and phrases. Iselina's voice fills with pride as she "reads" the class a Spanish story that she has memorized.

- Five-year-old Arran has just finished listening to a book about dinosaurs. The text presented several possible explanations for their extinction. Challenged to solve the puzzle, Arran combines these possibilities into a theory all his own. "I know why the dinosaurs died," Arran explains. "A big asteroid hit the Earth and it started a fire and lots of plants got burned up. Only poison plants were left. The dinosaurs ate those and they got sick and died."

Special times for reading, both at home and in child care, ensure that children gain familiarity with books through daily experience. Adults can choose books for particular purposes and can structure formal or informal learning experiences around them. For example, consider the following two scenarios:

Mr. Follow-Directions knows how important it is to read to toddlers. Every day at 10:00 a.m., he sets aside 20 minutes for reading. When Mr. Follow-Directions rings the bell, the seven 2-year-olds in his group race to get their books. He lets them climb into his lap one at a time—first come, first served—and he reads each child's story, real quick, before they have to line up for gym.

Ms. Sit-on-the-Floor, who runs a family child-care home, agrees that reading is important, but she does not like to be rushed. Ms. Sit-on-the-Floor likes to sit in the middle of the playroom, with a basket of books within easy reach. That way, she can watch what the children are doing, join them in pretend play, introduce books at appropriate times, and respond to the children's frequent requests for stories. Most days, Ms. Sit-on-the-Floor will read at least two books to every child, either individually or in a small group, but she does not worry too much if a child gets interested in other things for a while. Even the babies always seem to come back to the books.

Books are too important for young children and too valuable to their teachers and caregivers to be taken out only at "reading time." In settings that support emergent literacy, books are actively used for playtime, cuddle time, naptime, transition times, and alone time, as well as for intentional teaching.

Reading a story with a parent or caregiver can become a comforting ritual that eases a child's entry into child care each morning. Picture books can keep little hands and minds busy during waiting times and diaper changes; they can help children settle in to sleep or provide quiet activity for those who have given up their naps but still need down time. A well-chosen book can calm a child who is distressed or overexcited, or it can help a child cope with emotional challenges like jealousy, frustration, and teasing. A fiction or nonfiction story can spark a child's curiosity about people, places, and things beyond the realm of his experience; a true-to-life portrayal of familiar people, places, and things can help him feel good about himself and his heritage. A humorous book provides both entertainment and a new perspective. Lines that are easy to memorize and fun to recite can give a child a sense of mastery. Books that are looked at and listened to over and over can become trusted friends.

Information-rich nonfiction books are especially important for preschoolers. A rich, ever-changing collection encourages them to explore new interests.

CHOOSING BOOKS FOR CHILDREN

When selecting books for a classroom or group of children, it is important to pay attention not only to each individual book but also to the collection as a whole. The ages and interests of the children, the languages they speak and are learning, their ethnic and racial backgrounds, the topics in your curriculum, and your own preferences will all influence what books you choose for the collection.

For infants, books—like other toys—are things to touch, turn, shake, and put in your mouth. Well-chosen books can also provide valuable experiences with pictures, textures, sounds, and words.

- Infants enjoy touching the illustrations in books and are attracted to books that offer different tactile experiences.

- Board books, provided they are not too big for an infant to hold, have definite advantages. They can be wiped clean if an infant drools on them, they can withstand a bite or two, and the pages are easy to turn. Books that are made of cloth or vinyl have the advantage of being washable and sturdy, but the colors are not always vibrant and their pages can be difficult to turn.

- Babies love to see other babies. Close-up photographs are especially appealing. Choose (or make) books that show the racial diversity of the child's class or that contain photos or illustrations of children from different backgrounds.

- Older infants also enjoy books with familiar actions, routines, objects, and animals. They can learn to point to objects, animals, or body parts when you name them, and they can imitate the sounds of animals and vehicles.

- Infants enjoy listening to books with rhyming words and a steady rhythm. Books with nursery rhymes are always appropriate. Ask families to help you make books (and tapes) in their home language or dialect if you cannot find published versions of their traditional lullabies, chants, or nursery games.

In selecting books for toddlers, remember their need for active involvement and their desire to do things themselves. Classic toddler books such as *Goodnight Moon* (Brown, 1947), *The Very Hungry Caterpillar* (Carle, 1987), and Eric Hill's *Spot* books series (1985, 1986a, 1986b, 1989) owe their longevity as much to their illustrations and format as to their words.

- Toddlers like sturdy board books with colorful illustrations and interesting details. Children of this age have great fun finding items that are "hiding" in plain sight, for example, a little gray mouse who shows up in a different spot on every page.

- Toddlers love books with parts that they can play with—tabs to pull, flaps to lift, holes to peek through or poke fingers into, shapes to trace, buzzers that sound, and scratch-and-sniff features. Some of these books are too fragile to last long in a classroom, but others are sturdy enough to withstand repeated exploration.

- Children who are learning to talk enjoy books filled with pictures that they can name. Collections of land and sea animals, vehicles, construction machines, and foods tend to be popular.

- Older toddlers can follow a simple story line. Favorite plots involve separation and reunion: running away and being caught, hiding and being found, exploring and coming home, making a mistake and being forgiven.

- When the words and illustrations are simple, 2-year-olds love books that capitalize on their emerging sense of the absurd and their enjoyment of silliness.

- Toddlers like books with familiar main characters, so look for books that come in series. When you find authors or illustrators that your toddlers enjoy, add other books in the same style by the same authors and illustrators. Toddlers will welcome the new books as familiar family members.

- Well-chosen books can help toddlers cope with emotional issues and challenges such as toilet training, being a picky eater, making noise and messes, throwing temper tantrums, trying to be helpful, and learning to share.

- Although most toddler books feature animal characters or inanimate objects, toddlers also enjoy books about people. Make sure that your collection includes people whose backgrounds are both similar to and different from the children's, shown in positive, nonstereotypical roles.

When selecting books for preschoolers, think about building a diverse collection: books to read to groups of children and books that children can look at themselves; books that expand the themes in your curriculum and books that are just plain fun; books with few or no words and books with many words; books that are fiction and nonfiction, poetry and prose, newer books and classics.

- Take into account the physical features of the book, including its durability, size, shape, and length; the quality of the illustrations; the print size; and the number of words per page.

- Pay attention to the quality of the writing. Choose books that you enjoy reading aloud, including some that contain literary language that will stretch children's vocabularies. Include some books that capture the rhythm and cadence of different oral traditions and dialects.

- Select books that will capture children's interest and spark their imagination. Include books that match any special interests that the children may have expressed. For example, if the children get intrigued by an ant hole or a bird's nest, find several books about different kinds of animal homes.

- Look for books that make it easy for preschoolers to "help" with the reading. Choose some books with repeated elements that invite participation (e.g., "I'll huff and I'll puff and I'll blow your house down!" [Galdone, 1984]), and some with rhymes, surprise endings, or strong patterns (e.g., "Brown, bear, brown bear, what do you see?" [Martin & Carle, 1967]).

- Choose some books with simple story lines that are fun to act out with puppets or costumes.

- Choose some books that help young children cope with social and emotional challenges such as conflict with a friend, mixed feelings about a new baby, uncertainty about moving to a new home or school, or sadness over the death of a pet.

- Be sure to include some ABC books in your collection, along with counting books; color and shape books; and books that highlight color, shape, number, letters, or symbols in real world photographs.

- As you develop your ideas for curricular themes, make sure to include several children's books for each topic so children can investigate the elements that intrigue them. For example, a theme focusing on homes might include books about moving into a new house, books about animal homes, books about the homes of children who live in faraway places, and books about building homes. You might even choose a book as your central theme—such as Maryann Hoberman's (1978) *A House Is a House for Me*—and then look for books that expand it in different directions. These could include books by the same author, fiction and nonfiction books about different kinds of "houses," and books written in a similarly playful, poetic style.

- Be sure to select books that represent the culture and ethnicity of the children in your class and that do not reflect bias related to gender, age, or handicapping conditions. Books in which doctors and police are always male, where grandparents are depicted as old and feeble, or where children with disabilities are never included in groups are not appropriate for your collection.

- To counteract the stereotypes applied to people of color and the predominance of Whites in the images that children are likely to see on television, billboards, and in their general environment, the *Anti-Bias Curriculum* (Derman-Sparks, 1989) recommends that at least half the images of people in any preschool book collection be of non-Whites. For classes in which children of color predominate, the proportion of non-White images should be closer to three quarters. Look for books written in more than one language, especially if some of the children are bilingual.

You can never have too many books. Encourage children and families to bring in their favorites to share. Make a habit of going to your local or school library. Ask the librarian to help you select books for individual children and their families, as well as for the class as a whole.

BOOK-HANDLING BASICS

Once upon a time, most children's books were fragile, and children were taught to look but not touch. Today, books for young children come in both sturdy and fragile forms, and we recognize the benefits of encouraging children to handle books themselves.

When children not only can see but also can touch the pictures, they are more likely to be drawn into the story. For preschoolers,

Young toddlers love to hold books themselves, and can learn to turn the pages to find their favorite pictures.

seeing the words up close helps them begin to recognize that the print is what carries the specific message. Pointing to words as you read helps preschoolers make connections between the printed and spoken words.

When you read to a group of children, take the opportunity to teach some book-handling basics. Show the infants and toddlers the cover of the book. Read the title, and let the children touch the illustrations on the cover. In addition,

- Give each child an opportunity to hold and open the book.
- Help children to hold the book right side up.
- Let the children help you turn the pages.
- Talk about the importance of handling a book gently.

Preschool children are ready to learn more. When you read to a group of preschool children, you can provide more detailed information about the book and about book handling in general, such as:

- The cover has the name of the author and illustrator, and usually a picture that tells us something about the book. The pages of the book include illustrations and text.

- When we read a book in English, we need to start on the first page and turn the pages one by one until we get to the end. The words go from left to right, top to bottom.

- When we start to read a book, it is important to have clean hands so we will not get the book dirty. As we turn the pages, we need to be very careful not to tear them.

- When we finish reading a book, we take it back to the shelf or basket where it belongs so it will be easy to find when we want to read it again.

- Library books need special care because we have to return them so other children can use them.

Even with the best of care, well-loved books are bound to get battered. Some preschool teachers deal with the problem by designating part of the art or writing center as a "book hospital" and teaching children to help with the needed repairs.

SHARING BOOKS WITH CHILDREN

Whether you are reading to one child or to a group, sharing books with children is a multistep process. First, introduce the book and pique the children's interest, then read and discuss (or play with) the book together, and finally, extend the learning experience so that the children make connections to other aspects of their lives. Of course, each phase of this process does not require equal time with every child or every book. How you approach each phase and how much time you spend depends on the children's ages and interests, your own teaching goals, children's familiarity with the book, and how the book fits in with the rest of your curriculum.

Introducing the Book

Familiar books, like familiar people, need little introduction. New books, however, should be properly introduced so that children know the books' titles and have an idea of what to expect. Introductions should not be laborious, just enough to pique children's interest and get them thinking. Before you begin reading a book, tell the children the title of the book, the author, and the illustrator, pointing to these features for preschoolers.

In addition, talk with the children about the kind of book you will be reading and solicit their ideas. How much can the children tell from the title and the cover? Is it a story book? Is it a book of poems, rhymes, or riddles? Or is it a book that provides information about animals, plants, foods, people, places, how things work, or how things are made? Is it about things that are real or things that are just pretend? Is it about things that are happening today or about things that happened a long time ago? Is it about things that the children know about, like taking a bath or going to the doctor? Is it about things that happen in other places around the world?

Reading and Discussing the Book

There are all kinds of ways to read a story, and the choice of which ones to use depends on the book, the children, your teaching goals, and the response you are getting.

- Some books lend themselves to dramatic reading. You can use different voices as you play the parts of different characters, and you can use gestures and facial expressions to convey emotion and meaning.

- Some books are more about the pictures than the words. They lend themselves to interactive play, with children pointing to or naming pictures, finding hidden details, carrying out actions such as tracing the spider's web or blowing a kiss to the baby, identifying colors or shapes, counting objects, or telling what they see.

- Some books have strong story lines that may be conveyed through the pictures or through the words. You might stop at key points to ask children what they think will happen next or to talk about what the characters might be feeling.

- Some books have too many words for your audience or may contain sections that are violent or otherwise inappropriate. In these situations, you will want to abbreviate the text and tell your own story.

- Some books invite group participation. Children enjoy chanting repeated lines, filling in rhyming words, performing actions described in the text, or supplying sound effects.

- Some books are sources of information. You may want to focus on particular parts rather than read the whole book at once.

- Some books raise questions for children—these questions then become the focus of the discussion.

- Many of the books you choose will connect to important aspects of children's lives. A child may remember a similar story or event, may have shared a character's feelings or dilemma, may have seen something that looks like one of the illustrations, or may have had experiences that contrast with those portrayed in the book. These connections will help children understand the story; discussing these connections will also help children go beyond the book and get more out of the experience.

- Some children insist on uninterrupted, word-for-word reading of familiar texts. Encourage them to "read" along with you.

Effective story reading techniques catch and hold children's interest. When interest flags, it is time to shift techniques or to put aside the reading for another time. (See the box on the next page for an explanation of "dialogic reading," a specific technique for reading stories with children.)

When you finish reading the book, give the children a chance to talk about it:

- What did they like about the book? What do they remember?

- Did the book make them laugh? Did it teach them something new? Did it tell a good story or convey a message? Were they happy with the ending?

- Which illustrations did they like? Can they find them?

- Do they want to hear the story again?

DIALOGIC READING

Perhaps the most well-researched technique for reading stories with children is "dialogic reading," developed by Grover Whitehurst and his colleagues (Whitehurst et al., 1994) at the State University of New York at Stony Brook. This discussion technique was developed for parents working with individual children, but it can also be used by teachers working with individuals or with small groups.

The idea behind "dialogic reading" is to make reading a shared activity in which the child's role becomes larger and larger as the books become more familiar. At first, you might read a book through so a child can hear the story, or you might flip through the pages and tell a shortened version of the story based on the pictures. On second, third, fourth, and umpteenth readings, the book becomes a scaffold for structured conversations that expand vocabulary, extend concepts, and encourage expressive language. Whitehurst developed a simple mnemonic (PEER) to describe his technique for using a page of a familiar book as a conversation starter.

- **P**rompt the child to comment on the story or illustration: "Look. The pig is building his house. What's he making it out of?"

- **E**valuate the child's response, affirming what is correct or close and correcting any errors: "That's right. He's making his house out of hay."

- **E**xpand the child's response, adding new information or a more precise word. "Remember when we went to the farm and saw horses eating hay? Do you think that hay would make a strong house?"

- **R**epeat. Give the child a chance to repeat the new word or information or to introduce an expansion, question, or observation of

(continued)

DIALOGIC READING *(continued)*

her own. "So what kind of stuff is the little pig making his house out of?"

Of course, children who get hooked on a book are often eager to share their observations, story retellings, and ideas—with or without prompting—and may even prompt the parent.

For 2- and 3-year-olds, the prompts and conversations tend to focus on particular pictures or pages. Children are asked to name pictures, identify colors or shapes, find a character or object that is "hiding," tell what a character is doing, or say "night, night" to the teddy bear. Older children can focus on the story as a whole, predicting what will happen next, talking about characters' motivations or feelings, and drawing parallels with their own experience. Whitehurst uses another mnemonic (CROWD) to help parents remember the range of questions, or prompts, that they can use.

- **C**ompletion prompts encourage children to finish sentences, usually by supplying a rhyme or chiming in with a line that is fun to repeat: "I'll huff and I'll puff and I'll . . ."

- **R**ecall prompts ask children to recall information from previous pages or previous readings: "Remember what the wolf did to the first little pig's house?"

- **O**pen-ended prompts encourage children to use their own words to tell what is happening on a page or in a picture: "What's going on in this picture? What else do you see? How do you think the wolf feels now?"

- **Wh** prompts ask **who**, **what**, **where**, **when**, **why**, or **what** will happen next: "Where is that little pig going?"

- **D**istancing prompts ask children to make connections between the world of the book and the real world of their own experience and feelings: "Remember when we watched the masons building that brick wall? What did the bricks feel like?"

Extending the Learning Experience

Book-reading experiences can be extended in two ways: by going deeper and by reaching out. Going deeper means getting more out of the book itself: its words and illustrations; its literal and figurative meanings; and the author's and illustrator's purpose, style, and messages. For 4- and 5-year-olds who are showing an interest in letters, sounds, and "grown-up reading," going deeper also means directing their attention to the text and helping them connect spoken words with written words, letters, and word parts. Reaching out involves going beyond the book: retelling or reenacting the story in new ways, making comparisons with other books, or searching out and applying new information. There are some simple extension activities that toddlers and preschoolers enjoy, grouped by their teaching purpose.

Understanding and Learning From the Story. The following activities deepen children's understanding of the story.

- Have children join you in demonstrating key actions or making sound effects as you read a simple story. For example, they can blow out birthday candles, take their hats on and off, clap their hands, stamp their feet, nod or shake their heads, or pretend to go to sleep and snore along with characters.

- Make connections to real-world experience whenever you can. When you read about a garbage truck, for instance, talk about the real garbage trucks that pass by on the street and the people who collect the garbage. Likewise, when you see a real garbage truck, remind children of the trucks in their books. Encourage the children to point out similarities and differences and to ask questions.

- Have children take on roles and act out a familiar story as you narrate. In *Boys and Girls: Superheroes in the Doll Corner*, Vivian Gussin Paley (1986) describes how she uses this technique with stories that kindergarteners make up themselves. The teacher writes their words or helps them do so, and then the teacher or child reads back the story while other children act out the parts.

Attending to Words and Their Representations. The following activities can help children to expand vocabulary and make connections to printed words:

- When you come upon words that may be unfamiliar to some of the children, stop and see whether anyone knows the word or can guess its meaning from the context or from the pictures. Explain the meaning or point to an appropriate picture. With older children, you might also talk about what other words the author could have used and why the author might have chosen that particular word.

- Show children words in the story—for example, "Here's where it says 'Goodnight, Moon.'"

Remembering, Retelling, and Reenacting the Story. The following activities help children practice sequencing and story-telling skills.

- Make simple puppets that children can use to help retell a familiar story or to read along. You can make puppets by gluing paper plates to craft sticks or tongue depressors and letting children draw or glue on features. Or you can photocopy pictures from the book, back them with sturdy paper, and attach them to empty toilet paper rolls (these have the advantage of being able to stand up, so that children can also reenact the story in mini-play).

- Make tapes of children's favorite books so that they can "read" them themselves as they listen. Be sure to indicate when it is time to turn the pages.

- Provide children with costumes, props, and simple stage settings so that they can reenact favorite stories.

- Encourage children to retell favorite stories with flannel or magnet boards, and to create their own variations.

Appreciating the Author's Craft. These activities will help children tune in to the choices authors make and also become "authors" themselves.

- Read children some stories with strong patterns, such as *Goodnight, Moon* (Brown, 1947), *Brown Bear, Brown Bear, What Do You See?* (Martin & Carle, 1967), *The Very Hungry Caterpillar* (Carle, 1987), or *If You Give a Mouse a Cookie*

(Bond, 1985). After children have learned to retell or act out the story, have them create their own versions with different characters and events but a similar pattern. They can act out their versions (for example, by saying "good morning" to things in their classroom, making colored animal masks and taking turns telling what animal they see, or lining up play foods for their very hungry puppy dog to eat), or they can make their own books using stickers or drawings. (You can write the words they say or provide them with copies of the repeating words to glue into their books along with pictures and their own attempts at writing.)

- Read several variants of a folk tale. Talk with the children about what is the same and what is different in the retellings. Which parts of each version do children like best? Let children make their own books of these tales to take home or to add to your classroom library.

Applying Information and Concepts. Children can enhance what they learn by using the information in new and different ways, as in the following activities:

- Help the children work together to make a classroom museum or collection inspired by a fiction or nonfiction story. For example, *Hats, Hats, Hats* (Morris, 1993b) or *Bread, Bread, Bread* (Morris, 1993a) might prompt children to collect pictures or objects or to make their own drawings and photographs.

- Use story characters as role models. For example, children may identify with and emulate the heroine in *Amazing Grace* by Mary Hoffman and Caroline Binch (1991), or in *Corduroy* by Don Freeman (1968).

Investigating Print. The following activities can focus on printed words, enabling children to make direct connections to key words and letters:

- Point out words in a book's title or in the names of the authors, illustrators, or main characters that begin with the same letters and sounds as the names of children in the class.

- Read from a Big Book or chart, using a pointer to track the words as you read. With books that are very familiar and have simple, patterned text, let children who are interested take turns using the pointer as the whole class recites the familiar text with you.

- After reading a short page of a familiar story, challenge children to locate a key word you have read—for example, the name of the main character or the beginning of a refrain.

Loving Books Together.   The following activities can help children connect emotionally to others through books:

- Place some favorite dolls or stuffed animals in the reading corner. Encourage children to read to their real and pretend friends.

- Bring back some books that children used to enjoy when they were younger. Encourage them to reminisce together.

- Encourage parents to come in and read books to the children that they (the parents) loved as children.

- Encourage children to talk about their favorite books and what makes them special. You might even write down their "reviews" and keep them in a special place. That way, when you introduce a book to a new group of children, you can explain that it is a special favorite of a particular child and share what that child wants to tell them about it.

HOMEMADE BOOKS AND SOCIAL STORIES

Children love books about themselves and the familiar people, places, things, and events in their world. That is why some of the best-loved books are homemade.

For babies and toddlers, homemade books are simply photo albums, with pictures of themselves, family members, and pets. You can also cut pictures from magazines and catalogs and make books of familiar items such as foods, furniture, tools, toys, and vehicles that the children can name.

Older toddlers and young preschoolers can begin to make books of their own. They can select pictures that fit into various categories such as *my favorite things, things that are blue, things with wheels,* and *things that go up in the air.* They can also appreciate picture books that show a simple sequence such as *our trip to the zoo, my day in school,* or *making play dough.* They may even be able to help to put the pictures in order. With or without words, these books provide opportunities for shared storytelling that recall familiar experiences.

Homemade books can also help children cope with strong emotions and upsetting experiences. A child who is afraid of the dark, for example, might draw solace from a book in which she is the hero and chases away the monsters with her magic wand so that her dolls, stuffed animals, or action figures will not be scared anymore. The following scenario shows how a homemade book can support children in conflict:

Thomas, an artistic but not very verbal child who tried to act "tough," regularly picked on Kevin, a talkative classmate who was small and somewhat clumsy. Kevin usually ignored Thomas or told him to "buzz off." But one day, Thomas took it too far: He hit Kevin harder than usual, and Kevin surprised him by hitting back. Their teacher helped the boys write and illustrate a book together to remind them to use words, not fists. "Once there was a boy named Thomas who was very smart and very tough and very good at drawing. Thomas had a friend named Kevin, who was very smart and very fun and very good at Legos® One day, Thomas hit Kevin. It hurt! Then Kevin hit Thomas. It hurt! After that, Thomas and Kevin remembered to use their hands for drawing and making Legos®, but not for hitting."

The story that Thomas and Kevin wrote with their teacher is similar to what Carol Gray (2000) calls "social stories." Created especially for children who have difficulty reading social cues, Gray's social stories help children remember how to behave in new or recurring situations. They follow a specific formula, describing a situation, telling how the child responds or behaves, providing perspective on how others see or feel about the behavior, and ending with cues to help the child remember what to do next time. Such stories give children a sense of control and help them to use self-talk to guide their actions.

You do not have to be a professional author to make a book that can help a child cope with life's inevitable rough spots. The star of the story can be either the child herself or a favorite stuffed animal, imaginary friend, or TV character. This main character can encounter a challenging situation (such as not wanting to help at cleanup time or dealing with a classmate who will not share), try an ineffective strategy, find out how others feel, and learn a different way of acting that produces better results. Often, the point is best made with humor, and the story will read like a tall tale. For example, the classroom becomes such a mess that parents have to bring shovels so they can dig their children out to take them home, or a character waits so long for a turn that he falls asleep and snores so loudly that the reluctant sharer drops the toy to cover her ears. And of course, the story is most likely to be effective—and treasured—if the child participates in drawing the pictures and defining the solution.

LASTING GIFTS

The stories we give to children when they are young can be lasting gifts. Beautifully written phrases, poetic rhythms, and delightfully humorous illustrations linger in their memories. Storybook characters become friends. The lessons that children can learn from talking about books with the important adults in their lives can shape how children see the world and how they behave when faced with new challenges.

Vivian Gussin Paley, a kindergarten teacher at the University of Chicago Lab School, has explored the power of stories in her classroom and shares the results in her numerous books for teachers. In *The Boy Who Would Be a Helicopter* (Paley, 1991), she describes her attachment to children's books with these memorable words: "The poetry and prose of the best children's books enter our minds when we are young and sing back to us all our lives" (p. 44).

REFERENCES

Bond, F. (1985). *If you give a mouse a cookie*. New York: Harper & Row.

Brown, M. W. (1947). *Goodnight moon*. New York: Harper & Row.

Bus, A., van Ijzendoorn, M., & Pellegrini, A. (1995). Joint book reading makes for success in learning to read: A meta-analysis on intergenerational transmission of literacy. *Review of Educational Research, 65,* 1–21.

Carle, E. (1987). *The very hungry caterpillar* (2nd ed.). New York: Philomel Books.

Derman-Sparks, L. (1989). *Anti-bias curriculum: Tools for empowering young children*. Washington, DC: National Association for the Education of Young Children.

Freeman, D. (1968). *Corduroy*. New York: Puffin Books.

Galdone, P. (1984). *The three little pigs*. Boston: Clarion Books.

Gray, C. (2000). *The new social story book: Illustrated edition*. Arlington, TX: Future Horizons.

Hill, E. (1985). *Spot goes to the beach*. New York: G. P. Putnam's Sons.

Hill, E. (1986a). *Spot's first words*. New York: G. P. Putnam's Sons.

Hill, E. (1986b). *Spot looks at colors*. New York: G. P. Putnam's Sons.

Hill, E. (1989). *Spot counts from 1 to 10*. New York: G. P. Putnam's Sons.

Hoberman, M. (1978). *A house is a house for me*. New York: Viking.

Hoffman, M., & Binch, C. (1991). *Amazing grace*. New York: Dial Books for Children.

International Reading Association & National Association for the Education of Young Children (1998). *Overview of learning to read and write: Developmentally appropriate practices for young children, a joint position statement of the International Reading Association (IRA) and the National Association for the Education of Young Children (NAEYC)*. Washington, DC: National Association for the Education of Young Children.

Martin, B., & Carle, E. (1967). *Brown bear, brown bear, what do you see?*. New York: Henry Holt.

Morris, A. (1993a). *Bread, bread, bread.* New York: Harper Trophy.

Morris, A. (1993b). *Hats, hats, hats.* New York: Harper Trophy.

Neuman, S. B. (1998). How can we enable all children to achieve? In S. B. Neuman & K. A. Roskos (Eds.), *Children achieving: Best practices in early literacy* (pp. 18–32). Newark, DE: International Reading Association.

Paley, V. G. (1986). *Boys and girls: Superheroes in the doll corner.* Chicago: University of Chicago Press.

Paley, V. G. (1991). *The boy who would be a helicopter: The uses of storytelling in the classroom.* Cambridge, MA: Harvard University Press.

Scarry, R. (1998). *Cars and trucks and things that go.* New York: Golden Books.

Whitehurst, G. J., Epstein, J. N., Angell, A. L., Payne, A. C., Crone, D. A., & Fischel, J. E. (1994). Outcomes of emergent literacy intervention in Head Start. *Journal of Educational Psychology, 86*(4), 542–555.

CHAPTER

7

The "Outside-In" Domain

Jack Sprat

Jack Sprat, could eat no fat.
His wife could eat no lean,
And so between the both of them
They licked the platter clean.

—TRADITIONAL

Once upon a time, educators were split on how to teach children to read. One group argued that the way to teach children to read an alphabetic language was to start with phonics and to give beginners lots of practice in naming letters and their sounds and in "sounding out" short, regularly spelled words. A second camp, most recently called "whole language," argued that the meanings of the words and sentences were just as important as their sounds. Those who believed in this approach provided beginning readers with lots of practice in recognizing whole words and in reading along with simple stories that provided many context clues.

It turns out that both camps were right and that each method was most successful when it incorporated some of the other's techniques. Reading researchers Grover Whitehurst and Christopher Lonigan (2001) reframed the problem by describing two different domains of knowledge. "Outside-*in* units . . . represent sources of information outside the printed word that support a child's understanding of the meaning of print (e.g., vocabulary, conceptual knowledge, and story schemas). Inside-*out* units represent sources of information within the printed word that enable a child to translate print into sounds and sounds into print (e.g., phonemic awareness and letter knowledge)" (p. 13).

Reading with understanding is based on applying information from both the "outside-*in*" and the "inside-*out*" domains. Think about this sentence: "Mars is called the red planet." The child who uses only inside-out information will read the sentence word by word. When he sounds out the word "planet," he is likely to pronounce it as "plaint" and to have no idea what "plaints" are. The child who knows that Mars is one of the planets that go around the sun can read the word "planet" from the outside in as well as from the inside out. In fact, he is likely to guess the word from context and, therefore, to recognize it as "planet" without needing to sound out the whole word. Just as Jack Sprat and his wife, when eating together, successfully clean the platter, successful readers bring together outside-*in* and inside-*out* strategies.

The following "brain trick," which has been circulating on the Internet, demonstrates how both kinds of knowledge come together. Try it yourself:

Aoccdrnig to rscheearch at an Elingsh uinervtisy, it deosn't mttaer in waht oredr the ltteers in a wrod are, the olny iprmoetnt tihng is taht the frist and lsat ltteer are in the rghit pclae. The rset can be a toatl mses and you can sitll raed it wouthit a porbelm. Tihs is bcuseae we do not raed ervey lteter by itslef but the wrod as a wlohe and the biran fguiers it out aynawy.

The outside-*in* domain includes two basic kinds of knowledge: (a) knowledge about words, sentences, stories, and other literary forms and (b) knowledge about the real world. Both kinds of knowledge help children to decode words and to comprehend and interpret what they are reading.

This chapter begins with a section on helping children acquire real-world knowledge and underlying concepts of how things work. The next section focuses on deepening children's knowledge of words and their awareness of sentence and narrative patterns. The chapter concludes with examples of how curriculum topics or themes can provide a context for learning and the inspiration to seek new knowledge from books.

LEARNING ABOUT THE WORLD AND HOW IT WORKS

The world is an exciting place for young children, who have much to learn about how it works. Ideas and connections that we take for granted are new and exciting for them. Sometimes it seems as if every day is filled with new discoveries.

A young baby bats at a mobile—and learns that her batting can make it swing. A toddler steps in a puddle—and learns that by stepping harder, he can make a bigger splash. A preschooler watches water evaporate on a sunny day and wonders where it went.

Through their own efforts, explorations, and questions, children gradually build a repertoire of knowledge about objects, people, and processes. This knowledge provides a foundation for understanding the stories and information in books, which in turn contribute to the child's expanding knowledge base.

Babies: Developing Fundamental Concepts

Babies have an amazing capacity to learn through experience. Although they are born with the ability to see, hear, smell, taste, touch, and feel, it is only through experience that they can grasp the meaning of the information they receive through their senses. As we provide babies with a range of developmentally appropriate experiences, we enhance their ability to understand their world.

The Explorations and Discoveries of Infants

From birth to 3 months, the baby's primary focus is on the development of self-regulation. Her interactions with the world outside of herself are focused on taking in information. She explores the world with eyes, ears, hands, and mouth, and continues to make new discoveries.

By the age of 3 months, the baby is ready to explore her world in a more active way. Her behavior becomes action oriented, and she becomes a prime mover in a responsive environment. She initiates responses from family and friends, seeking out faces, smiling and babbling, and making the world smile back. Who can resist smiling when a baby looks at you and smiles?

Between the ages of 6 and 12 months, babies make an important discovery. They discover that people and objects continue to exist even when they do not see them. This is the age when babies love to play peekaboo. The caregiver covers his head with a blanket and emerges seconds later with a resounding "peekaboo!" The baby laughs out loud, delighted that her caregiver has not really disappeared. The baby has discovered "object permanence." Her caregiver still exists even when he is out of sight, and a ball still exists even if it has rolled behind a shelf.

A second discovery that babies make between the ages of 6 and 12 months is that things can fit inside other things. The caregiver places a few wooden blocks inside a box, tips the box over, and the blocks fall out. After a few demonstrations, the baby turns over the box, watches the blocks as they fall out, and one by one puts them back in the box. The baby has discovered the relationship between the container and its contents. For several months the baby will keep busy, emptying, filling, and emptying again.

Activities That Provide Babies With Opportunities to Explore and Experiment

Here are just a few of the many things you can do to encourage babies to explore and experiment.

- Let the baby touch your face and put his hands on your lips as you sing a lullaby. He is learning that people make interesting noises, and he is investigating where the noise is coming from.

- Each day, let babies spend some time on the floor and some time on their backs. They need to see the world from different perspectives.

- Take babies outside for a part of the day whenever the weather permits. If there is a light breeze, let the babies sit under a tree so they can hear the rustle of leaves and watch clouds drift by overhead.

- Attach mobiles to both sides of the baby's crib. He will look from one side to the other, comparing the difference between the two visual displays.

- Blow bubbles when babies are outside, and let them watch the bubbles as they float through the air.

- As babies get older and more mobile, their explorations are more extensive. Let the babies creep over different surfaces and experience different sensations. Place toys in different places around the room, and let them discover where they are.

The Ways That Babies Learn About Cause and Effect

Between the ages of 3 and 6 months, babies first show an interest in making things happen. They bat at a cradle gym, and they watch the rings as they spin and jingle. Then, as soon as the rings are still, they bat the gym again. Reaching and grasping are two important skills that babies acquire during these 3 months. When you show the

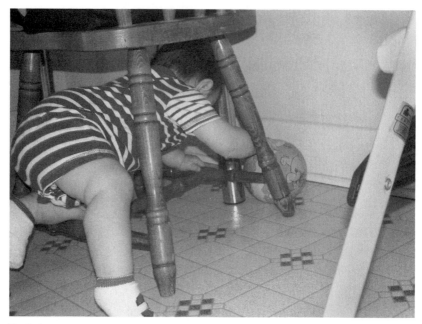

Retrieving a ball that has rolled behind a chair presents a new crawler with a problem that is both intellectually and physically challenging.

baby a rattle, he reaches out and grasps it. When he holds the rattle he shakes it, listens to the jingling sound, and then shakes it again. The baby has learned that he is an agent of change. He can cause things to happen. In other words, the baby has grasped the concept of cause and effect.

Between the ages of 6 and 12 months, babies are fully aware of their ability to make things happen. They are fascinated with toys that have moving parts and with pop-up toys that have levers they can push down to make different figures pop up. As babies become more mobile, they have many more opportunities to make interesting things happen. They can open drawers and cupboards and take out whatever they find. They can turn the knobs on a VCR or television set, making moving pictures appear. They can drop things into the toilet and make delightful splashing sounds. They can pull papers off a desk and tear them into small pieces. They can pull a book down from a shelf and find colorful pictures inside.

Activities That Help Babies Learn About Cause and Effect

As you watch babies discovering how to cause effects, make sure to talk with them about what they are doing. The following activities will provide ample opportunities for babies to explore the concept of cause and effect:

- Bounce the baby on your knee as you recite a nursery rhyme or sing a familiar song. When you reach the end of a stanza, stay still. If the baby tries to keep on bouncing, he is sending you a signal: "I want more." Respond to this signal by resuming the song and bouncing the baby on your knee.

- When the baby has mastered reaching and grasping, sit him in a baby chair and give him a rattle with a handle. At first he will shake the rattle a few times, touch it to his mouth, and let it drop. Over the course of several months, the baby will learn more things that he can do with the rattle. He passes it from hand to hand, bangs it against the floor or the table, hides it under the blanket and retrieves it, or initiates a back-and-forth game with you, offering you the rattle and immediately taking it back.

- Give the baby a roly-poly toy that straightens up after it is pushed down. The baby is likely to keep on batting the toy until it tips over and then to stop and watch as it rights itself. He will delight in his ability to make the roly-poly perform.

- During the same period of time, the baby is learning to use his fingers and thumb in opposition (pincer grasp). When the baby is sitting at his feeding table, put a few small crackers or cereal rings on the table. See whether the baby can pick up a cracker or a ring by using a pincer grasp rather than by scooping it up with his fingers. Using this pincer grasp is a good skill for babies to practice while they are waiting to be fed. When the baby has mastered crackers and cereal, try more challenging foods such as spaghetti, ice cubes, and Jell-o.

- Hide a toy in your pocket and let the baby reach in your pocket to retrieve it.

- Put a toy inside a pot and see whether baby can find it by lifting up the lid.

How Babies First Learn to Use Tools

Toward the end of the first year, babies begin to learn how to use a tool to accomplish a goal. As they manipulate tools, babies are extending their knowledge of cause and effect. Their first tool is likely to be a spoon. In the beginning, they grasp a spoon and use it much like they would use another toy, shaking it, banging with it, passing it from hand to hand, and putting it in their mouth. As they continue to hold the spoon while they are being fed, they begin to recognize that the purpose of a spoon is to pick up food and put it in their mouth. Babies' first attempts to eat with a spoon are likely to be disastrous. Instead of ending up in their mouth, the food lands on the floor, on their clothes, and in their hair. But they do grasp the idea that we use spoons to eat with and, every once in a while, a spoonful makes its way to their mouth.

Sensory and water play also provide babies with early opportunities to use tools. Babies use shovels to scoop up the oatmeal in their sensory bin, and they use sponges or washcloths to bathe a baby doll in the water-play tub. Occasionally, a baby will use a brush to fix a teddy bear's hair, a precursor of pretend play.

Activities That Encourage Babies to Use Tools

Take advantage of the following activities to supply babies with plenty of practice using tools:

- Give the baby a large spoon rather than a baby spoon while you are feeding her. Even though the spoon may not fit inside her mouth, she will become increasingly more adept at getting the food up to her mouth.

- Tie a piece of ribbon to a toy when the baby is at her feeding table. See whether she can learn to pull the ribbon to retrieve the toy. She is more likely to be successful if you show her how it is done.

- Give the baby a sponge so she can help you wash off her table.

- Give the baby a wooden spoon and an upside-down pot. See whether she can use the spoon to bang on the pot.

Toddlers: Making Connections and Solving Problems

As you plan activities for the toddler classroom or for a mixed-age group, it is important to keep in mind the kinds of problems that toddlers are trying to solve, the level of skills the toddlers have, and the kinds of feats the toddlers are trying to accomplish. Toddlers, like infants, enjoy toys and activities that give them an opportunity to accomplish their goals. Between the ages of 1 and 3 years, toddlers recognize cause-and-effect relationships and are especially interested in discovering ways in which they can have an effect on both objects and people.

Exploring, Experimenting, and Making Discoveries

Toddlers are continually carrying out experiments to discover how things work, what new things they can accomplish, and what new things they can learn. They have the unique ability to find the one new toy that has been placed in the room, and a hassle will likely result over who gets to play with it first.

Toddlers are known for their tendency to get into things, and they have no trouble finding trouble. Rather than spend much of your time saying "No," "Be careful," "Don't touch," or "Blocks are not for throwing," caregivers are well advised to "toddler-proof" the room on a daily basis, putting everything out of reach that they don't want toddlers to touch.

Toddlers are especially interested in discovering how they can make objects change. What would happen if I dropped the dish on the floor? How can I make things move? What would happen to the cracker if I threw it on the floor and trampled on it? What things that I throw on the floor will bounce, roll away, or come apart? What is inside the mat, or the sandwich, or the chest of drawers? How can I make the riding toy go really, really fast? How can I push the chair across the room? How can I get the insides to come out of the teddy bear?

Although toddlers may have the reputation of being difficult to manage, most toddlers are fun to watch, and even their mischief makes us laugh. They are very good at finding the things we do not want them to find or at making a mess when we have just cleaned up. Their curiosity leads them into trouble as they search for answers to questions they cannot ask with words. What will happen if I throw the paint into the fish bowl? How big a pile can I make if I take everything off the shelves? How many beans can I fit in my ear? How loud a noise can I make when I shut the door? What's inside the pillow, and how much of it can I pull out?

Two-year-old toddlers are learning to use words to ask their questions. Tanya and Absalom were sitting beside each other comparing the color of their arms. Tanya asked the teacher how she could turn brown like Absalom. Timothy, whose dog had died over the weekend, also had a question for the teacher. "Can Blackjack get undead?"

Toddlers use their fast-growing motor skills to learn about spatial relationships and position in space. Young toddlers are learning the advantages of moving around on two legs. They can walk and carry things at the same time. They can toot the horn of their riding toy with one hand and use their feet to scoot across the floor, experiencing the fun of moving fast. They can turn their head to keep track of the position of the toy that they are pulling. They can climb into a big chair, assume a sitting position, and manipulate a toy or "read" a picture book.

Older toddlers are confident walkers who are able to use their new skills to make more discoveries and increase their understanding of movement, position, speed, and distance. They can walk forward and backward, climb up stairs, extend their reach by standing on a stool, and balance on one foot long enough to kick a ball across the room. They can run across the playground, chasing or escaping from other children. Walking and running are no longer just skills to master—they are a means of achieving a goal. When 2-year-olds go for a walk through the park, their focus is on what new discoveries they can make. They rub their hands over the trunks of the trees, pick up acorns or interesting rocks, watch squirrels jump from tree to tree, and bend down to smell a wildflower.

Activities That Encourage Toddlers to Explore, Experiment, and Make Discoveries

Here are some good ways to encourage toddlers' explorations, experiments, and discoveries. Be sure to talk with toddlers about the goals they are trying to accomplish, the strategies they try, and the discoveries they make.

- Rather than buy new things for the toddler room, think about adding recycled materials. Spindles from toilet paper, film cans, small plastic bottles with tops too big to be swallowed, wrapping paper, paper towel rolls, used greeting cards, old playing cards, carpet pieces, shells, cloth swatches, odd mittens, catalogs, unmatched socks, empty juice bottles, and cell phones that do not work (and that have the batteries removed) are just a few of the items that you could collect.

- Provide young toddlers with cars or trucks that they can zoom along the floor.

- Provide toy vans and trucks that toddlers can load up with blocks, or empty boxes and small chairs that they can push around the room.

- Fill a basket with small (but not small enough to swallow) items such as odd puzzle parts from a wooden puzzle, plastic or rubber animals, alphabet blocks, squeak toys, or miniature plastic boats. Toddlers will have fun emptying and filling the basket. (Do not be surprised, though, if they end the activity by emptying rather than filling!)

- Give young toddlers pop-up toys or spinning tops so they can watch what happens when they push down their levers. (It is a good idea to buy two similar pop-up toys because toddlers typically like to play alongside a friend and are not very good about sharing.)

- Create a filling and emptying toy for young toddlers by making a hole in the cover of a box. Give the toddlers plastic chips, craft sticks, or ping-pong balls and show them how to drop the items into the slot. When they run out of items, show them how to take the cover off the box, take out the items, put the cover back on the box, and play the game again.

- Give young toddlers a spindle toy and help them learn to put the rings on the spindle.

- Provide young toddlers with large pegboards and pegs. Putting pegs in a hole is a fine filling and emptying activity. Toddlers practice their small motor skills as they adjust the orientation of the pegs to fit them in the holes of the pegboard.

- Put out three pots and three lids. After some practice, toddlers will learn to match each lid to its appropriate pot.

- Make a house out of a discarded appliance box. Cut out doors and windows. Older toddlers will enjoy crawling through the door, standing up inside and peering through the windows.

- Give 2-year-old inset puzzles that have 6 to 10 puzzle pieces with knobs. Toddlers learn to orient the pieces so they fit into the appropriate spot. If you buy a rack of knob puzzles, be sure to limit the number of puzzles you put out on the shelf. If you have too many puzzles on the shelf, toddlers are likely to take all the pieces out of every puzzle, ending up with a heap of mixed puzzle pieces.

- Two-year-olds are usually ready to string large beads. Begin with a short string so they can accomplish the task without getting frustrated.

- Toddlers enjoy block tables such as the Lego® tables that combine the fun of building with the fun of filling.

How Toddlers Learn About Cause and Effect

Toddlers are quite aware of their own power to make things happen. They continually seek ways to manipulate toys, furniture, and especially people. Toddlers are insistent about doing things by themselves and making their own decisions. "I'm always late for appointments," one mother explained. "Teresa insists on putting her jacket on by herself, and it takes her forever!" Another parent explained why she missed family night: "I was all ready to bring Tina, but she insisted on wearing her bathing suit and absolutely refused to put anything on over it. How could I bring her to a meeting in her bathing suit?"

Asserting themselves is a major goal of older toddlers. They want to feel powerful, grown up, and independent. They love to stand in front of the mirror and watch themselves make faces. They make sure that they have an audience when they get ready to do a stunt, and they wait for the audience to applaud when the stunt has been executed.

Activities That Provide Toddlers With Opportunities to Learn About Cause and Effect

Because toddlers can learn very quickly, make sure to refurbish each area when toddlers need more challenging tasks. Engage toddlers in activities such as the following that provide them with opportunities to make interesting things happen:

- Give older toddlers a large paper or plastic cup. Provide a pail of potting soil. Let each child shovel soil into his cup until it is a quarter full. Pass out some fast-sprouting and hardy seeds (grass seed works quite well, as do radishes).

- Give toddlers an opportunity to make Jell-O® or play dough.

- Let toddlers play with wind-up toys or miniature cars.

- Give toddlers a cardboard or plastic tube and let them blow through it.

Toddlers Use Tools to Achieve Goals

Toddlers understand the concept of using a tool to achieve a goal and have learned to use several tools successfully. They are likely to have a favorite tool that they carry around everywhere. Alfonso's aunt gave him a toy screwdriver for his second birthday. For several months, he took the screwdriver to bed with him every night. One night, he misplaced the screwdriver. After both parents spent a good

15 minutes searching in vain for the screwdriver, his mother tried to convince him to put his nice cuddly teddy bear in his bed. Alfonso protested, "I gotta have my screwdriver. It makes the dinosaurs scared."

Toddlers use tools to perform a variety of tasks. Young toddlers eat with a spoon, pour milk from a pitcher, bang with a hammer, wipe off the table with a sponge, sweep the floor with a child-sized broom, and use a stick to retrieve a toy that rolled under the sofa.

By the age of 2 years, toddlers use a wide variety of tools for many different purposes. They use a crayon to make a mark on a paper or on the wall. They use a fork to spear their food, a toothbrush to clean their teeth, a rolling pin to flatten clay, a hammer to pound down a peg, a shovel to dig a hole in the sand, a key to attempt to unlock a door, and a fly swatter to chase away a fly. They use paste, paper clips, or staples to keep papers together, a leash to walk the dog, and a mouse to make pictures move on a computer.

Activities That Help Toddlers Learn to Use Tools

The following activities will challenge toddlers to enhance their tool-using skills:

- Give young toddlers a variety of tools that they can use in the sandbox, including shovels, scoops, funnels, molds, sieves, and rakes.

- Place a variety of tools in the water table. Watering cans, squeeze bottles, cups of different sizes, funnels, strainers, egg beaters, and sponges add to fun of water play. Put a rubber doll in the water-play area, and let the children use the sponge to wash the doll.

- Give older toddlers a tool bench with a hammer, wrench, screwdriver, and pliers. Let them use the screwdriver to tighten the screws on the bench and the wrench to loosen the bolts.

- Give older toddlers a xylophone or a set of musical bells. Let them experiment with making different sounds.

- Give older toddlers a pair of safety scissors and a strip of colored paper. With some direction, older toddlers can learn to cut a strip of paper in two.

How Toddlers Learn Concepts Related to Quantity, Color, Shape, and Size

Although many 2-year olds can count up to 10 by rote, their concept of quantity is usually limited to sets that contain two or three items. They have no problem recognizing that they need to find two mittens before they go outside, three candles on their cake (two because they are turning 2 and one more to grow on), and three chairs at the snack table (so that both of their friends have a place to sit). They are also perfectly aware of *more* and *less* and will shout "no fair" if the teacher gives another child more juice than they got.

Very few 2-year-olds can name colors, but many know how to choose a favorite book by the color of its cover or how to sort according to color. They can also complete a shape puzzle with three

Finding pictures of a yellow yo-yo, a red car, and an animal with a long, curly tail is a fun activity for a toddler who is mastering concepts of color, shape, and size.

or four different shapes, although they may not be able to name a circle or a triangle. Sorting according to size is a relatively easy task, and most 2-year-olds will happily join in at cleanup time when they are given the task of putting the long blocks, medium-sized blocks, and short blocks on the appropriate shelves.

Preschool Children: Building Knowledge and Understanding

While infants and toddlers learn basic concepts about the world and how they can make things happen, preschool children are developing knowledge that will have a direct effect on their reading performance. The information base, the vocabulary, the expectations about consequences of actions, and the understandings of what makes people tick—all of which they acquire through an emergent literacy curriculum—will help them to decode words, predict what will happen in a story, and interpret what they read. A rich and diverse array of concept-building experiences lays the groundwork for a successful experience in kindergarten and first grade, when learning to read is the heart of the curriculum.

Learning About Cause and Effect

Preschool children, like toddlers, enjoy doing experiments. Some of these experiments are their own inventions; others are teacher directed or are inspired by the way teachers have laid out materials. At first, preschool children carry out experiments to answer the question, "What would happen if . . . ?" As they gain more practice in carrying out experiments, they begin to guess or "hypothesize" what the outcome of their experiment will be. They may begin a sink–float experiment by hypothesizing that heavy things will sink and lighter things will float. They drop a pebble into the water and it sinks, then they drop a dried bean into the water and it floats. So far, their hypothesis is supported. Next, they drop a safety pin in the water and it sinks, then they drop a large piece of wood and it floats. Much to their surprise, their hypothesis is refuted.

Children are likely to continue dropping items into the water in hopes of finding out why certain objects sink and others float. Although they are unlikely to come up with the word *density* without help from their teacher, their guesses will become more accurate. As children try out different activities and carry out different experiments, they begin to grasp basic scientific principles.

The following scenario provides an example. Timothy and Rosio were playing in the science area of the classroom where the teacher had set up a tray of small objects and a large pan of water.

Timothy:	(*holding up a small rock*) I bet this is gonna sink. (*Drops it into the pan.*) See, I'm right.
Rosio:	(*holding up a moon shell*) This shell is pretty heavy. It's gonna sink too.
Teacher:	(*giving Timothy a long piece of bark*) Try this. What do you think will happen?
Timothy:	It's gonna sink. (*Drops it in the pan.*) Nah—it floats.
Teacher:	Why do you suppose it floats?
Timothy:	Cause it's long, I guess.
Teacher:	(*giving Timothy a long piece of chain*) Try this.
Timothy:	(*sounding surprised*) It sinks! I guess it's too heavy to float.
Teacher:	(*giving Rosio a pencil*) Now try this.
Rosio:	(*Drops the pencil in the pan.*) It floats. Is that 'cause it's wood?
Teacher:	You both have done some good thinking. I'll bring in some more objects tomorrow so you can keep on experimenting. For now, let's put all the things that floated on the red plate and all the things that sank on the blue plate.

As children continue to experiment with sinking and floating objects, they learn that whether an object sinks in or floats on water depends on the object's density; when they encounter that word in reading or science class, they will be able to understand its meaning because they have a basic, intuitive grasp of the concept. The more concepts of this kind that children learn in their early years, the easier it will be for them to understand what they read and to learn new ideas and information. In addition, the habits of prediction, observation, inference, and analysis that they develop through their real-world experimentation will help them to decode words, to figure out which of several possible words or meanings makes sense in a particular sentence, and to follow the logic of a story, explanation, or argument.

Activities That Help Children Learn About Cause and Effect

By challenging children to think about the characteristics and properties of things they play with every day, you can help children learn important ideas about cause and effect as well as related concepts. Consider the following activities:

- When children play on the playground slide, ask them to think about why they can slide down faster than they can climb up. Then throw a ball up in the air and ask the children what made it come back down. Through their own direct experiences and the kinds of questions they are asked, children begin to grasp the concept of gravity.

- When children are building a house out of blocks, ask them to try putting a big block on top of a small block or ask them to see how long they can stand on one foot. As you give children physical challenges, you are helping them learn concepts related to balance.

- When children are playing on a swing, ask them whether it is harder to begin pumping the swing or to keep the swing in motion once it is in the air. When the children are pulling each other around on a wagon, ask them whether it takes more strength to get the wagon going in the first place or to keep it going once it is in motion. Through activities and questions like these, you can help children explore concepts of acceleration and inertia.

Learning to Use a Variety of Tools

Because of their increased dexterity, preschool children become adept at using a variety of tools to perform different functions. They learn to use tools such as rakes, brooms, scoops, or sponges to gather material; tools such as knives, scissors, strainers, or hoes to separate materials; and tools such as glue, paper clips, needles and thread, brads, nails, or staples to attach one piece of material to another. Like toddlers, preschool children discover that tools increase their ability to make things happen. As they make things happen and talk about the process and results, they expand their vocabularies and their repertoires of concepts.

Activities in Which Preschool Children Learn to Use Tools to Accomplish Different Goals

Learning to use tools requires practice—even for adults. Children not only can develop skills through practice but also can continue exploring their world through the following activities:

- Place a variety of tools in the sand table, including scoops, shovels, sifters, spreaders, funnels, and cookie cutters. Provide several different containers such as muffin tins, plastic bowls and dishes, cake pans, and cookie sheets. Ask the children to see how many different things they can do with the sand.

- Give each child a large sheet of paper. Put out crayons, markers, scissors, paint brushes and paint, Q-tips®, pencils, and eyedroppers. Challenge the children to create a picture using three different "tools."

- Divide the children into three groups. Give each child a sheet of paper. Put out staples, brads, a hole puncher, yarn, scissors, and tagboard sheets. Ask each small group to make their own book using some of these materials.

Extending Concepts of Shape, Size, Time, and Quantity

Although children develop rudimentary concepts of shape, size, time, and quantity in the early years, these concepts become more sophisticated in the preschool years when children spend a good proportion of their time categorizing, sequencing, and identifying relationships. These concepts contribute to their understanding of mathematics and science as well as to their ability to identify and form letters, retell events in a logical sequence, and follow and construct narratives. *Concepts of shape* include the ability to name, sort, and categorize commonly seen shapes such as circles, half circles, squares, rectangles, triangles, octagons, and pyramids. They also includes the identification and naming of different number and letter shapes and the use of prepositions to describe spatial relationships. *Concepts of size* include the ability to sort and sequence according to size and to use some type of measure to compare the size of objects or people. *Concepts of time* include an understanding of past and present, a differentiation of the immediate past from the distant past, and a differentiation of the near future from the distant future. Concepts of time also include an understanding of the ways in which time is measured. *Concepts of quantity* include the ability to name and sequence cardinal numbers (1, 2, 3) and ordinal numbers (first, second, third), the understanding of one-to-one correspondence (each number counted is associated with one thing), and the recognition of the different ways in which quantities are measured.

Activities That Help Children Acquire Concepts of Shape

The following are just a few of the many activities you can organize that will help children expand their knowledge of shapes:

- Organize the classroom blocks by shape and "label" the places where they go with appropriate pictures. As children put away the blocks, they will learn to attend to the shape of each block and put it in the right place on the shelf.

- Give children lots of opportunities to play with geometric shapes and to fit them together in patterns and pictures. For example, they can make shapes with rubber bands on a geoboard; play with pattern blocks and tangrams; make a picture using magnetic shape blocks or Colorforms®; fold paper to make rectangles, squares, and triangles; put together a shape puzzle; or trace the shapes of puzzle pieces as templates and draw around them.

- Challenge children to make shapes from other shapes. Can they make a square out of triangles? a rectangle out of squares? a triangle out of a square and two triangles?

- Help children recognize that some shapes with the same name can look quite different. For example, rectangles can be tall and skinny; they can also be square. Triangles can be tall and narrow like witches' hats or equilateral like the triangle instrument that children play. In addition, they can be oriented with a point at the top like an **A** or at the bottom like a **V**. Some triangles even contain an angle that is greater than 90 degrees.

- Read shape books with the children and help them make their own shape books. They can stamp copies of a shape with a rubber stamp or with a stamp cut from a vegetable or sponge. Then they can paste on pictures that depict or contain that shape, cut from magazines and toy catalogs.

- Give the children opportunities to sort plastic letters or numbers, or challenge them to find the letters that are in their first name or the numbers that are in their telephone number or street address.

- Go on a shape walk in which children name and identify the different shapes they see on the playground or in a walk around the block.

Activities That Help Children Acquire Concepts of Size

The following activities allow children to explore the idea of size:

- Let children sort blocks, buttons, miniature animals, or small vehicles according to size.

- Give children sequence puzzles, stacking blocks, spindle toys, or measuring cups that involve self-correcting ways of ordering according to size.

- Line the children up according to height.

- Read books that illustrate size differences, or let the children make their own books. The daily newspaper is likely to have advertisements about cars, and children have fun cutting out pictures of small, medium, and large cars or trucks and pasting them into their homemade books.

- See how many words the children can think of that are related to size (e.g., *small, tiny, itsy-bitsy, miniature, skinny,* and *short*—or *big, tall, large, huge, giant, enormous,* and *humongous*).

- Hang a tape measure or chart on the wall and give each child a turn to get measured. Put a mark on the chart with the date and the child's name. Measure the children six months later so they can see how much they have grown.

- Engage the children in a cooking activity that involves measuring the ingredients.

Activities That Help Children Acquire Concepts of Time

Children can begin to comprehend concepts of time through the following discussions and activities:

- Make a point of using time words with children. Talk to the children about what they did yesterday or what they did last summer and what they are planning to do—tomorrow, on their birthday, or during their next vacation. Use words and phrases such as *hurry up* and *slow down*, walking *slowly* and running *fast, ahead of time* and *late*.

- Talk about the difference between seconds, minutes, hours, days, weeks, months, years, and centuries.

- Read books to children about things that happened a long time ago—for example, books about people who traveled in horses and buggies and books about dinosaurs. Do not expect children to grasp the difference between prehistoric and historic time, but help them to understand that some past things happened at about the same time and some happened much, much earlier. "This story happened a long time ago, even before I was born. People did not have computers then, or even TVs or cars." "Dinosaurs lived a very, very, very long time ago, way before there were even any people on earth."

- Talk about animals that are alive today and about animals that are going to be born or eggs that are going to hatch.

- Put a calendar on the wall and have the children make an **X** on each day they are in school.

- Talk about plans for future events.

Activities That Help Children Acquire Concepts of Number

Once you are certain that children can count by rote, give the children practice with counting objects. Start by lining up three to five objects in front of the child and asking him to count them. Make sure that he counts one and only one number for each object as he touches it (which indicates a knowledge of one-to-one correspondence). Make the task more challenging by adding more objects, by letting the child be the one to put the objects in a row, or by putting objects in a different arrangement such as two lines or a **V**.

- Use egg cartons to help children practice counting with one-to-one correspondence. As they drop one small object in each hole, they can say a number. Later, they can use the egg cartons to help them count by twos or threes.

- Seize teachable moments to talk about mathematical ideas such as *more, fewer, enough, how many,* and *one for each.* For example, as a child is helping you pass out the snack, you can figure out together how many plates you need or whether you have enough crackers.

- Read number books with a child, letting him count the number on each page. Show him the numeral that stands for each number. Give children lots of opportunities to create sets of objects. Start with sets of three and continue until children can create sets of 10. Show children how to combine two smaller sets to create one larger one.

- After children have created a small set of objects, cover up some of them. See if the children can tell how many you are hiding by looking at how many are left.

- Place five carpet squares in a row on the floor. Ask one child to sit on the first square. Ask the next child to sit on the second square. Continue until there is a child sitting on each of the five carpet squares.

- Play a clapping game with the children. Let them begin with one clap and continue until they can clap five times in a row.

- Help children count out rhythms when they use musical instruments.

- Bring a doctor's scale into the classroom. Weigh and measure each child. Talk about how many pounds they weigh and how many inches tall they are.

- Let the children create their own books of number sets. Help the children write numerals up to the numeral 6 on each page of their number book. Give the children stickers. Let them place one sticker on the first page, two on the second page, and so forth, until they reach the last page.

- Talk about things that come in twos (shoes, hands, twins), threes (tricycle wheels, triangles' lines, traffic lights), fours (table legs, car doors, butterfly wings), and fives (star points, fingers, buttercup petals). Help children find pictures to go with each number and make a class display or number book.

- Let children count their own fingers. Teach them finger plays and rhymes such as "Five Little Pumpkins."

- Teach the children how to play a card game such as "Go Fish" or "Old Maid." Begin by putting only aces, deuces, threes, and fours in the set.

- Collect picture books with mathematical themes, such as *Ten, Nine, Eight* (Bang, 1983) and *Too Many Tamales* (Soto, 1996).

Mathematical understanding, or numeracy, is as important to develop in the preschool years as is emergent literacy. The NAEYC position statement (2003), "Early Childhood Mathematics: Promoting Good Beginnings" will give you a good overview as you seek professional development opportunities to help you support children's learning about all aspects of mathematics.

GAINING KNOWLEDGE ABOUT WORDS, SENTENCES, AND STORIES

Like knowledge about the real world, knowledge of words, sentence patterns, and stories is gradually built through everyday interactions. As you play, converse, read, and sing with babies, toddlers, and preschoolers, you have many opportunities to help them build these key literacy foundations.

Building a Knowledge of Words

The relationship between the size of a child's vocabulary and her reading performance is well-documented in the literature, as described in Chapter 5. Building vocabulary begins in infancy when infants tune in to the sounds of language, engage in back-and-forth cooing conversations, and learn to associate phrases with actions such as waving in response to adults asking them to "Wave bye-bye." Between the ages of 1 and 2 years, the typical toddler develops a vocabulary of between 50 and 100 words and can follow simple directives such as "Find the picture of the kitty" or "Show me your shoes." Between the ages of 2 and 3 years, toddlers typically experience an exponential growth in vocabulary and learn to speak in two- and three-word sentences. During the preschool years, children not only continue to learn new words with remarkable ease but also recognize that the same word can have more than one meaning and that different words can be used to express the same idea.

But all this learning does not simply unfold. As we saw in Chapters 4, 5, and 6, children learn vocabulary by using it in interesting conversations with their parents, teachers, and peers; as they listen to books and talk about them; as they engage in pretend play; as they hear and tell stories about past, future, or imagined events; and as they participate in the celebrations and rituals that are important in their community. The more opportunities they have to hear and use language in ways that are meaningful to them, the more that language connects with and extends their real-world experiences, the more it includes rare words and refers to things beyond the here and now, and the more it includes open-ended, cognitively challenging questions, then the richer their vocabularies are likely to be.

Young children do not need specific vocabulary lessons, but the adults in their lives can help them to fall in love with words. Consider the words that the following three children have chosen:

"Here, Nona," said Emmett (age 22 months) as he handed his grandmother a flower he had picked. "Black-Eyed Susan."

Three-year-old Lyle seemed a little shy when he came in for his checkup, so his doctor asked him a question that he knew Lyle could answer. "What color are my eyes?" Lyle stared at the doctor's eyes for a long time, then finally replied: "Turquoise."

"Stay still, Muffy," said 4-year-old Kathryn, addressing a stuffed puppy. "You know I'm the veterinarian. I'm not going to hurt you. I just have to listen to your heart with my stethoscope and then I'm going to give you your injection."

Small children such as Emmett, Lyle, and Kathryn enjoy using big words. Emmett could have said, "flower," but he was intrigued by the idea that his flower had an eye and also a name. Lyle could have said "blue," but he had been playing with his older sister's crayons and liked having a precise word for each color. Kathryn loved playing veterinarian, and the big words her teacher had taught her were an important part of the role.

Activities That Help Infants Have Fun With Words

Consider trying the following activities to enhance infants' awareness of words:

- Talk about what you are doing as you take care of the infant, speaking slowly and clearly and in a high-pitched voice. "I'm washing your hand."

- Tell the baby what she is doing. "You are holding the rattle."

- Repeat simple rhymes as you and the baby play together. "This little piggy went to market." "See-saw, Margery Daw."

- Sing songs and read stories to the baby.

- Show the baby a picture of his family, naming each member: "Mommy," "Daddy," "Nana."

- Read a picture book with familiar illustrations as you hold the baby in your lap. Help her touch each illustration as you name it. "Cracker, bottle, car, spoon."

Activities That Help Toddlers Have Fun With Words

Use interesting words with toddlers; do not feel that you have to talk down to them or use only familiar words. In addition, try the following activities with toddlers to help them focus on words:

- Talk about words themselves, especially compound words. "I wonder why this is called a mailbox? Do you know why?"

- Talk about the names of people and of favorite storybook characters. For example, you might tell the children, "Violet and Daisy are girls, but their names are the same as the names of flowers," or "Ted has a long name, Theodore, and a short name, Ted, just like his father."

- Sing songs such as "Head, Shoulders, Knees and Toes" or "Old MacDonald" that give you an opportunity to introduce new vocabulary words as you make up new verses.

- Put a collection of miniature animals in a paper bag and let a small group of toddlers select an animal from the bag. If a toddler picks out the pig, for example, ask the toddler to tell you what animal he picked. Then tell all the children to make noises like a pig. Continue to let the children choose an animal until none are left in the bag.

- Read a Big Book to three or four toddlers. Touch one of the illustrations in the book and ask the children to tell you what it is. If they do not know, label it for them. Next, ask them to tell you the name of another object. Then, go back to the page with the first object, and ask the children to point to it. Continue to play the game until you finish the book.

Activities That Help Preschoolers Have Fun With Words

An intentional focus on words as a fun part of a preschool curriculum can have a dramatic effect on the size of young child's vocabulary. Consider trying the following activities with preschoolers to help them enjoy words:

- Play games with opposites.

- Help children notice details. Find something the same and something different in two photographs or between one page of a storybook and the next.

- Talk about homonyms, words such as *right* and *write* that sound alike but have a different meaning. Use two words that sound alike in the same sentence. "I ate eight pancakes for breakfast." "I am going to write my name in the right place." Ask the children to find the words that sound the same but have different meanings. See whether they can come up with other examples on their own; you may need to help them by giving suggestions such as *red* and *read*, *threw* and *through*, *one* and *won*, or *plain* and *plane*.

- Read the book *Amelia Bedelia* (Parrish, 1983). Ask the children to tell you why Amelia was silly.

- Play a game with picture cards of flowers, animals, tools, or other objects related to a theme. Put the cards in a pile with the picture side down, and give each child a turn to pick up a card and name its picture. Encourage children to help one another come up with precise names. (Supply names and details yourself if the children do not know them. "Yes, that's a bird. It's a Baltimore Oriole.")

- Read a book with some words that are unfamiliar to the children. When you come to an unfamiliar word, tell the children what it means. Then, before you continue reading, ask the children to use the word in a different sentence.

- Recite a familiar rhyme or song, using a synonym for one of the words (e.g., Jack and Jill went up the *slope* to fetch a *container* of water).

Learning Sentence Patterns

Do Not Jump in the Puddles

It was a rainy, rainy day.
I wanted to go out and play.
"Okay," said Mom. "Put your raincoat on,
But do not jump in the puddles."
I jumped on the sidewalk and I jumped on the rocks.
I took off my shoes and I jumped in my socks.
But I did not jump in the puddles.
I walked in the puddles, I ran in the puddles.
I took off my coat and I swam in the puddles.
But I did not jump in the puddles.

—BETTY BARDIGE AND MARILYN SEGAL (1990)

Poems such as this one are fun for preschoolers because these poems play on children's intuitive understanding of sentence patterns. The child in the poem knows what her mother means, but the child takes the words literally. As she describes actions that follow the letter of the law but violate its principle, she substitutes prepositional phrases for "in the puddles" and verbs for "jumped."

By the age of 5 years, most children have mastered the syntax, or grammar, of their first language. The patterns are intuitive, and they know when they have been violated. If you say to a child who has developed an ear for English syntax that "the dog black is in the pet store" and ask him to repeat the sentence, he is likely to say either "The black dog is in the pet store" or "The dog named Black is in the pet store." An ear for syntax helps children anticipate the word that is coming next in a sentence and, at times, to decide how a word should be pronounced or interpreted. For example, the child who reads the sentence, "I read a book yesterday," knows that *read* must be pronounced like *red* and not *reed*. If, instead, the sentence were "I read a book every day," then the syntactically attuned child would realize that, this time, *read* could be pronounced as either *reed* or *red*, depending on whether the activity is in the past or present.

Children who are learning two languages are usually quite good at keeping the syntax straight. Although they may import a vocabulary word from one language to another, they rarely confuse rules such as whether the adjective comes before or after the noun in the language they are speaking.

Children who speak an English dialect or who hear one from their teachers have a more subtle challenge. The basic rules of the oral and written languages they are using are the same, as is most of the vocabulary. But some of the rules are different. For example, some of the poems in Eloise Greenfield's (1978) book *Honey, I Love* are written in dialect. They contain lines such as "Ain't got it no more" and "Wasn't scared of nothing neither" that form negatives according to the rules of African American Vernacular English. Although some parents may insist that their children associate only with people who "talk right" and other parents may be uncomfortable having their children in settings where everyone "talks White," being able to switch from one dialect to another ultimately gives children an advantage in life.

Overgeneralizations such as "I goed to the store" or "The food falled off my fork" indicate that a young child is learning the rules of grammar and should not be "corrected." Similarly, it is both inappropriate and counterproductive to "correct" a child who is using syntactical forms that are perfectly correct in his dialect. Children who either exclusively or predominantly hear Standard American English forms will learn to expect and use those forms. Children who get lots of practice with both dialectical and standard forms will eventually master both.

Learning Narrative Skills

Narrative skills, or story schema, refer to those skills that children acquire as they listen to books read to them by fluent readers. When children become familiar with the structure of sentences in familiar books, they are able to anticipate how a sentence will be completed or to interpret the meaning of words within a sentence or a paragraph that they have never heard before. They will also be able to recognize when a sentence is grammatical without being taught grammar.

Grover Whitehurst, in a speech given at the White House Summit on Early Childhood Cognitive Development, said "Children who have listened to adults tell stories, have read picture books, and have overheard and participated in oral descriptions of events come to understand the general script for that type of language use" (2001). This script, Whitehurst explains, includes the introduction of characters, the description of a goal or motive, some sort of action or happening, and a resolution of the problem that ends the story.

Knowledge of the story script helps children comprehend a story. They can anticipate the sequence of events, which makes it easier to interpret and retell a story. They are also able to act out the story using puppets or assuming the role of one of the characters.

Activities That Help Children Acquire Narrative Skills

The following activities are examples of ways that teachers can give children opportunities to develop narrative skills:

- Read a book or a poem with words that are unfamiliar to the children. See if the children can guess the meaning of each new word from either its context or an illustration.

- Give the children stick puppets that represent the characters in the story. When a particular character is mentioned in the story, let each child hold up the puppet that represents that character. When the story is completed, let the children use the puppet characters to retell the story. This activity works well if different children take a turn telling the story while the other children hold up the puppets.

- Give the children props that help them retell the story, or put out a sequence of pictures that represent the events that occurred.

- Show children pictures of totem poles, and explain how artists used these to help people remember important stories. Help children create their own story poles by drawing pictures to represent important characters or events in a folktale or other story, then cutting out the pictures and pasting them in order on a paper towel spindle. Encourage them to retell the stories to their friends and families, using their story poles as cues.

Using Themes as a Context for Learning

Beginning in the toddler years, children acquire information about the world, which, like the development of concepts, fosters reading comprehension. To comprehend what they read, children need to acquire specific information that will enable them to relate what they are reading about to what they already know. A child-care program, whether it is housed in a home or a center setting, provides ongoing opportunities for a child to acquire this information. The kind and extent of the information that children acquire is determined in large part by the quality of the curriculum and the skill and expertise of staff members.

An established way of planning a content-rich curriculum is to use a thematic approach. When a class uses a theme such as "Me and My Family," "Weather," or "Transportation" to structure the curriculum, then information and concepts that are introduced in one interest center or in one activity are reinforced and expanded in different centers within the child-care setting and in different activities scheduled throughout the day. The choice of themes either can be determined at the beginning of the program year or can emerge in the course of the year in accordance with events that occur in the community, the interest expressed by the children, or both. A theme such as "Me and My Family" may be selected as the first theme of the year as a way to help children learn about one another and to create a bridge between home and school. The theme of "Weather" might be selected if the children have just experienced a scary event such as a hurricane or a tornado.

Ways to Use Themes

Transportation is a favorite theme in many child-care programs. The teacher might begin the day with a morning circle time. After talking with the children about different kinds of transportation, the teacher might ask the children about the vehicle they used to come to school or the kinds of vehicles they saw on their way to school. They might sing a song such as "The Wheels on the Bus" or read together *The Little Engine That Could* (Piper, 1978) and look at other books about airplanes, boats, trucks, trains, or beasts of burden. In the course of the day, the children might spend time in the creative art center making paper boats or airplanes, they may put together transportation puzzles in the manipulative play center, or they may play Travel Agency in the pretend play center. At the end of the day, a parent who is a firefighter, truck driver, police officer, taxi driver, or bus driver might be invited to bring his vehicle to school and show it to the children. The unit might continue for several days or even for a month as children learn more about vehicles and use their new words and knowledge to make a pretend gas station, race course, or highway construction project.

When themes are used appropriately and flexibly, they give children an opportunity to expand the scope of their knowledge and encourage the teacher to continue to use his creativity to keep the curriculum vital and varied. As the children try to assimilate new information and represent it in their artwork, pretend play, and conversation, new questions often emerge. The transportation theme might lead to an exploration of things that fly or float, ways to travel through mud or on snow, or ways by which people got around in the days before automobiles.

Themes can be related to experiences that the child is likely to have at home, thereby allowing parents to talk with their children about the theme or engage their child in activities related to the theme. Themes also provide children with the opportunity to be experts and to share knowledge with their parents. "We're studying about bears!" 4-year-old Kimby announced proudly. "Did you know they can get cavities from eating too much honey?" "I didn't know that," replied her duly impressed father, "I wonder how they clean their teeth?" These kinds of conversations send parents, children, and teachers to the library or to the Internet for more information.

Themes for Toddlers

Introducing a theme in a toddler classroom is a good way to capture their interest and provide them with new information. Themes that can be used effectively in a toddler room relate to topics with which they are already familiar—for example, their families, food, houses, and grocery stores. They also enjoy themes about animals, cars and trucks, babies, and holidays or celebrations. However, flexibility is key with toddlers. Consider the following scenario:

M iss Full-of-Enthusiasm decided that the toddlers in her class should know about community helpers. She spent her entire weekend planning how she would arrange the classroom and writing out lesson plans for the month to teach the children about doctors, nurses, ambulance drivers, firefighters, letter carriers, and sanitation workers:

Week One
Theme: Letter carriers.
Objective: Support emergent literacy by helping children understand how letters are sent and delivered.
Classroom Additions—A puzzle of a mail truck, a mail bag, a postman's hat and satchel, a collection of brochures from the post office, a mailbox, a collection of stickers to use as stamps, catalogs, advertisements and postcards, stationery and envelopes, and a book about the merry postman.
Activities—Circle time discussions about how mail is delivered and collected; a walk to the post office; teach the children to sing "A Tisket, a Tasket"; give each toddler a turn writing a letter, putting it in an envelope, putting a sticker on it, and then putting it in the mailbox.

Miss Full-of-Enthusiasm shared her plans with Miss Been-There-Done-That, a seasoned teacher. Miss Been-There-Done-That praised

Miss Full-of-Enthusiasm for having so many creative ideas and for recognizing the objective for carrying out each activity. She explained, however, that with a toddler class, it is better to go with the flow, letting the themes emerge from the spontaneous interests expressed by the toddlers. She told Miss Full-of-Enthusiasm about a pet unit that she had developed with her young toddler group when one of the mothers in the class brought in a kitten and let the toddlers take turns petting it. She provided the following description about the pet unit:

> "After this mother's visit, the toddlers started talking about their own pets. These ranged from big dogs, to goldfish, to a variety of stuffed animals. I decided to select pets as our classroom theme. I asked the parents to send pictures of their pets to school so the children could show the pictures to the class. I was lucky enough to find several toddler-level books about pets, and I shared them with the children. When one child brought his teddy bear to school, we expanded the theme further. I invited the other children to bring in their stuffed animals. We made them "homes" from blocks and boxes and made sure that they all had enough to eat. I also showed the children pictures of different animals, including dogs and cats, and asked them to make the animal sounds that went with each picture. The children talked about their pets for several days."

Themes for Preschoolers

During the preschool years, themes can be used in the classroom as a way of providing children with new information, encouraging conversation, and broadening their knowledge base. It is important to remember that themes are not the curriculum. They are a way to organize and integrate the curriculum and to give children the opportunity to reflect on, demonstrate, and practice what they learn.

Themes that are appropriate for preschoolers include themes about families, familiar and faraway places, plants and animals, culture, seasons, weather, the arts, transportation, jobs, school, health, safety and nutrition, holidays and celebrations, clothes, houses, collections, community helpers, farms, stores, dinosaurs, the beach, and outer space. Selecting a theme that can be reinforced through a field trip is always an appropriate approach. Make sure that there are many different books associated with each theme you select.

Reflection

Select a theme that would be appropriate for either toddlers or preschoolers. Think of at least five activities that you could plan in the course of one day that would provide these children with new information that would increase their fund of knowledge.

REFERENCES

Bang, M. (1983). *Ten, nine, eight.* New York: Greenwillow Books.

Bardige, B., & Segal, M. (1990). Do not jump in the puddles [poem]. In CompassLearning [multimedia publisher], Tapestry Early Learning Programs. [Software and curriculum package]. San Diego, CA: CompassLearning.

Greenfield, E. (1978). *Honey I love and other love poems.* New York: HarperCollins Children's Books.

Jack Sprat. [Traditional nursery rhyme.]

Parrish, P. (1983). *Amelia Bedelia.* New York: HarperCollins Children's Books.

Piper, W. (1978). *The little engine that could.* New York: Grosset and Dunlap.

Soto, G. (1996). *Too many tamales.* New York: Puffin.

Whitehurst, G. (2001, July 26). Address by Grover J. (Russ) Whitehurst, Assistant Secretary of Education for Research and Improvement, U.S. Department of Education. White House Summit on Early Childhood Cognitive Development.

Whitehurst, G., & Lonigan, C. (2001). Emergent literacy: Development from prereaders to readers. In S. Neuman & D. Dickinson (Eds.), *Handbook of early literacy research*, pp. 11–29. New York: Guilford.

CHAPTER 8

The "Inside-Out" Domain

Katie Can!

Katie can do lots of things
Now that she is six.
She can shoot a basket
And do a lot of tricks.

She can feed her kitten.
She can fly a kite.
And when her pet gets sleepy
She kisses him goodnight.

She can say the alphabet
Or sing it as a song
And when Ms. Kelly reads a book,
Katie reads along.

Katie know her letters
And she can write them, too.
And if you write what Katie says
She'll read it back to you.

Katie practices each day
So soon she'll hear her father say
"Everybody, shout 'Hooray!' "
'Cause Katie can read!"

W e've all heard of very young children who suddenly burst into reading without any formal instruction, but, like the child depicted in this verse, most children must be taught to read. They must learn to recognize and name the letters of the alphabet, to identify the sounds and parts of words and to "blend" word parts together, and to associate particular sounds with particular letters. With lots of practice, they learn to combine their knowledge of sound, print, and meaning to "break the code." With a lot more practice, they learn to process the printed words quickly and automatically so that they can focus their attention on the message.

In English-speaking countries, a major portion of the curriculum in kindergarten, first grade, and second grade is devoted to reading and writing skills. By the time children reach third grade, they are expected to have mastered these skills. Unfortunately, many children reach third grade without having mastered the basics, and a disproportionate number of these children come from low-income, non-English-speaking, or African American homes (Barbarin, 2002).

Children who enter school with a strong emergent literacy foundation and who receive excellent early reading instruction generally learn to read without too much difficulty. However, many children from African American or non-English-speaking backgrounds or from low-income families cannot count on receiving excellent instruction in the primary grades. It is therefore doubly important for their early childhood teachers to see that they are well prepared.

In the early days of Head Start, many educators and policymakers were convinced that the way to prepare 4-year-olds was to teach them academic skills before they entered primary school. Alphabet strips were placed on the walls and teachers were trained to stand up in front of the class, hold up a flash card with an *A*, and ask the class to repeat in a loud voice, "A is for Apple." The second day, the teacher would hold up both the *A* and the *B*, continuing to add a letter a day until they finished alphabet. When the research showed that the gains made by 4-year-old children who had experienced a highly structured, academically oriented curriculum could not be sustained, Head Start programs did an about-face. The alphabet strips were stripped off the walls, and teachers were mandated to adopt a "developmentally appropriate," play-based curriculum.

In the mid- and late-1990s, new and more sophisticated techniques for measuring outcomes were developed, and the pendulum in Head Start swung back, but not all the way. The alphabet strips went back on the walls, but the approach to teaching alphabet skills became more play-based and developmentally appropriate. "Educators are beginning to look critically at curricula to expand their notion of the key demands of early education. Goals for early literacy are now comfortably placed alongside those for language, cognition and social, emotional and physical development" (Strickland, 2002, p. 66). Informed early childhood educators, responsible for designing curricula and training teachers, are stressing both the inside-*out* and the outside-*in* domains.

Educators and caregivers do not need to bring the kindergarten and first-grade curriculum down into the preschool to make sure that children have a strong foundation in the inside-out domain. At the same time, their learning cannot be left to chance. Children from highly educated, literacy-focused families often learn inside-*out* skills at home through both informal and deliberate instruction. Children from less literacy-oriented backgrounds profit from early education experiences that focus intentionally, yet playfully, on inside-*out* skills. And research shows that basic inside-*out* skills, generally taught to 5- and 6-year-olds, can be taught just as easily to 4-year-olds (Dorval, Joyce, & Ramey, 1980).

So, what inside-*out* skills should children learn before kindergarten? Basically, they fall into three areas: tuning in to the sounds that make up words, letter naming or alphabet skills, and writing. Children who can name some letters, who can recognize words that rhyme or that begin with the same sound, and who can blend word parts together can understand the "alphabetic principle"—the idea that letters and letter combinations represent the sounds that make up words. Later, they can learn to sound out regularly spelled words by applying their knowledge of letters and their associated sounds as well as their understanding of how these sounds are likely to be combined.

Writing is important because it helps children to make the link between the written and spoken word and to tune in to the way in which words are constructed. As they see the words they say represented on paper, children make the critical link between the spoken word and its representation in writing. As they try to communicate with the marks they make and then by writing "real letters," children work out the alphabetic principle for themselves.

In fact, in the Home School Study of Language Development in low-income toddlers and preschoolers (reported in *Beginning Literacy with Language*, Dickinson & Tabors, 2001), researchers found that the presence and active use of a "writing center" was a key factor that distinguished preschools whose graduates went on to do well in reading in the primary grades from programs whose graduates were less successful. Although many of the classrooms had writing centers, far fewer of them had teachers who took the time to support children's early writing efforts (Dickinson & Sprague, 2001, pp. 263–280). The most successful teachers intentionally incorporated some inside-*out* teaching into their curricula and encouraged children's active involvement in both reading and writing efforts.

Tuning in to the Sounds That Make Up Words

In ordinary conversation, we focus on the meanings of words and pay less attention to their sounds. To read a language that is written with an alphabet, however, we need to identify the sounds, or phonemes, that make up the words. To understand how children hone this ability and what their teachers can do to help them, it helps to distinguish among some closely related concepts (see box on this page).

CONCEPTS ABOUT SOUNDS AND PHONEMES

Sound awareness is the ability to recognize and differentiate sounds. (The sound of a horn is different from the sound of a siren.)

Phonological awareness is a general awareness of or attention to the sounds of language, as distinct from their meaning. For example, a young child who is developing phonological awareness may recognize rhymes and enjoy word-play games like "banana-fana-fo-fana." He may realize that *bowtie* has two parts—"bow" and "tie"—and that *paper* is made up of "pay" and "per."

Phonemic awareness is a subset of phonological awareness and involves its more sophisticated skills. Phonemes are the individual sound units of words that are represented by the letters of the alphabet (or by letter combinations such as *qu, sh,* or *th*). A child who is developing phonemic

(continued)

awareness may be able to recognize that *cat* and *kitchen* both begin with a /k/ sound and may be able to combine d-o-g into "dog."

Phonics refers to instructional methods that highlight systematic connections between speech sounds and their representation by letters or letter combinations.

The *alphabetic principle* is the idea that letters (and letter combinations) represent the individual phonemes that make up words.

Tuning In to Sounds

Although most children are not ready to learn about the sounds that letters or clusters of letters make until they are at least age 4, sound awareness—which is the logical precursor of phonological awareness—is acquired at birth or perhaps even earlier. Newborns with intact hearing are sensitive to similarities and differences in sounds and can differentiate between background noises and their mother's voice. By the age of 6 months, most infants have learned to babble, repeating strings of speech sounds in rapid succession—for example, *pa-pa, da-da,* or *ba-ba.* Linguists are able to identify the language spoken in the baby's home by the babble sounds she can utter.

Over time, the infant's brain undergoes a pruning process. The baby's capacity to identify and reproduce the sounds of his home language remains intact, but he will have difficulty identifying and reproducing the sounds of a new language. When an older child or adult learns to speak a second language, he may become fluent in that language, but he will most likely speak with an accent from the first language.

In addition to individual sounds, or phonemes, babies tune in to the rhythms and cadences of speech as well as learn to recognize those that are typical of the language (or languages) they hear. Indeed, they often produce strings of gibberish that sound like sentences before they learn to say meaningful words.

Many of the "games" that adults traditionally play with babies help foster an awareness of sounds. We imitate their babbles and encourage them to imitate ours. We recite nursery rhymes with a strong rhythm and encourage them to clap along or to act out key words (e.g., "Patty cake, patty cake baker's man. Bake me a cake as fast as you can."). We amuse them with games like "Pop Goes the Weasel" in which they learn to listen for and anticipate the "Pop." We teach them to imitate animal sounds; indeed, *moo* and *peep* are often among the first words of toddlers who have never seen a cow or a baby chick.

Developing Phonological and Phonemic Awareness and Oral Memory

Children as young as 2 years begin to develop phonological awareness. They notice ways in which words are alike and different in their sounds, and they begin to play with rhyme, rhythm, and compound words. A 3-year-old may be able to clap out the syllables in his name, repeat a simple tongue twister, or supply a rhyming word to fill in the blank in a familiar poem or nursery rhyme. Beginning at about the age of 4, children learn to take words apart into component phonemes— not just component sounds—and to put them back together again.

During the preschool years, children also develop their oral memories. They are likely to memorize the repeated refrains in familiar stories (e.g., "I'll huff and I'll puff and I'll blow your house down"), to recite nursery rhymes and chants as well as learning songs, and even to memorize significant chunks of favorite books. Knowing the words that they see "by heart" enables children to concentrate on how the words look and also to "read" a familiar text with fluency. As their phonemic awareness and letter knowledge develops, their pretend reading may grow imperceptibly into real reading of familiar, and then unfamiliar, material.

Activities That Support the Development of Phonological Awareness

Use the following activities to help children develop phonological awareness.

- Play clapping games to help children (ages 2 to 4) count the syllables in a word. In circle time, let children clap on each syllable of a child's name as you point to each child in the circle. Explain that some names get three claps, some names get two claps, and some names get only one clap.

> I see Mar-y sitting on the floor
> I see Tim sitting on the floor
> I see Fran-cis-co sitting on the floor.

- Read a picture book that is written in rhyme to a group of children (ages 2 to 4)—for example, *Brown Bear, Brown Bear, What Do You See?* (Martin & Carle, 1967), *Goodnight Moon* (Brown, 1947), or a Dr. Seuss book. Read the first line of a rhyming couplet. When you come to the second line, pause when you come to the rhyming word and let the children complete the rhyme.

> I saw a little monkey that was sitting in a tree.
> I looked up and waved to him, and he waved back to ___.

- Sing or recite in unison a familiar song, chant, or nursery rhyme such as "Twinkle, Twinkle Little Star," "Jack and Jill," "Shake It to the East," or "Five Little Monkeys." Ask the children (ages 2 to 4) to raise their voices and clap to emphasize the rhyming words.

- If you can read Spanish with accurate pronunciation or if a parent or other adult could help you, use a book like *Pio Peep!* by Alma Flor Ada (2003) or *Las nanas de abuelita/Grandmother's Nursery Rhymes* by Nelly Palacio Jaramillo to teach children (ages 2 to 5) nursery rhymes in English and Spanish.

- Seat a small group of children (ages 4 to 5) in a circle for a game called "Rhyme Around." Begin the game by saying a word such as "cat" for which it is easy to find a rhyme. Ask the child on your right to find a word that rhymes with *cat*. Ask each child, in turn, to come up with another rhyme for *cat* until you run out of rhymes. Then start another word, such as *frog, cake, tree,* or *book.* Can you get all the way around the circle? Which rhyming word family gets you the furthest? Can the children think of good words to start with?

- Encourage children (ages 4 to 5) sitting in a circle to play a rhyming game with one another. Begin the game by holding a ball, saying a word like "cat," and passing the ball to one of the children. The child who catches the ball has to say a word that rhymes with *cat*. If he cannot think of one quickly, he can ask the class for help. After they have jointly come up with a rhyme, he then says a word with a different sound—for example, "fast," and passes the ball to another child, who tries to think of a word that rhymes with *fast*. Continue the game until every child has a turn catching and throwing the ball.

- Make a set of rhyming picture cards: *bat-cat, phone-cone, fan-can, moon-spoon, shell-bell,* and *key-bee*. Ask the children (ages 4 to 5) to sort the pictures by putting together those that rhyme. You might give a small group of children different cards and ask them to find their partners. You can also put matching designs on the backs of rhyming pairs so children can turn the cards over to check their matches.

- Say a compound word such as *cupcake, lipstick,* or *thumbtack*. Challenge the children (ages 4 to 5) to find two words that are inside the one word. Give the children an opportunity to think of a different compound word. Write the words the children suggest on a whiteboard or flipchart and see how long a list they can create.

- Challenge children (ages 4 to 5) to say a word leaving out the first or last sound. "Try saying 'sailboat' without the 'sail.'" "Try saying 'carpet' leaving out the 'car.'"

Activities That Support the Development of Oral Memory

The following activities can help children between the ages of 2 and 5 to strengthen oral memory skills:

- Play a follow-the-leader game. Recite the following verses and ask the children to repeat each verse after you.

  Fee-Fie-Foe-Fum: Should I sing or should I hum?
  Or should I beat it on my drum?
  Fee-Fie-Foe-Fout: Should I whisper it or shout?
  Or should I try to clap it out?

**Fee-Fie-Fout-Foe: Should I shout it high or low?
Raise your hand if you don't know.**

- Reread a familiar book or recite a familiar rhyme. Say one word wrong and let the children correct you.

  "Rudolph the green-nosed reindeer"
  **"Peas, porridge hot, peas porridge cold. Peas porridge in
     the garbage can, nine days old."**
  "The itsy bitsy crocodile went up the water spout."

- Tell a story with a repeated refrain and see how quickly the children learn to say the refrain with you. *The Three Little Pigs* (Galdone, 1984), *Goldilocks and the Three Bears* (Marshall, 1998), and *The Little Red Hen* (McQueen, 1947) are familiar stories with refrains that children enjoy saying.

- Read books with repeated refrains that incorporate fun-to-say names and nonsense words—for example, *King Bidgood's in the Bathtub* (Wood, 1985), *Tikki Tikki Tembo* (Mosel, 1968), and *Chicka Chicka Boom Boom* (Archambault & Martin, 1989).

Activities That Support the Development of Phonemic Awareness

To help children recognize alliteration, use words that have the same beginning sounds in activities such as those listed below. (*Note:* These activities are best for children who are 4 years of age or older, although 2- and 3-year-olds may enjoy listening to the recommended poems and stories).

- Read books with alliterations in their titles or in key lines— for example, Mary Ann Hoberman's *The Seven Silly Eaters* (2000), Maurice Sendak's *Alligators All Around* (1991), and *Really Rosie* (1986), or Deborah Guarino's *Is Your Mama a Llama?* (which is also fun to read in Spanish). See if the children can identify the alliterations and tell you which sound is repeated.

- Teach children alliterative nursery poems in languages other than English. You might ask parents either to make tapes of the poems they learned as young children or to come in and teach these poems to the class; alternatively, you might ask a child who knows the poems by heart to teach the others.

- Recite Mother Goose rhymes that are built on alliterations—for example, "Wee Willie Winkie," "Diddle Diddle Dumpling," and "Goosey Goosey Gander."

- In addition, children might also enjoy the following new alliterative rhymes:

Bean Bag Ball

Bean bag ball
We play it in the hall.
You catch a bean bag with your toes
In bean bag ball.

Bean bag ball
We do not let it fall.
Balance the bean bag on your nose
In bean bag ball.

Rainy Day Song

Pitter, patter
Pitter, patter
Pitter, patter
Pit

The rain that pounds
My window pane
Puts polka dots on
It.

Pitter, patter
Pitter, patter
Pitter, patter
Pat.

The rain plays
My umbrella drum
Just like
That.

Tommy Turtle

*Tommy Turtle tickles me
With his tiny toes.
But if I try to tickle him—
In his shell he goes.*

To help children learn the sounds of letters that begin a word, use activities such as the following:

- Help children isolate and identify beginning letter sounds.

- Pretend that the names of all the children begin with a *b* sound. Call the roll, pronouncing each child's name as if it begins with the same sound. "Barry, Bohn, Bimothy." Ask the children to say their own name as if it begins with a *b* sound.

- Recite a familiar rhyme, changing the first letter of a key word—for example, "Tack and Till went up the hill." Ask the children to correct your mistake by saying "It's not Tack and Till. It's supposed to be Jack and Jill!" Determine whether they can tell you what letter Jack and Jill start with and which letter you stuck in instead.

- Teach children the trick of separating and blending the sounds in words. Start by giving lots of clues. "Meow, said the c-at. Do you know what a c-at is? Who can guess what a d-og might be?" When children get good at this game, see if they can quiz you by taking words apart and asking you to put them together.

WHAT ABOUT ACCENTS AND DIALECTS?

So far, our discussion of phonological and phonemic awareness has made the implicit assumption that everyone is saying and hearing the same sounds in the same ways and, therefore, that it makes sense to associate particular letters with these sounds in a regular way. But of course, this assumption is not always valid.

Young children who learn one language at home and another one in school or in the community are unlikely to speak the second language with an "accent" that reflects their first language. However, people who learn a second or third language as adults are likely to have difficulty speaking or even hearing sounds that are not in their primary language (or languages). For example, some Japanese speakers have trouble distinguishing the /l/ and /r/ sounds in English.

Children's pronunciation of English words and their use of grammar is, of course, influenced by the way that English is spoken in their homes and communities. They may be hearing a dialect such as African American Vernacular English with well-developed sound patterns and grammar, or they may be hearing Standard American English pronounced in ways that are highly influenced by the sound patterns of their parents' and grandparents' home languages.

Teachers of young children may be speakers of Standard American English, with regional or ethnic accents that match those of the community in which they work or that reflect their sojourns in other parts of the country. They may also, however, be English learners, or they may speak dialects that are markedly different from Standard American English with respect to how words are pronounced. Some teachers are adept at code-switching and can shift readily from one system of pronunciation and grammar to another. Others speak only one language or dialect and would have great difficulty matching the speech patterns of the children and families with whom they work.

What do all of these differences mean for children's language and emergent literacy—and especially for their phonemic awareness? English spelling is a very imperfect mirror of spoken English, so all children must struggle to some extent with the differences between the sounds they hear in words and the way that these words are conventionally represented in print. Children who do not hear critical distinctions, such as the difference between /l/ and /r/ sounds, may have an additional challenge. When they get to first grade, those children who habitually hear words with "extra" or "missing" sounds such as the dropped /r/ sounds of a "Boston" accent or the added /h/ sounds of Jamaican patois (*okay* is pronounced "hokay" and *art* is pronounced "hart") may also need to learn that these words are not written the way they say and hear them.

Languages and dialects are living systems of communication. "Correcting" a child's grammar and pronunciation—or your own—is not useful if it detracts from the conversation. However, a teacher who is aware of language and dialect differences can introduce poems and songs that highlight sounds and distinctions that children may have difficulty hearing and can take care to enunciate these sounds clearly.

LEARNING CONCEPTS OF PRINT AND ALPHABET SKILLS

In a society where literacy is pervasive, young children learn a lot about reading and writing long before they can read and write on their own. They see print on signs and billboards, in books and magazines, on labels and mail, even on television. If adults repeatedly direct their attention to the print itself, they learn a lot about how it works. They learn to distinguish print or writing from

Directing children's attention to print helps them realize that the print represents the words we say when we read.

other graphics and come to recognize that print is what is read and that it corresponds to the spoken word.

At the same time, children who see adults reading and writing learn much about the functions of print. They learn that signs and labels help people identify things; that recipes and directions tell you how to make something; that notes and lists can help you remember things; and that cards, letters, and e-mail are ways of sharing information with other people. They come to recognize which part of a package has a label, where to find the title on a book, and the beginning and ending of a story.

With more experience, children learn that print in English is read from left to right and from top to bottom and, perhaps, they also learn that some languages use different alphabets that are read in a different direction. They learn that words are made up of letters, which are different from numbers, and that they are separated from one another by spaces. They learn that the same letter can be written in upper- or lowercase and that, although people form letters differently, the forms that appear in print are fairly standard. Often, well before they can name a letter, they can distinguish its standard written form from a rough approximation. They also learn that a group of words that make a statement or ask a question is called a sentence, that a sentence begins with an uppercase letter and ends with a dot or other mark, and that a story can contain many sentences. Children who come to kindergarten knowing many of these "concepts of print" have an advantage in learning to read.

The key to writing English—and many other languages—is, of course, the alphabet; thus, learning the ABCs is an important part of learning to read and write. Knowing the names of the letters helps children understand reading and writing instruction. It also helps them to figure out the sounds that the letters represent, as most letters stand for sounds that are similar to their names.

Children are introduced to letters and to concepts of print in many ways. They may wear a t-shirt with words on it, watch their teacher point to the words as she reads a story, or see their own name written on the picture they drew at school. They pretend to write by drawing a squiggly line or by drawing letter-like shapes that only they can "read." They learn to recognize oft-seen symbols: a big M means McDonalds, the buttons in an elevator tell it what floor to go to, and a big red sign means stop. They may read ABC books, play with alphabet blocks, and learn to sing the ABC song. Young children are likely to recognize the first letter in their name and may assume that anything that has their letter on it belongs to them. These early discoveries prepare children to learn alphabet concepts.

Learning the names of the letters and their sounds used to be a central task of the kindergarten or first-grade curriculum, but today, children are expected to recognize at least 10 letters before they get to school. They may also be expected to know some letter sounds and be able to identify objects whose names begin with commonly used consonants such as *b, d, g, l, m, n. p, r, s,* and *t.*

Activities That Help Children Learn Concepts of Print

The following activities can help children learn concepts of print:

- Talk about a book before you begin to read it to the children.

- Show the children how you hold the book right side up.

- Show the children the cover of the book and talk about the title of the book, the author, and the illustrator.

- Show the children how you read the book one page at a time and let them help you turn the pages.

- As you read, underline the words with your fingers so children can learn that the printed words tell the story.

- Point to important words in the book—for example, the names of the people or the animals. This visual guidance will help children recognize that words are made up of letters and that the same word always has the same letters in the same order. After a while, they will be able to find familiar words.

- Write children's names on their drawings as they watch. Let them help if they want to.

- Ask children to dictate a few words to go with a drawing or to tell a simple story. Write down the words they say (or type them on a computer). Have the children read back the words with you or by themselves.

- Point out the labels on food packages, toys, and classroom shelves. "This says 'blocks' to help us remember that the blocks go on this shelf."

- Let children see you read and write. Talk with them about what you are doing. "I'm writing a note to your Dad to tell him what a good helper you were today. It says 'Javon helped Andre clean up the paint that spilled. He is a very good friend.'"

Activities That Help Children Learn to Identify and Name Letters

Older toddlers and preschoolers will enjoy and benefit from the following activities, which will help them learn to identify and name letters.

- Sing the alphabet song and recite the alphabet with the children to familiarize them with the names of the letters.

- Read an alphabet book to the children to help them learn that every letter has its own name.

- Take out three sets of plastic uppercase letters. Give each child a pile of letters, with three of a kind in each pile. Challenge the children to put the letters that are the same shape together. Name the letters as the children show you their piles. Continue the game until the children have had a chance to sort out all the letters.

- During circle time, put an alphabet strip in the middle of the circle. Give each child one or more plastic letters. Let the children take turns putting one of their letters in the right place on the alphabet strip.

- Write the first name of each child on a strip of tag paper and give each child his own name. Put out a row of plastic letters with the first letter of each child's name. Let each child find the letter that begins her name. If any of the children want to find all the letters of their name, find the letters for them and help them put the letters down in the correct order.

- Read an alphabet book to the children. Give the children a chance to guess the names of the letters as you come to them.

Activities That Help Children Learn the Sounds That Letters Make (Symbol–Sound Correspondence)

The following activities help to focus children's attention on relating letter sounds to letters:

- Read an alphabet book with the children. When you come to a letter that they can name, ask them to name the objects in the book that begin with the sound of that letter. Do they know anyone whose name begins with that letter or sound?

- Send the children on a scavenger hunt around the room, looking for objects that begin with the sound of the letter (begin with letters such as *b* and *d*, which are the beginning sound of many of the objects in the room).

- Put out two or three small boxes with a letter on the cover. Fill the boxes with objects that begin with the letter written on the box. For the letter *B,* you could add a small ball, a button, a barrette, a miniature boat, a bean, a bell, a miniature baseball bat, and a bead. If you cannot find enough small objects, then use pictures of the objects pasted onto cards.

PUTTING IT TOGETHER—THE ALPHABETIC PRINCIPLE

U nderstanding the alphabetic principle—that words are written with letters that represent their component sounds (phonemes)—is the key to reading an alphabetic language. Children cannot "break the code" without understanding the principle on which the code is based. Of course, the alphabetic principle is not something that beginning—or even expert—readers can recite; it is something that they intuitively understand and use.

At first glance, the alphabetic principle seems like a simple idea. To grasp it, however, children need to be able not only to identify and blend the phonemes in words but also to identify letters. To understand and use the alphabetic principle, they need to put these two kinds of knowledge together.

In a series of experiments, Byrne and Fielding-Barnsley (1989, 1991, 1995) taught either phonemic or alphabet skills to young children who did not know their letters. That is, children learned either (a) to segment words into component sounds (say "s-at" for *sat*) and to recognize words that began with the same sound (e.g., *mat* and *moon*) or (b) to recognize letters such as *m* and *s* and to name the sounds that these letters make. Neither ability by itself was sufficient for children to understand the alphabetic principle and use it to decode simple words. After being taught "mat" and "sat," for example, children were asked which word said "mow," *mow* or *sow*. Children needed both phonemic awareness and letter–sound association skills to answer these types of questions correctly. The Committee on the Prevention of Reading Difficulties in Young Children explains:

> Because phonemes are the units of sound that are represented by the letters of an alphabet, an awareness of phonemes is key to understanding the logic of the alphabetic principle. Unless and until children have a basic awareness of the phonemic structure of language, asking them for the first sound in the word *boy*, or expecting them to understand that *cap* has three sounds while *camp* has four, is to little avail (National Research Council, 1998, p. 54).

Phonics involves instruction in how sounds are represented by letters and letter combinations. In kindergarten and first grade, children are often taught common spelling rules as well as patterns and are drilled in phonics so they can quickly recognize the sounds associated with initial consonants, the consonant combinations like *bl* and *str*, and common word endings like *–an*, *-ing*, and *–ock*. At the same time, children learn to spell words that are represented phonetically and to recognize and spell some common words such as *could* and *enough* that violate phonetic patterns. Children with strong phonemic awareness and the ability to recognize some letters are well prepared for these lessons.

Preschoolers with good phonemic awareness and a strong interest in letters, words, and learning to read can enjoy some of the phonics games and activities that are more typical of kindergarten and first-grade classrooms:

- Read poems and short stories that use a lot of short, regularly spelled rhyming words. *Green Eggs and Ham* (Seuss, 1960) is a good example. See if children can point out some of the rhyming words after you have read a short section.

- Introduce children to the concept of word families (rhyming words in which the rhyming part has a standard spelling) and let them play with different letter combinations to see what words they can make. A fun way to do this activity is with a word strip or word wheel in which part of a word is written on a fixed piece and part appears in a window. Children pull the strip or turn the wheel to change what appears in the window. So, for example, an *–at* wheel or strip can allow children to see *bat, cat, fat, hat, mat, pat, rat, sat,* and *vat*. An *–et* wheel or strip would show *bet, get, let, met, pet, set,* and *wet*. Alternatively, children can keep the beginning constant and see different endings, as in *back, bat, bet, big,* and *bug*.

- Help children sort their names into groups of names that begin with the same sound. Which ones start with the same letter or letters? Which ones use another letter or letter combination to make the same sound?

- When children can recognize some little words, help them find these words in longer words. For example, can they find the "tree" in *street*, the "pill" in *pillow*, and the "can" in *candle*? (Make sure to choose examples where the sounds do not change. The "here" and "her" in *there* can be very confusing.)

- Make some puzzles with letters on the front and a picture on the back. When the child puts the two pieces together to make a word (for example *c* and *ar*), the two pieces of the picture fit together.

THE QUIRKS OF ENGLISH SPELLING

A nyone who has ever tried to learn English spelling as an adult or to explain English spelling to a non-native English speaker knows that the phonetic patterns of English are anything but simple. A common letter such as *a* has different sounds in simple words such as *cat, car, way,* and *war.* Furthermore, *way* can be written as *weigh* and *war* as *wore,* but then they are different words with different meanings. A common word such as *right* has a strange spelling that includes two silent letters; words with the same sound include the logically spelled *rite* as well as *write* and *wright.* English words come from many languages, and their spellings often reflect earlier pronunciations.

Children's names create similar complications. Philip, Phoebe, Fatima, and Frank all have names that start with a /f/ sound, but they are spelled differently. Cindy and Candy start with the same letter, but they sound different. Jorge's name starts with an /h/ sound similar to Horatio's, but Jimmy's starts with a /j/ sound similar to George's. Caitlyn and Kaitlin have the same name, but they spell it differently. Nguyen's name is pronounced like "win," and Ntozake's begins with a sound combination that is not used at the beginning of English words.

Still, children's own names are usually the first words that they learn to write, and the names of their classmates are likely to be among the first words that children can recognize. Pointing out the similarities and differences helps children see that letters stand for sounds, even if, sometimes, different letters can represent the same sound and the same sound can be represented by different letters. As they begin to write for themselves, they will produce closer and closer approximations to conventional English spelling.

HELPING CHILDREN LEARN TO WRITE

A s with the development of phonemic and alphabet skills, the precursors of writing skills are acquired by very young children. To learn to write, children must develop the small-muscle skills and the eye-hand coordination required to draw a line in the sand with their finger or to make a mark on a sheet of paper with an instrument. In the first days of life, the infant learns to track a moving object as it is moved back and forth in front of her eyes. In the next few months, she learns to grasp a rattle, give it a few shakes, and then pass it to the other hand. During the toddler years, children continue to improve their hand–eye coordination and develop their small-muscle skills. Two- and three-year-old children learn to draw pictures on a piece of paper. At first, their drawings consist of lines drawn in different directions, but before long, children learn to draw circles as well as lines and to use crayons or markers to create a piece of abstract art.

After a while, children may decide to sign their drawings or to write messages on them. At first, these signatures and messages may just be squiggly lines. If you encourage children to tell you what they "wrote," they will often beam with pride and continue their efforts to make their writing look more like the real thing. When children are encouraged to write with a purpose, they often progress from squiggly lines to letter-like forms, and finally to the attempted production of real letters.

As they figure out the alphabetic principle, some children begin to use invented spellings that include some of the sounds that they hear. For example, a child may write "gr" for *girl* or "pnabtr" for *peanut butter*. Other children will want to write words "the real way" and may ask you to help or to provide models that they can copy. Both paths lead to competent writing and spelling. Writing words "their own way" can help children figure out the alphabetic principle and express their ideas on paper. As children progress in elementary school, they will need to learn correct spellings.

Activities That Help Children Develop Eye–Hand Coordination and Small-Muscle Skills

Toddlers and preschoolers will enjoy engaging in these activities that will help them develop eye–hand coordination and small-muscle skills:

- Play a tracking game with 2- and 3-year-olds. Ask the children to sit on the floor and turn toward one of the walls. Turn off the lights. Turn on a flashlight and challenge the children to follow the beam as it zigzags across the wall.

- Give toddlers paintbrushes and water and let them "paint" the playground.

- Give toddlers large beads and a shoelace and let them string the beads.

- Give toddlers dressing frames that give them practice fastening with zippers and buttons.

- Give toddlers lock-boxes that give them practice turning keys and closing different kinds of locks.

- Give toddlers pegboards with large pegs, inset puzzles, building blocks, and snap blocks.

- Encourage toddlers to finger paint or to make designs with shaving cream on a smooth, washable surface.

- Sing action songs such as "Itsy, Bitsy Spider" or "Where is Thumbkin?" that give children an opportunity to isolate and exercise each of their fingers.

- Give the children the opportunity to use different tools, including hammers, screwdrivers, blunt scissors, shovels, forks, hole-punchers, and glue sticks.

- Do finger plays such as "Here is the Church" that help children practice tricky hand and finger movements.

- Put out plastic jars and lids and ask the children to find the lid that goes with each jar. As the children screw on the lids, they are developing eye–hand coordination and are practicing wrist swivels.

- Let the children use a tongs or tweezers to transfer grains of rice or other small objects from one container to another. This activity helps develop the pincer grasp that is used to hold a writing utensil.

- Let children use an eyedropper or squeeze bottle to add food coloring to play dough or glue or to add a few drops at a time in a color-mixing experiment.

- Provide children with clay or play dough. Rolling pins, cookie cutters, craft sticks, recycled birthday candles, and other small items help children make interesting creations. Children may also enjoy making imprints with plastic letters and with objects that have different textures.

- Give children Legos®, Tinkertoys®,Duplos®, or other snap-together building toys and encourage them to build.

- Give children a hole puncher, a paper plate, and some yarn. Show them how to use the hole puncher to make holes around the rim of the plate and, then, how to thread the strand of yarn through the holes.

- Give children glue and a variety of materials such as scraps of paper, glitter, stickers, buttons, spaghetti, or confetti, and let them decorate paper cups or make abstract designs on a paper plate or sheet of paper.

- Provide children with crayons, markers, pencils or chalk, and white or colored paper, and encourage them to draw whatever they would like. When they finish drawing, ask the children if they would like you to write their name on the picture.

Activities That Help Children Recognize the Different Functions of Writing

These simple activities will support children in recognizing that writing is used for various purposes:

- Ask the children to help you make a list of all the things they will be able to do when they learn to write. This list might include writing their name on things that belong to them, writing notes to their parents, sending out invitations to their birthday party, making lists of things that they would like to buy in the store or that they want for their birthday, writing letters to their friends and relatives, writing stories, and writing down the things they want to remember.

- Place pads of paper, pencils, and crayons in pretend play centers.

    —Ask the children to tell you what sorts of things they would like to write down when they are pretending to make dinner. Do they need to make a shopping list, to write down messages when they answer the phone, to write out recipes, or to label the foods that they put in the refrigerator?

—What would they want to write down if they were playing doctor, hospital, animal hospital, fire station, bank, supermarket, or restaurant?

Ways to Help Children Learn How to Write Lowercase and Uppercase Letters

Preschool children can learn how to write lowercase and uppercase letters with the following support from you:

- A good way to help children learn to write letters is to let them begin with the first letter of their own name. Using plastic letters or letter cards, let each child find the first letter of their own name. Then show the children different ways of learning to write the letter. (Obviously, every child does not have to go through every one of the following steps; as soon as a child feels that he or she can do it, let him or her jump to the last step.)

  —Pass your index finger over the letter beginning at the top.

  —Write the letter with your finger in sand, shaving cream, or finger paint.

  —Trace over the letter with a crayon when your teacher writes it for you or use a letter stamp and trace over the letter that you have stamped on the paper.

  —Copy the first letter that is written on your name card.

- Once children have learned to write the first letter of their name in uppercase, show them how to write the rest of the letters in lowercase.

- Once children have learned to copy their first name, encourage them to copy their last name.

- Suggest that they write their name on their drawings or on a nameplate.

- If children show an interest, help them learn to write other letters.

- Do not correct children if they write their letters backwards. They will either figure it out themselves or learn when they get to kindergarten. In the preschool years, writing is just for fun!

STOCKING THE WRITING CENTERS

Whether you create a dedicated "writing center" or place writing materials strategically throughout the environment or both, it is important to ensure that toddlers and preschoolers have easy access to writing materials so they can experiment with writing and can make the things they need for pretend play and other purposes.

For toddlers, a writing center can be very simple. You will want to include paper and crayons, collage materials, stickers, rubber stamps and stamp pads, and plastic or wooden letters. You might also include a keyboard, old memo pads, a play telephone, and some cards, junk mail, and envelopes so children can imitate the writing tasks in which the adults in their lives engage.

Preschoolers will appreciate having many kinds of paper and writing materials as well as scissors and paste, some folded paper for "books," recycled cards and envelopes, stickers, alphabet and picture stamps, name tags, labels, and an alphabet strip. Be sure that you and other adults spend time in the writing center so you can help and encourage the children.

Another way to encourage writing is to make a classroom mailbox. Children can help you to decorate a carton for this purpose. Encourage them to create pictures and notes for classmates and to put them in the mailbox. You can facilitate the addressing by making sheets of stick-on labels with the names of children in the class.

A well-stocked and well-used writing center is one of the best ways to support emergent literacy. This child is making a name-tag for her friend.

A computer can be a wonderful tool for teaching the alphabet, writing, and concepts of print. A simple word processing program, set to write in a large font (e.g., 24 point), will give children opportunities to connect upper- and lowercase letters, pretend to write or actually write messages, and make all kinds of "secret codes," labels, and important signs (such as "Do Not Touch" or "SAVE") for block buildings and other creations. Children's reading and writing programs can enable children to hear, play out, and retell stories; write with rebus pictures and words; make picture books (and, in some cases, hear the words they have written or attempted to write read back by computer software that "speaks"); or flip back and forth between rebus symbols and the words they represent.

With printing and graphics software or access to the Internet, children can use a computer to make all sorts of items for pretend play: menus, placemats, recipes, shopping lists, tickets, maps, blueprints, banners, traffic signs, newspapers, badges, certificates, and awards. Of course, most of these things can be created without a computer, but children enjoy making items that look like real print.

BUILDING A BALANCED PROGRAM

Ms. Gung-Ho wanted to be sure that all of the 4-year-olds in her class would be well-prepared for kindergarten. Each week, they studied a new letter. Ms. Gung-Ho helped the children make a list of 10 words that started with that week's letter. Then, the children had to copy the list into their notebooks. If they could not make all the letters, then Ms. Gung-Ho would write the words for them and then let them trace the letters. By the end of the year, several of the children in Ms. Gung-Ho's class could copy the lists themselves and read back the words. But many of the children still did not know all of their letters and could recognize only a few words. The next year, Ms. Gung-Ho decided to work more on phonemic awareness. She taught the children lots of alliterative poems and tongue twisters, played games at circle time like "Banana-fana-fo-fana" and "guess my rhyme," and made phonics games and puzzles where children had to match a letter with a picture of a word that started with it. The children got good at the new games, but some of them still did not learn all of their letters by the end of the year, and others still had trouble writing and recognizing words.

Ms. Wait-a-Bit grew up in a country where children did not begin formal schooling until they were 7. They would read stories and play games in their nursery schools, of course, but no one would have dreamed of teaching them letters or numbers before they got to school. Ms. Wait-a-Bit was convinced that her 4-year-old charges were too young for formal instruction. Instead, she focused on dramatic play. She filled the classroom with all kinds of materials for making costumes, props, and stage sets, and read the children lots of stories to inspire their imaginations. She helped them make tickets, signs, invitations, shopping lists, and sometimes even scripts for their productions. Ms. Wait-a-Bit was very surprised when some of the children in her class started reading, in spite of her best efforts not to teach them. Many of the children, however, could not name all the letters or sound out simple words, just as Ms. Wait-a-Bit expected.

Ms. Gung-Ho and Ms. Wait-a-Bit have sharply different expectations of the children they teach. They also differ in the emphasis they place on formal instruction and in their theories of how children become successful readers. Reading researchers and early childhood education experts can point to strengths and missing pieces in both teachers' methods; these researchers recommend a more balanced approach for most children. The box on this page describes this approach.

A BALANCED APPROACH TO LITERACY LEARNING

During the preschool years, young children need developmentally appropriate experiences and teaching to support literacy learning. These include, but are not limited to, the following:

- Positive, nurturing relationships with adults who engage in responsive conversations with individual children, who model reading and writing behavior, and who foster children's interest in and enjoyment of reading and writing.

- Print-rich environments that provide opportunities and tools for children to see and use written language for a variety of purposes, with teachers drawing children's attention to specific letters and words.

- Adults' daily reading of high-quality books to individual children or small groups, including books that positively reflect children's identity, home language, and culture.

- Opportunities for children to talk about what is read and to focus on the sounds and parts of words as well as the meaning.

- Teaching strategies and experiences that develop phonemic awareness—for example, songs, finger plays, games, poems, and stories in which phonemic patterns such as rhyme and alliteration are salient.

- Opportunities to engage in play that incorporates literacy tools—for example, writing grocery lists in dramatic play, making signs in block building, and using icons and words in exploring a computer game.

- Firsthand experiences that expand children's vocabulary—for example, trips in the community and exposure to various tools, objects, and materials.

(continued)

A Balanced Approach to Literacy Learning **(continued)**

Adapted from *Learning to Read and Write: Developmentally Appropriate Practices for Young Children*, a Joint Position Statement of the International Reading Association and the National Association for the Education of Young Children (1998).

Reflection

What can you remember about your first "reading lessons?" How have ideas such as phonemic awareness, concepts of print, and emergent writing changed our approach to preparing children to be successful readers?

How might you strengthen the inside-*out* component of your emergent literacy program?

How can you be sure to keep it in balance with other critical elements?

References

Ada, A. F. (2003). *Pio peep!: Traditional Spanish nursery rhymes*. New York: HarperCollins.

Archambault, J., & Martin, B., Jr. (1989). *Chicka chicka boom boom*. New York: Simon & Schuster.

Barbarin, O. (2002). The black-white achievement gap in early reading skills: Familial and socio-cultural contexts. In B. Bowman (Ed.), *Love to read: Essays in developing and enhancing early literacy skills of African American children*. Washington, DC: National Black Child Development Institute.

Brown, M. W. (1947). *Goodnight moon*. New York: Harper & Row.

Byrne, B., & Fielding-Barnsley, R. (1989). Phonemic awareness and letter knowledge in the child's acquistions of the alphabetic principle. *Journal of Educational Psychology, 81*(1), 313–321.

Byrne, B., & Fielding-Barnsley, R. (1991). Evaluation of a program to teach phonemic awareness to young children. *Journal of Educational Psychology, 83*(3): 451–455.

Byrne, B., & Fielding-Barnsley, R. (1995). Evaluation of a program to teach phonemic awareness to young children. A 2- and 3-year follow-up and a new preschool trial. *Journal of Educational Psychology, 87*(3), 488–503.

Dickinson, D. K., & Sprague, K. (2001). The nature and impact of early childhood care environments on the language and early literacy development of children from low-income families. In S. B. Neuman & D. K. Dickinson (Eds.), *Handbook of early literacy research,* pp. 263–280. New York: Guilford.

Dickinson, D. K., & Tabors, P. O. (2001). *Beginning literacy with language.* Baltimore: Paul H. Brookes.

Dorval, B., Joyce, T. H., & Ramey, C. T. (1980). *Teaching phoneme identification skills to young children at risk for school failure: Implications for reading instruction.* Unpublished manuscript, University of North Carolina, Chapel Hill.

Galdone, P. (1984). *The three little pigs.* Boston, MA: Clarion Books.

Guarino, Deborah. (1997). *Is your mama a llama?* New York: Scholastic.

Hoberman, M. (2000). *The seven silly eaters.* New York: Voyager.

International Reading Association & National Association for the Education of Young Children (1998). *Overview of learning to read and write: Developmentally appropriate practices for young children: A joint position statement of the International Reading Association and the National Association for the Education of Young Children.* Washington, DC: National Association for the Education of Young Children.

Jimenez, G. (2000). Reading lesson. In B. Brenner (Ed.), *Voices: Poetry and art from around the world* (pp. 24–31) [translated by Kristie Franklin]. Washington, DC: National Geographic Society.

Marshall, J. (1998). *Goldilocks and the three bears.* New York: Puffin Books.

Martin, B., & Carle, E. (1967). *Brown bear, brown bear, what do you see?* New York: Henry Holt.

McQueen, L. (1947). *The little red hen.* New York: Scholastic.

Mosel, A. (1968). *Tikki tikki tembo.* New York: Holt, Rinehart, & Winston.

National Association for the Education of Young Children. (1998). *Learning to read and write: Developmentally appropriate practices for young children: A joint position of the International Reading Association and the National Association for the Education of Young Children.* Retrieved October 5, 2004, from www.naeyc.org/resources/position_statements/psread2.htm

National Research Council. (1998). *Preventing reading difficulties in young children.* Committee on the Prevention of Reading Difficulties in Young Children, C. E. Snow, M. S. Burns, & P. Griffin, (Eds.). Washington, DC: National Academy Press.

Palacio Jaramillo, N. (1986). *Las nanas de abuelita: Lullabies, tongue twisters, and riddles from South America/Grandmother's nursery rhymes.* New York: Henry Holt.

Sendak, M. (1986). *Really Rosie.* New York: HarperCollins Juvenile Books.

Sendak, M. (1991). *Alligators all around.* New York: Harper Trophy.

Seuss, Dr. (1960). *Green eggs and ham.* New York: Random House.

Strickland, D. S. (2002) Bridging the gap for African American children. In B. Bowman (Ed.), *Love to read: Essays in developing and enhancing early literacy skills of African American children.* Washington, DC: National Black Child Development Institute.

Wood, A. (1985). *King Bidgood's in the bathtub.* Orlando, FL: Harcourt Barnes.

CHAPTER
9

Creating an Environment That Enhances Emergent Literacy

Twinkle, twinkle, little star
How I wonder what you are.
Up above the world so high,
Like a diamond in the sky.
Twinkle, twinkle little star
How I wonder what you are.

—TRADITIONAL

F or young children, the world is filled with wonder. Everywhere they look, there is something new to discover, and each discovery gives rise to new questions. Children use what teachers in Reggio Emilia, Italy, refer to as "one hundred languages" to share their wonder and their questions with us. In addition to the words of their language(s), young children use gestures, manipulation, drawing, sculpting, dance, pretend play, music, and even misbehavior to tell us what they know and what they wonder about. As they get older, spoken and written words become more important. The other "languages" feed into and support emergent literacy.

An environment that enhances emergent literacy gives children a sense of trust and assurance even as it excites their wonder and invites them to explore. Whether it is in a home, a school, or a community setting such as a library or play space, an environment that supports emergent literacy is full of possibilities for imagining and opportunities for pretend play. It provides children with not only a wealth of spoken and written words but also many opportunities to engage in reading, writing, singing, and storytelling activities.

Setting up these kinds of environments for infants, toddlers, preschoolers, or mixed-age groups is usually a three-step process:

1. Create a safe and comfortable setting that supports relationships and invites exploration. Rooms for toddlers and preschool children should include spaces for quiet and active play, for intimate gatherings, and for larger group activities.

2. Furnish the rooms with equipment, books, and materials that are appropriate for the developmental age or stages of the children.

3. Make the environment "print rich." Add decorations and learning materials that demonstrate various functions of print and that provide the children with multiple opportunities to explore print in various forms. Post signs and symbols that show children and adults what the environment offers and that invite their participation, reflection, conversation, and play.

CREATING AND FURNISHING ENVIRONMENTS THAT SUPPORT RELATIONSHIPS AND INVITE EXPLORATION

A ll young children appreciate environments that are organized, uncluttered, interesting, and attractive. Whether you are setting up a classroom, a family child-care home, or a space for child-and-parent activities, you will need to make sure that the space is cozy and welcoming for both children and adults. Here is a basic checklist of recommended features for indoor environments:

☐ The environment is safe for young children to explore. It is free of hazards and meets all licensing and fire department standards. Everything is in good repair.

☐ The environment is easy to keep clean and to maintain.

☐ The environment includes different kinds of spaces that are appropriate for different kinds of activities: active play, messy play, quiet concentration, large-group activities, private conversation, eating, sleeping, book sharing, building, and pretending.

☐ Flooring is appropriate for the children's ages and activities. Washable mats, area rugs, vinyl remnants, quilts, etc. are used as needed to create inviting, easy-to-clean surfaces for sitting, crawling, toddling, active play, cooking and eating, and messy play.

☐ Public spaces and work spaces are light and bright, but not glaring. Walls are painted in attractive colors such as beige, light green, or light blue that are neither somber nor overly bright.

☐ The environment is well organized. An environment that is cluttered is confusing to children and can be overstimulating.

☐ The environment is interesting at a child's eye level.

☐ Toys and books that children use are attractively displayed where children can reach them. High shelves and childproof cabinets hold spare materials, toys that have temporarily been taken out of circulation, and things that children should not have access to without adult supervision. It is easy to tell where things belong. Like items and items that are used together are grouped in logical ways. Shelves, bins, or baskets may have labels or pictures that indicate their contents. Some labels reflect overarching categories such as "farm animals," "vehicles," "doll clothes," "furniture," or "tools."

☐ The environment reflects the children's cultures. Books, commercial and homemade toys, wall displays, artifacts, nature and science collections, foods, sleeping spaces, dolls, pretend-play materials, furnishings, and gathering spaces welcome children and their families, draw from their traditions, and help them feel at home while also teaching about a wider world.

☐ The environment embraces children's home languages. Books, bulletin board displays, communications to parents, charts and schedules, and other environmental print reflect all of the languages that children and their parents use.

☐ The environment celebrates children's identities and show-cases their products. Photographs of the children and their families are on display. Children see their names on their personal spaces and artwork as well as in other displays.

☐ The environment works not only for the children who use it but also for the adults.

Teachers take into account their own needs as they set up their classroom. Frequently used adult materials are easy to access but beyond children's reach or safely locked away. Materials that are used only occasionally can be put on higher shelves or in storage.

　　—Teachers and adult visitors have safe places to keep purses and other private possessions that are out of the reach of children.

—Adults have comfortable places to sit while working with an individual child or group or while just observing. A space for infants or toddlers contains a rocker, glider, or swing that an adult can use to comfort or feed a baby.

—A bulletin board either outside the door or near the entrance keeps parents abreast of what is happening in the classroom and of community events and resources that might be of interest to them.

Environments for Infants

The Happy Land Child-Care Center, at the urging of parents, had decided to add an infant room to their child-care center. They hired two caregivers, Mrs. Cuddles and Miss Bright-Eyes, to care for eight babies, ages 2 months to 12 months. The caregivers' first task was to plan the physical layout of the room that they would share. Unfortunately, these two caregivers disagreed from the beginning on how the room should be set up. They decided that, rather than argue with each other over each decision, they would write out their separate ideas and present them to the director. The director, they hoped, could help them develop a layout with which both would be comfortable.

Mrs. Cuddle's List
Room décor and furnishings: Paint the walls light blue, and install wall-to-wall carpeting; space eight standardized cribs far apart so the babies will not disturb one another and will not share germs; use incandescent lighting so the room will not be too bright; add two adult rocking chairs, two changing tables, one playpen with a washable mat, two baby windup swings, and a bulletin board for tracking each child's day.
Toys and equipment: CD player, a collection of lullabies, foam blocks, rattles, wind chimes, mobiles that attach to the sides of the cribs, an unbreakable mirror, baby swings, soft squeak toys, music boxes, cloth books, a fabric ball and washable stuffed animals, and soft covers to put over the bottles.
Miss Bright-Eyes' List
Room décor and furnishings: Sky-blue or white walls, tile floor with area rug, three feeding tables, a changing table, wall mirrors with pull-up bars, an infant play pit, a water-play table that

could be filled with water or sand, a crawl-through tunnel, a rocking boat, mats for climbing over, a small bookcase, low shelves for manipulative toys, colorful wall hangings and large family photos, eight small cribs grouped together on one side of the room, a baby bounce chair, and a rocking chair for adults. *Toys and equipment:* Cardboard blocks, board books with bright illustrations, busy boards, dolls and stuffed animals, pop-up toys, a beach ball, containers for filling and emptying, water-play toys, sponges, cake pans and wooden spoons, knob puzzles, stacking rings, stacking cups, a pot with a lid, a tape player with a collection of Raffi tapes, shape puzzles, trucks, jack-in-the-box toys, and pull toys.

Mrs. Moderation, the director, pointed out that although both lists were different, they were not incompatible. Mrs. Cuddles was most concerned with creating an environment that was quiet, healthful, and parent-friendly and that would meet the needs of very young infants and of infants who might be overwhelmed by too much stimulation. Miss Bright-Eyes wanted to create a more stimulating environment that mobile infants would enjoy and that would give them opportunities to develop their physical, cognitive, and emergent literacy skills. Fortunately, the two caregivers were able to recognize and respect each other's point of view, and with guidance from their director, they became an effective team.

As you arrange and equip an infant classroom, remember that every baby is unique. Infants differ from one another in developmental age, temperament, and prior experiences in child care and their home environment. As you plan a developmentally appropriate environment, make sure that the room arrangement you select is both safe and flexible and that the furnishings and toys you select will be appropriately challenging for babies of different ages with differing capacities, needs, and preferences. Most important, the environment you create should be safe, healthy, and comfortable and should make each baby feel at home.

Room Arrangement and Furnishings That Support Infant Development

When setting up an environment for infants, take the following steps to ensure a setting that will support infant development:

- Make certain that the furniture, equipment, and toys that are placed in the classroom can be washed and disinfected on a regular basis.

- Make sure that the floor coverings can be washed and that there are no loose rugs on the floor that would cause a person to slip.

- Arrange the furniture so that the caregiver has a clear view of every infant.

- Arrange the cribs in the sleeping area so that babies can see and watch one another. Make sure that they are at least 18 inches apart and that the caregiver can have full view of every infant.

- Create protected areas where infants who are not yet crawling can see one another as they play on the floor and where an adult can comfortably join them. In a mixed-age group, arrange these areas so that infants can also watch and interact with older children without being in the middle of the fray.

- Create safe but interesting spaces for crawlers, using tunnels, peepholes, furniture to pull up on and peek over, mirrors, low windows, different surfaces to touch or traverse, and toys and displays at floor level.

- Provide a play area with an easily cleaned surface in a defined space—for example, a corral, empty wading pool, or giant playpen, where two or more older infants can play together. Make sure that a variety of books and toys are within easy reach.

- Provide a changing area where running water and all supplies are within reach so that the caregiver can use changing time as a special opportunity to interact with the infant. A mirror, board books, and a few toys will help make changing time a time for conversation and play.

- Provide a quiet area with a rocking chair where infants can be quieted, soothed, comforted, nursed, or given a bottle. Place a collection of board books and some soft toys or fabrics nearby.

- Develop a flexible schedule that recognizes individual differences, and provide transition markers such as dimming the lights, going outside, or playing lullabies to establish a daily rhythm.

Toys and Equipment That Support Infant Development

As you acquire and organize toys and equipment for the infant area, take the following steps to support infant development:

- Provide toys and equipment that take into account the developmental characteristics of young and older infants.

- Provide opportunities for infants to see, hear, feel, and manipulate interesting things.

- Provide a CD player with different types of music, including lullabies, classical music, baby songs, and songs with a strong rhythm (You can use different musical selections to mark transitions within the day.)

- Provide infants with opportunities to experience handling different textures and to lie on different surfaces.

- Provide visual displays such as mobiles and wall hangings that give babies different visual experiences.

- Provide toys that change shape or produce an interesting effect when infants manipulate them.

- Provide washable dolls and stuffed animals.

Environments for Toddlers

Miss Set-in-Her-Ways, who had been the teacher of the 4-year old group for 6 years, was reassigned to a toddler classroom with children ranging from 14 months to 3 years. She began by rearranging the toddler room into interest centers, with a center for pretend play, a center for building and constructing, a science center, a math center, a reading and writing center, a social studies center, a music center with a piano and drums, and an art center. She equipped the pretend play center with a structure that could be used as a store or an office. She put small tables and chairs in the other areas, with the exception of the block center, where she put nothing but a big shelf for the large, wooden unit blocks. When the director came into the room, she looked horrified. Miss Set-in-Her-Ways could not understand why the director was so upset.

Can you help Miss Set-in-Her Ways understand the problems with her layout?

Between the ages of 1 and 3 years, toddlers are making important developmental strides. They need environments that encourage active exploration, conversation, friend making, and pretend play.

Toddlers are learning new physical skills such as walking forward and backward, squatting to pick up a toy, carrying heavy objects, climbing on play structures, going up and down stairs and slides, pulling wagons, pushing big toy trucks, racing around on riding toys, opening and closing doors, throwing balls, and moving small chairs from place to place.

Toddlers are interested in playing with manipulative toys that enhance small-muscle skills and encourage problem solving. They love building toys and enjoy stacking up blocks and knocking them down, putting puzzles together, playing with stacking toys, busy boards, dressing frames, lock-boxes, pegboards, and small objects that they can sort. They can use a variety of tools and are progressing from imitative play to pretend play.

Toddlers are learning language at a rapid rate and love to listen to stories being told and books being read. They enjoy singing songs, participating in finger plays, scribbling and painting, pretending to write, participating in book reading, reciting ditties, drawing pictures, and engaging in mini and maxi pretending.

Arrange the rooms in interest areas that differentiate the kinds of play that the area invites. For example:

- Consider dividing the room into an area for greeting parents, an area for climbing and active gross motor play, a "house corner" for pretending, an area for sensory play such as water and sand play, and an area for quiet play that includes a soft surface and a cozy place for reading books, as well as low tables or hard surfaces for art activities, mini-play, and puzzles.

- Use double shelves, walls, or low, sturdy dividers to designate the boundaries of an area.

- Provide play materials that take into account the developmental needs of the toddlers in your group.

Developmental Needs of Young Toddlers

Consider these developmental needs and interests as you set up areas for young toddlers:

- As 1-year olds learn to walk, they develop a special interest in pushing, pulling, and carrying things around. Provide purses, carrying bags, and large beach balls that they can carry; rolling toys such as corn poppers, carpet sweepers, and toy strollers that they can push; and small wagons and trucks with short ropes attached that they can pull.

- In addition, 1-year-olds are interested in discovering the relationship between containers and the things they contain. Favorite activities include pulling toys off a shelf, emptying and filling containers, and throwing objects into wastebaskets or toilets. We can capture this fascination with containers and their contents either by filling small containers with ice cubes and letting toddlers take out the ice cubes and put them in a second container or by filling a bin with oatmeal and letting the toddlers scoop the oatmeal into different-sized containers.

- As we engage young toddlers in activities that encourage manipulation, they are learning about the different properties of objects and discovering their own capacity to make interesting things happen. The discoveries that young toddlers are making enable them to gain real-world knowledge that provides the basis for language learning.

- Young toddlers are great imitators and like to have child-sized versions of the items that their parents use. As toddlers imitate talking on the telephone, sweeping the floor with a broom, or feeding a cracker to a teddy bear, they are repeating acts that they have watched adults perform. As they grow older, this imitation turns into pretending. If the appropriate prop is unavailable, an older toddler may, for example, use a square block as a cup or a long block as a telephone. The toddler is using the blocks as stand-ins for real objects, making the leap into symbolic thinking.

Developmental Needs of Older Toddlers

Consider these developmental needs and interests as you set up areas for older toddlers:

- Although young toddlers spend much of their time actively exploring their environment and discovering the kinds of things that they can make happen, 2-year olds also are developing a special interest in playing with other children. Favorite activities include stacking cardboard blocks together and then knocking them down; rolling, pounding, and making snakes or pancakes out of clay and showing them to one another; riding beside one another on push cars or trucks; climbing, jumping, and chasing one another through tunnels in a primitive version of follow the leader; or hiding together in cozy places and reading books together.

- In addition, 2-year-olds also enjoy spending short periods of time sitting with a friend or two at a small table. They like to put together knobbed puzzles; play with stacking rings; manipulate sorting toys; complete form boards; string beads; make designs with giant pegboards; make chains out of snap-together blocks; finger paint; or tear, paste, and scribble on paper.

- By the time a child is 2 years old, we usually see the emergence of genuine pretending. The 1-year-old will simply babble into a toy telephone; the 2-year-old will carry out a sequence of events—making a ringing sound, putting the receiver to his ear, babbling or saying "Hi, Daddy," and hanging up the phone. The child will repeat this same sequence over and over again.

- Another way that 2-year-olds' pretending is more sophisticated than that of a 1-year-old is that the 2-year-old is learning to share her pretending with another child. Two-year-olds may decide to bake a birthday cake together, then sing

"Happy Birthday", blow out the candles, take a pretend bite of birthday cake, and, once again, blow out the candles.

- Because 2-year-olds enjoy routines and can attend to a whole-group activity for a short time, it is a good idea to set up a part of the room for "circle time." It is also helpful to follow a simple daily schedule that provides blocks of time in which children can experience different types of activities. For example, a full-day program might have an arrival time routine, a mid-morning playtime, outdoor play, lunchtime, naptime, mid-afternoon playtime, outdoor time, and good-bye circle. However, unhurried time is one of the best gifts we can give young children, so the schedule should not create pressure to rush.

Environments for Preschoolers

An exciting learning environment for preschoolers does not have to look like a classroom, but it should offer a variety of play and learning experiences as well as different types of activities. It should affirm children's identities by reflecting their cultures, languages, and interests. It should encourage creativity, support language, and inspire pretend play. It should also be flexible, taking on different shapes and appearances as children's interests evolve and as the curriculum shifts from one theme to another.

Preschoolers like to participate in shaping their environments. With just a bit of encouragement, they will build "forts" with pillows, sheets, and furniture; set up obstacle courses; and construct myriad other settings for their pretend-play scenarios. They also enjoy making things, and they love to see their work on display.

An environment for preschoolers must also take into account the different temperaments, learning styles, and activity patterns of individual children. Some children will tend to flit from activity to activity; others will concentrate intently for long periods of time. Some will prefer the intimacy of a small group and a quiet setting; others seek the excitement of a larger group and of active, often noisy, play.

Interest Centers for Preschoolers

One way to create a flexible environment that accommodates children's varying needs is to set up interest centers that provide settings and materials for different types of learning and play experiences. The interest centers can be arranged to separate areas for quiet play from areas for active or noisy play. While supporting other aspects of physical, cognitive, and social–emotional development, each interest center should also contribute directly to the enhancement of emergent literacy skills in the following ways:

- Each interest center should provide opportunities for extending children's vocabulary. A science center, for example, can provide opportunities to introduce words such as *magnet, attract, repel, float, sink, balance, seed, germinate, roots, dissolve, absorb, melt*, and *evaporate*, along with names of plants, animals, rocks, seashells, and other natural objects. A math center can provide opportunities to introduce the names of different shapes, numbers, operations (*plus, take away, cut in half*), measures (*foot, minute, pound, teaspoon*), and measuring tools as well as ordinal numbers (*first, second*), sizes, and terms of comparison (*greater, less than, equal, more, longer, fastest*).

- Each interest center should include materials that encourage pretend (and real) reading and writing. An imaginary play center could include pencils, pads, and ledgers or appointment books for playing store, restaurant, or doctor's office; a math or science center could include charts, graph paper, lab notebooks, a calendar, and a weather log. An art center could include crayons, clay, markers, tempera colors, and finger paint along with a variety of cutting, drawing, painting, and stamping tools that give children opportunities to practice hand–eye coordination, improve their finger dexterity, and begin to form letters or words.

- Each interest center should include picture books. These can be related to the center's ongoing purpose or to a current theme or project.

- Each interest center should display attractive signs with the name of the center and a representative symbol. Of course, these signs can change if the block center turns into a city or the pretend play center becomes a spaceship or a bodega.

The following paragraphs represent one example of a set of interest centers that encourage preschoolers to explore, converse, pretend, and learn. This set of interest centers is noteworthy because it is balanced; together, the areas provide opportunities for children to learn and practice a broad range of information and skills.

The Imaginative Play Center. This interest center provides opportunities and materials for symbolic play. It may include the following features:

- Kitchen units, small table and chairs, doll bed and highchair, shopping cart.

- Multicultural dolls, stuffed animals, bibs, telephones, play coffee makers and toasters, dishes, cups and glasses, pots and pans, empty food packages, cookbooks or recipe cards, play food, placemats or tablecloths.

- Toys that encourage restaurant and store play, including cash register, balance scales, paper for writing shopping lists, paper bags, play money, coupons, menus, tablecloths, and play food.

- Toys that encourage doctor play, including a doctor's kit, BAND-AID® boxes, diplomas, eye charts, flashlights, empty medicine bottles, spoons, and a prescription pad.

- Items for dress-up, including a variety of hats, masks, mirrors, wallets, keys, credit cards, shirts, dresses, shawls, scarves, boots, and shoes.

- Picture books to read to the baby; books about doctors, veterinarians, restaurants, marketplaces; etc.

The Constructive Play Center. The constructive play center provides opportunities and materials for representational play. It may include the following features:

- Basic building materials such as unit blocks, interlocking blocks, and blocks with interesting shapes.

- Recycled objects that can be used for building—for example, cardboard tubes, floor tiles, and boxes of various sizes.

- Fences, bridges, and ramps.

- Miniature toys such as vehicles, traffic signs, doll furniture, people, and zoo and farm animals.

- Materials for building machines, vehicles, and "inventions," including wheels, gears, gizmos, and magnetic toys.

- Shelves and storage bins labeled with pictures and words.

- Interesting spaces such as a low table that a group of children can build on or around, a mirrored corner, or a box turned on its side that can serve as a parking garage.

The Move and Grow Center. This interest center provides opportunities for physical activities, dance, and musical activities that help children develop and practice large-motor skills, relieve stress, regulate their energy and activity level, express themselves through music and movement, and share in active group activities. It may include the following features:

- A large area that allows children to move about without disturbing children in the other areas of the room and that can accommodate a group.

- Exercise materials such as tumbling mats, skipping ropes, balance toys, Hula Hoops®, and beanbag games.

- Music and dance materials such as rhythm instruments, CDs or tapes, scarves, sets of bells, song books, and a large pad and easel for writing favorite songs.

- Other materials that encourage children to collaborate in creating performances, games, and obstacle courses—for example, low platforms, flashlights, large foam or cardboard blocks, and carpet squares.

The Create and Discover Center. This interest center provides opportunities to learn science concepts and includes materials that encourage experimentation, observation, and data collection. It may include the following features:

- Materials that introduce children to concepts about the natural world, including aquariums, butterfly gardens, worm and ant farms, plants, and terrariums.

- Materials that encourage experimentation—for example, water and sand tables with sieves, basters, funnels, pitchers, bottles, balance scales, measuring cups, prisms, magnifiers, and egg beaters.

- Materials that encourage data collection—for example, a plant-growing center with pots, seeds, rulers, shovels, graph paper, labels, and notebooks or a computer so that children can dictate or record daily observations.

The Creative Art Center.   This interest center provides opportunities and materials for arts-and-crafts activities. It may include the following features:

- Materials that encourage children to explore a variety of media, including finger paint, water colors, poster paint, markers, crayons, colored pencils, dough, clay, chalk, pipe cleaners, craft sticks, and wood scraps.

- Materials that provide opportunities for creative expression—for example, paint, clay, art materials, a variety of collage and woodworking materials, paint brushes, sponges, glue, scissors, different types of paper, wood chips, stencils, pompoms, glitter, pipe cleaners, felt sheets, craft sticks, and yarn.

- Materials that encourage children to practice writing skills—for example, finger paint and soft play dough with which children can practice making letters; an alphabet or set of name cards so that children can copy their names; rubber stamps with letters and pictures; and templates to encourage children to make materials such as diplomas, tickets, menus, and various signs (such as *Open, Closed, In,* and *Out*) for use in pretend play.

- Magazines and books containing project ideas.

- Posters or picture books about artists and their work, including both fine art and traditional crafts from different cultures (including those of the children in the class).

The Reading, Writing, and Language Center.   This interest center provides children with opportunities to enhance language development and to foster early reading and writing skills. It may include the following features:

- Language and vocabulary games such as picture cards, lotto games, and table and floor puzzles.

- Small toys to sort and categorize (with accompanying labeled boxes or storage bins) or to use in mini-play and storytelling activities.

- ABC books as well as alphabet and reading games such as inset puzzles, matching cards, pictures dominos, lotto games, rhyming cards, and sound- and letter-matching games.

- A variety of writing materials such as magnetic letters, writing utensils, stencils, crayons, slates, chalk, paper of various kinds, envelopes, blank books and book-making materials, and a computer or an old keyboard.

- A reading nook that includes a book display shelf with a collection of age-appropriate books, beanbag chairs or rocking chairs, pictures, posters, dolls, stuffed animals, and puppets.

- A storytelling and listening area with tape recorders, books and tapes, flannel boards, puppets, and a place for an adult to take dictation.

The Math Center. This interest center provides children with opportunities to learn mathematical concepts, including sorting, classification, sequencing, spatial relationships, measurement, and number skills. It may include the following features:

- Materials that encourage children to sort and classify—for example, rocks, shells, attribute blocks, buttons, beads, miniature zoo and farm animals, artificial fruits, dinosaurs, and vehicles of different colors and sizes.

- Materials that encourage children to sequence—for example, measuring cups and spoons, sequence puzzles, stacking toys, and nesting blocks.

- Materials that help children learn about shapes and spatial relationships—for example, parquetry blocks, shape sorters, pegboards, puzzles, and attribute blocks.

- Materials that help children learn about measurement—for example, balance scales, yardsticks, tape measures, thermometers, and clocks with movable hands.

- Materials that encourage children to learn number skills—for example, a variety of objects for counting, number cards, number puzzles, counting cubes, sandpaper or tactile numbers, number lines, dominoes, play money, and cash registers.

- Counting books and other math-themed picture books, including books that the children have made themselves.

CREATING A PRINT-RICH ENVIRONMENT FOR TODDLERS AND PRESCHOOLERS

A print-rich environment is one in which words and symbols play key roles. In a home setting within a highly literate culture, we would expect to see books, newspapers, and magazines. We would also see mail of all kinds; instruction manuals; and informative labels on foods, clothing, medicines, and other products. We might find notes on the refrigerator or on a bulletin board; scrapbooks and personal records; and special places set aside for writing, including desks, computers, or even a home office. Numbers and letters would be abundantly found on clocks, timers, telephones, scales, remote control devices, calendars, keyboards, monograms, thermostats, stamps, and money.

In the course of a day, a young child might watch his parents read and write as they choose his breakfast cereal, checked its ingredients and nutritional value, get news of the world from television and newspapers (or the Internet), pay bills, follow recipes or directions, read for pleasure, jot down or look up phone numbers, make lists, check the calendar, look at a clock or watch, thumb through a catalog, and leave a note for the baby-sitter. A toddler might handle printed objects as he opens a box of crackers, selects a book or videotape, pushes buttons on a play phone or cash register, scribbles on used envelopes, looks at a scrapbook or photo album, plays with the soap in the bathtub, and reads books with his parents. On any outing, he is likely to see street signs; logos of familiar stores and products; license plates, posters and advertisements; trucks with the name of a brand, product, or company; and people using various forms of print as they find their way around, make purchases, and exchange information.

A playroom or classroom for young children can also be an environment that invites children to participate in the world of print. The key to successfully creating this type of environment is meaningful use and communication. Labeling every wall, toy, or piece of furniture would be unnatural in a home and could create visual clutter in a classroom or public play space. That kind of labeling would not have much communication value because children who could recognize the labels would already know what the labeled items were. However, a different kind of environment—for example, a pretend play area that had been set up as a hair salon—would be enhanced by a barber pole, empty labeled shampoo bottles, magazines, an appointment book, and a cash register. Moreover, a bulletin board display showing captioned pictures of a recent project would spark conversations among parents, children, and teachers.

Making relevant print visible and accessible to the children can strengthen almost every classroom area and teaching activity. The following paragraphs provide some examples.

Imaginative Play. Opportunities abound for using various forms of print in imaginative play:

- Incorporate print into scenery, as appropriate. For example, you might have a sign for a store or restaurant, a mailbox and welcome mat at the entrance to a home, a sign that says "Tickets" on a ticket booth, or an "Emergency" sign at the hospital or animal hospital.

- Incorporate props that contain real print—for example, empty food packages in the grocery store or kitchen; post-cards, maps, and travel brochures for the airport or travel agency; train schedules, newspapers, subway maps, and tickets for commuters; numbered jerseys, team caps, programs, score cards, and autographed items for ballplayers.

- Solicit parents' help in collecting labels or packaging from products that their children use at home, especially items that reflect their home languages and cultures.

- Use print on costumes, hats, nametags, and badges.

- Provide appropriate writing materials and props such as ledgers, envelopes, checkbooks, prescription pads, order blanks, chalkboards, and trip logs.

- Encourage children to make their own props such as menus, placemats, play money, treasure maps, tickets, invitations, valentines, crowns, flags, banners, street signs, and sports insignia, using art and writing materials or a computer.

Constructive Play.   Print-related elements are easily incorporated into constructive play:

- Provide children with street signs, labeled buildings, and labeled vehicles to use in building cities, towns, farms, and imaginary worlds.

- Provide inspiration through books and posters showing real cities, farms, bridges, and buildings.

- Provide measuring and planning tools such as tape measures, rulers, graph paper for drawing plans and maps, blueprints, and schematic drawings.

- Take pictures of children's constructions for their portfolios or scrapbooks or to post in the block area.

- Take *before, during,* and *after* pictures of a construction project, and let children put them in order as well as dictate captions.

- Provide signs such as "Don't Touch" or "Leave Up" that children can use to temporarily protect their constructions.

Art and Writing.   Activities involving art and writing are naturally conducive to using lots of print forms:

- Recycle all kinds of print materials—envelopes, greeting cards, egg cartons, calendars, magazines, catalogs, newspapers, junk mail, and so forth for use as art and collage materials.

- Encourage children to make their own books.

- Encourage children to sign their creations.

- Encourage children to write or dictate captions and stories to go with their creations.

- Provide alphabets, letter stamps, stencils, plastic letters, and so forth for children to copy or to print with.

- Put up an alphabet chart, and post children's first names on removable cards next to the appropriate first letter. (They can be attached with magnets or Velcro or slipped into slots or envelopes. If you do not have room for a chart, you can put a hook under each letter of an alphabet strip and let the children hang up their names.)

- Have children decorate nameplates for their cubbies and make or decorate other useful signs for the room.

- Make a classroom message center or mailbox.

- Provide attractive display spaces for children's individual artwork. Include the artist's name, title, and date, as in a gallery or museum.

- Create a class mural that relates to your curriculum theme, with appropriate captions or labels.

Music, Dance, and Active Play.   Materials using print can also be effectively used in music and dance activities as well as in active play:

- Use chart paper, Big Books, or songbooks to prompt children as they sing familiar songs and to record children's made-up songs and song variations.

- If you can read music, let children see you do so as you sing or play an instrument.

- Use signs saying "Stop," "Go," "Walk," "Don't Walk," and "Yield" to enrich running games and to control riding-toy traffic.

- Make a scoreboard for team games, races, and pretend sports.

Science, Math, Cooking, Discovery, and Sensory Play. Activities involving science, math, cooking, discovery, and exploring the senses provide other avenues for using print materials:

- Use chart paper to display the steps in recipes or experiments. You can use rebus pictures or even real objects to make them easy for children to follow.

- Provide measuring instruments for scientific investigation, cooking, construction, as well as sand and water play. These items can include rulers, tape measures, measuring cups, measuring spoons, a scale or balance, a level, and a compass. Choose instruments with large, easy-to-read numbers.

- Provide guidebooks and posters to help children identify and learn about plants and animals in their environment.

- Provide display space for labeled collections of natural objects and other "treasures."

- Provide drawing and writing materials so that children can document their observations.

- Record and display children's questions, inferences, insights, and conclusions so that parents can see how their children's thinking is developing.

- If you have a class pet, make a nametag for its cage. Post care and feeding instructions near its food, using words and rebuses as appropriate.

- Use tape, chalk, or paint to create a large number line on which children can step or jump forward and backward.

- Display charts and graphs that children have helped to create.

Puzzles and Games. Whether homemade or commercial, puzzles and games can be a rich source of print-related activity:

- Choose some puzzles and games that contain letters, numbers, words, and symbols.

- Make puzzles from book jackets, captioned photos, and children's names by gluing them to heavy cardboard and then cutting them into pieces.

Schedules, Safety Procedures, and Daily Routines. Items such as schedules, safety procedures, and daily routines provide regular and practical opportunities to relate to print:

- Post a classroom schedule (with icons) and a class calendar.

- Post fire drill instructions and other safety information, including any instructions for children with severe allergies or other special medical needs.

- Create an attendance sign-in chart where children can place their names on a hook or in an envelope under the labeled picture of "home" or "school."

- Keep a weather log with the children. Include signs of seasonal change.

Crowd Control, Clean Up, and Chores. In addition to being practical, the various tasks and ways of managing groups can provide real-world experiences with forms of print:

- Label shelves and containers with pictures, words, or both to help children put things away in the appropriate places.

- Make signs saying "Open" and "Closed" to post on doors, gates, or cabinets that may be temporarily closed or off limits.

- Use symbols such as stars or footprints to show how many children an area can accommodate.

- Create a chart with removable names to show whose turn it is to help with each classroom job. Ways to help children recognize their own (and one another's) names include giving each name its own color and pairing each name with a geometric shape, symbol, or distinctive fabric pattern that is also used on a cushion for circle time.

- Post rules that children have helped to create for their space.

Curriculum Planning. Involving children in helping to plan what they want to learn not only will involve using print forms but also will help children feel empowered to make decisions about their learning:

- Involve children in planning projects and thematic units. Use chart paper to record children's questions about a topic or to list what they know and what else they want to know.

- Brainstorm with children the materials or props they will need for a long-term project. Let them watch as you write down their ideas.

- Help children put their names in books and other items that they bring from home to enhance classroom units.

- Help children put stickers on a calendar to indicate upcoming events.

Field Trips, Guests, and Special Events. Exciting activities such as field trips, visits from guests, and other special events provide unique opportunities to relate to print:

- Use chart paper to record children's words as they brainstorm questions, make plans, recall details, or write collective "thank you" letters.

- Create wall displays and scrapbooks using photographs, brochures, ticket stubs, children's drawings, and other memorabilia.

Communication with Parents. Using print to communicate with the key people in their lives will be especially appealing to children:

- Put up a "Welcome" sign. Children might add messages such as "Come see the books we made" or "Please visit our animal hospital."

- Create a message center and a parent bulletin board.

- Make a special spot for sturdy home–school journals or scrapbooks that both teachers and parents can use to record developmental milestones and to share with children. (Older children can keep their own picture journals or contribute to a home–school scrapbook.)

- Post children's interesting comments and questions where parents and children can see them.

- Create displays at children's eye level to show what children have been working on and what they have learned or created. Encourage parents to read the captions aloud as they reflect on the displays with their children. (Be sure to use children's home languages as well as the language or languages that you use for instruction.)

Administration, Record Keeping, and Assessment.   Children can even benefit from relating to print as you use it to take care of administration, record keeping, and assessment:

- Do some of your administrative tasks in a public space so that children can see how you use reading and writing to plan, order materials, remember important information, and keep track of what they are learning.

- Create portfolios for children where they can keep their best work. Let them participate in designing the covers, writing their names, and choosing items to include.

- When you take time to do formal observations, explain to children what you are doing. You might use a special notebook or clipboard or wear a sign that says, "I am kid-watching."

Reflection

Look around your classroom or family child-care home.

- How have you used print and symbols to help organize space, scheduling, objects, and activities? What might you add to the environment that would help children keep things in order and see print as an organizing tool?

- How does the environment reflect the children's backgrounds, interests, insights, and creations? Are children's home languages used throughout the environment and for many different print functions? Are children's names and words visible? Are their creations attractively displayed in ways that promote conversation? What words, pictures, and artifacts can you add to help children see the space as their own and celebrate their emerging identities?

- How have you incorporated books, signs, directions, numbers, and other meaningful print into the various classroom areas? What else can you do to encourage children to look at print up close and make it part of their work and play?

- If you have reading, writing, or listening centers, are they actively used? What can you do to make these centers more attractive to children and to keep them fresh and interesting?

- What settings and routines have you created that enable children to see you reading and writing for various purposes? How can you make your own use and enjoyment of literacy more visible to the children?

- How does the environment encourage parents to get involved in the program and to enhance their children's emergent literacy? How do parents use the spaces, books, toys, information exchange systems, and displays as they interact with you, the children, and one another? What changes might you make to better accommodate parent needs? What can you do to encourage parents to linger, converse, and forge stronger links between home and school? What new opportunities might you create for parents to contribute to the environment?

REFERENCE

Edwards, C. (1998). *The hundred languages of children: The Reggio Emilia approach, advanced reflections* (2nd ed.). Toronto: Ablex.

CHAPTER
10

Fostering Literacy Through Art, Music, and Pretending

*The wind was bringing me to school
And that is the fast way to get to school.
So why don't you let the wind bring you to school just like me?
And you will be to school on time, just like I was.*

—JAMES SNYDER, age 6 (1981)

Т he words of this 6-year-old child capture the challenge that all early childhood teachers face. How do we create the "wind" that propels a child to enter school prepared and eager to learn? It is relatively easy to make a list of the outside-in and the inside-out skills that we want children to acquire. The challenge is to make learning exciting so that children want to learn and feel good about each new accomplishment. Maria Montessori, an Italian early childhood education pioneer, spoke a profound truth. For a child, Montessori tells us, learning is play and play is learning. In this chapter, we describe how children learn emergent literacy skills through art, music, and imaginative play.

FOSTERING EMERGENT LITERACY THROUGH ART

В illie, a young Seminole boy, was standing at an easel, engaged in painting a picture. His teacher, who reported the scene, was standing beside him. "I paint me," Billie announced, as he brushed red paint across the paper. "Going fishing," he continued, adding a diagonal stripe and a blotch of orange to the painting. "Big alligator coming. Goin' to bite me," he continued, brushing on a glob of green paint. "Bash im, smash im" Billie shouted, crisscrossing the painting with bold red slashes. "I killed im dead," he announced triumphantly, as he covered the paper with black paint. "That was a great picture story" his teacher commented, as she helped Billie untie his smock.

Billie's teacher was perfectly correct. Painting a picture was Billie's way of telling a story. Billie's imaginative story of his battle with the alligator was depicted symbolically in a series of visual images. Anne Dyson (2001) describes drawing as a "key resource in enacting a symbolic world" (p. 129). Although Billie used language to tell his story to his teacher, his story was crafted from visual images in his mind. For Billie, as for most young children, drawing is akin to writing. As Dyson explains, "Pictures may be used in ways that foreshadow the use of written language" (p. 130).

As children engage in drawing, painting, or creating forms out of clay, they are laying the groundwork for writing in more than one way. In addition to helping children tell a story, artistic activities like drawing, painting, working with clay, or making crafts provide children with opportunities to develop the small-muscle dexterity and the hand–eye coordination that enable a child to form letters.

When children first make marks on a paper with crayon or marker, they are learning to hold the tool between their thumb and forefinger and maintain a pincer grasp while simultaneously moving their hand along the paper. Judith Schickedanz (1999) describes these early attempts to make marks as experiments. The child is trying to find out what the marks would look like if he moved his hands up and down, stabbed the paper with the point of the tool, or moved his hand in a circular motion. Schickedanz quotes Eleanor Gibson, who says that, although "scribbling seems to be its own reward ... [i]t furnishes an unparalleled opportunity for learning the relations[hips] between the finger movements that guide the tool and the resulting visual feedback" (Gibson, 1975, p. 293).

After their early attempts at scribbling, children become more adept at making different kinds of lines and at organizing the lines on the paper in a way that pleases them. As children become more proficient with scribbling, they move from the design to the representational stage. Their drawings depict a picture that is in their mind; nevertheless, what they draw and what it represents may not be easy to recognize.

As children become adept with writing implements, they often add "writing" to their drawings. At first, this "writing" is likely to be just a series of small, squiggly, generally vertical lines. In most cases, the child uses these squiggles to claim authorship of his picture story by "signing" his name. In the drawing, the child may also use a row (or rows) of squiggles to label elements such as "me" and "my house" or to "write" a greeting or message.

Children who draw squiggly lines to represent writing are demonstrating their grasp of concepts of print. English writing consists of individual letters that are usually vertical in orientation and placed along a horizontal line, proceeding from left to right. Spaces between scribbles indicate a nascent understanding that a group of letters represent a word and that a space after a letter signifies the beginning of a new word. After a while, children introduce letter-like forms into their lines of scribbling. Soon, they are able to form actual letters, usually beginning with the initial letter of their first name. At first, almost any letters will do; gradually, however, the random letters and letter-like squiggles give way to invented spellings and serious attempts at conventional writing.

Not all children go through these stages in the same way. Most begin with drawings and picture stories, but some learn writing as an entirely separate process. They may begin by typing random letters on a computer, arranging magnetic letters, or attempting to copy letters and words.

Art Activities That Build a Base for Reading and Writing

Art activities can serve as a foundation for developing reading and writing skills as well as for fostering a broader appreciation of literacy. The following activities can build a base for these skills:

- Encourage children to use a wide range of art materials, including paint brushes, markers, crayons, finger paint, and pens or markers that can make fine lines.

- Encourage children to draw and "write" on a large scale, using large paper taped to an easel or wall. Their movements will be more fluid and their representations bolder than when using smaller pieces of paper.

- Encourage children to draw and "write" on cards, notebook paper, drawing paper, and envelopes as well as in "journals" or "books" and in clay. At this smaller scale, children practice fine-motor skills and also may be prompted to "write" because they are making books, letters, or cards.

- Set up opportunities for children to draw together. They might use two sides of a double easel, work at adjacent easels or at the same table, or collaborate on a large drawing or mural. Drawing with a friend tends to encourage conversation, especially when the children are sharing drawing space or materials.

- Always encourage children to sign their drawings. Ask them whether they would like you to write their name for them, to let them do it themselves, or to provide assistance.

- Encourage children to tell you about their pictures, either as they are working (as Billie's teacher did) or after they have finished. Write the words of their stories or their labels for their drawings either on a separate piece of paper or, with their permission and participation, on the drawing itself.

- Display children's artwork in the classroom. Talk with children about the stories that their pictures represent.

- Create a portfolio for each child where she can keep her favorite pictures. When she adds a new picture, you can look together at some of the old ones and retell the stories or talk about the colors and shapes as well as the drawing and writing techniques that she used.

FOSTERING LITERACY SKILLS THROUGH MUSIC

T hree-year-old Wan Leigh was a bright little girl who seemed to have problems with oral memory. She could never remember the names of the characters in a book or learn a simple rhyme. When it was time for the class to put on a show for the parents, the teacher wanted all the children in the class to participate. Because Wan Leigh was a vivacious child, the teacher selected her to open the show. She tried to get Wan Leigh to repeat the lines, "Welcome to our show tonight. We are happy that you are here." Wan Leigh tried hard to remember, but she could never get past the first line. Then her teacher got an idea. Wan Leigh had had no trouble learning her ABCs when they sang the alphabet song. Maybe she could teach Wan Leigh a song that would help her memorize her lines. Using "Mary Had a Little Lamb" as a tune, the teacher composed this song. "Welcome to our school tonight, school tonight, school tonight, welcome to our school tonight, we are glad you're here." The teacher's idea worked. Wan Leigh had no problem learning the song and got a round of applause when she opened the show.

Many children, like Wan Leigh, can learn new material more easily when it is set to music. The rhythm and cadence of a song and its accompanying movements or gestures make retention easier and more fun. Shelley Ringgenberg (2003) suggests that story-songs—existing or original stories that are set to simple, rhythmic, and repetitive melodies—offer a "fun and effective way to hold children's attention and help them learn" (pp. 76–79). Just as we teach children the ABCs by teaching them the alphabet song, we can use familiar tunes to help children retain other concepts related to emergent literacy.

Helping Children Learn Symbol–Sound Correspondence

If children are developing symbol–sound correspondence, we could support their efforts by using a song like "Mary Had a Little Lamb" to teach children a variety of letter-to-sound correspondences:

> *Did you know that B is for ball, B is for ball, B is for ball?*
> *Did you know that B is for ball, and B is for baby and bat?*
> *Did you know that C is for car, C is for car, C is for car?*
> *Did you know that C is for car, and C is for carriage and cat?*

Helping Children Develop Phonemic Awareness

Substituting a beginning consonant in a song with one that is different helps children tune in to the beginning sounds of a word and, at the same time, lets them have fun as they listen to the silly words they are creating. Try changing the beginning sounds in the first line of "Row, Row, Row Your Boat." Show the children a card with the substitute letter on it while you sing the song.

> (Hold up the letter B.)
> *Bow, bow, bow your boat, gently down the beam . . .*
> (Hold up the letter D.)
> *Dow, Dow, Dow your doat gently down the deam . . .*
> (Hold up the letter F.)
> *Fow, fow, fow, your foat gently down the feam . . .*

Another way to help children tune in to the beginning sounds of words is to change the words to the classic children's song, "Old MacDonald Had a Farm." Change the words so that the children can refer to any object that is found on the farm, and in the place of what would have been an animal sound, substitute the first phoneme of the object's name:

Old MacDonald had a farm, ee i ee i o.
*And on that farm there was a **barn**, ee i ee i o.*
*With a **b-b** here and a **b-b** there,*
*Here a **b**, there a **b**, everywhere a **b-b** . . .*

Connecting Sung and Written Words

The connection between songs and emergent literacy is strengthened when children can see the words to the song in print. Some children may know that songs can be written down because they will have seen adults using hymnals, songbooks, or sheet music. For others, seeing songs in print may be a new experience.

One common technique that emergent literacy teachers use is to write the words of a song on a large sheet of chart paper. Once children have learned the song, the chart can be used like a Big Book. As the children sing the song together, the teacher—or a child—can use a pointer to point to each word as it is sung.

With a substitution song such as "Old MacDonald," children can tape pictures to cue the verses. For example, the chart might say "and on that farm he had a _____." Children could decide which picture to put in the blank. Or, you could put up several pictures and use the pointer to indicate which one the children should sing in each verse.

Mary Renck Jalongo and Deborah Ribblett (1997) suggest using picture books of familiar songs for a wide range of literacy activities. Often, these books contain both words and music, accompanied by appropriate illustrations. *Over the River and Through the Woods* (Gurney, 1992) and *Frog Went A-Courting* (Langstaff, 1955) are two good examples. Jalongo and Ribblett (1997) point out that these types of books merge two literacies—literacy in music and literacy in print—helping children connect singing with reading and writing songs with writing stories. They foster emergent literacy in five discrete ways:

- *Build on familiarity and enjoyment*—Song picture books motivate children to read by encouraging them to look at the words that describe a well-known and much-loved song.

- *Provide repetition and predictability*—Because many of the familiar and best-loved songs include choruses that are repeated over and over again, children learn to identify the words of the chorus.

- *Expand vocabulary and knowledge of story structures*—Some songs include words that children sing without knowing their meaning. "Jack and Jill," for instance, includes *fetch* and *crown*. When the teacher reads those words in a story picture book, he has an opportunity to talk about their meaning. Other songs such as "There Was an Old Woman Who Swallowed a Fly" have a sequential order of events that familiarizes children with story structure.

- *Promote critical thinking and problem solving*—Children can be challenged to think of ways to change the pictures or the words in a book. "How would we sing 'Old McDonald Had a Farm' if the first picture were a lion instead of a cow?" or "How could we change the words of 'Old McDonald Had a Farm' if we were to draw pictures of objects like bells or drums instead of pictures of animals?"

- *Foster creative expression and language play*—After children have read several story picture books, they love to create their own picture storybooks based on their own favorite songs.

FOSTERING EMERGENT LITERACY THROUGH PRETEND PLAY

Encouraging pretend play is perhaps the most effective means of promoting emergent literacy. McLane and McNamee (1991) describe two ways in which pretend play links to emergent literacy:

First, as a symbolic activity, pretend play allows children to develop and refine their capacity to use symbols to represent experience and to construct imaginary worlds, capacities they will draw on when they begin to read and write. Second, as an orientation or approach to experience, play can make the various roles and activities of people who read and write more meaningful and hence more accessible to young children. (p. 3)

In other words, pretend play gives children the opportunity to represent, repeat, and share stories. It also provides opportunities for children to pretend to read and write as they imitate the actions of adults. In the course of activities such as these, children practice and hone storytelling, book handling, and other emergent literacy skills that they will use as readers and writers.

The Emergence of Pretending

Pretend play, similar to emergent literacy, does not emerge all at once. The ability to pretend has its roots in infancy, when the baby first demonstrates her capacity to imitate. It reaches a height in early childhood, when it takes center stage as a dominant mode of play, socialization, and learning. And of course, people who continue to develop their pretend-play skills beyond childhood can go on to adult careers as actors, directors, puppeteers, and teachers.

Young infants are able to imitate facial expressions. When their caregiver smiles, they will smile back, and when their caregiver suddenly frowns, they, too, will change their expression. By the age of 2 or 3 months, babies can imitate a sound or an action that is in their repertoire. A baby who has learned to make cooing sounds will engage in a back-and-forth cooing conversation. A baby who has learned to bang with a toy will repeat his banging when a familiar adult starts banging. Infants are also able to reenact a familiar behavior when they are cued by an object—for example, if they see a blanket or a pillow on the floor, they may put their head on the pillow or pull the blanket over their body as if they are going to sleep.

At the age of 1 year, the baby's imitation is more sophisticated. When given an appropriate prop, a 1-year-old may imitate the way that she has seen that prop used. She will wipe the table if you give her a cloth or will babble if you bring a toy telephone up to her ear. As they approach their second birthday, many 1-year olds will invent their own props. If they want to feed their teddy bear and they do not have any real or play food, they may act as if a plastic ring were a cookie and put it up to a teddy bear's mouth.

By the time a child is 2 years old, we see the emergence of genuine pretending. The 1-year-old will babble into a toy telephone, but the 2-year-old will carry out a sequence of events such as making a ringing sound, putting the receiver to his ear, babbling or saying "Hi, Daddy," and hanging up the phone. This same sequence will be repeated over and over again. The following vignette characterizes this early pretending:

> One morning, Danny insisted that he be given a coffee cup just like his daddy's. Danny grasped the empty cup, brought it to his mouth, and began to blow into it. After breakfast, he went outside to play in the sandbox with his next-door buddy. The two boys decided to make a birthday cake. They shaped a mound of sand into a "sort of" circle and stuck a few twigs into the mound. Pleased with their product, they sang their own rendition of "Happy Birthday" and puffed on the sticks. Next, they each picked up a shovel and pretended to eat the cake. After putting down their shovels, they blew out the "candles" again. As far as Danny and his buddy were concerned, it was perfectly fine to resume their blowing even if they had already "eaten" the cake.

There is a recognizable difference between the way a typical 2-year-old pretends and the way a typical 3-year-old does. At 3 years old, most children like to plan before they begin to play. Like 2-year-olds, they often play out the same scenarios over and over. However, instead of working with whatever props are at hand, they decide in advance what props they will need and begin their play by gathering them. A second and important addition to their play is the use of language both to plan and to sustain the play. The following scenario involving Rosita and Consuelo, cousins who often play together, provides an example of this use of language:

Rosita:	Let's play picnic. I be the mama and you be my little boy.
Consuelo:	No, I be a daddy.
Rosita:	Okay. Daddy, go get the towels. I get the picnic basket.
Consuelo:	We need food.
Rosita.	The picnic basket has lots of food. Just pretend.
Consuelo:	Let's go. I wanna eat.
Rosita:	Gotta get the beach ball and the sand pails.
Consuelo:	I wanna eat.
Rosita:	We're in the car. Zoom, zoom, zoom, we're at the beach. I'm going swimming. Help, help, there's a shark!
Consuelo:	There ain't no shark. Gotta eat the picnic.

By 4 years of age, children's pretend play gets more varied, more elaborate, and more creative. It reflects their individual interests, concerns, and questions, but it also occurs in a social and cultural context. Play themes, playmate choices, preferred toys and props, group sizes, and play locations often reflect the gender stereotypes of children's cultures. However, 4-year-olds also tend to be quite flexible; if adults encourage it, boys and girls will play together and will enjoy both "girl" and "boy" pretending.

Four-year-olds engage in several different types of pretend play. At times, they engage in mini-pretending, manipulating props and talking for various miniature animals, dolls, or action figures. Girls and some boys enjoy playing with a dollhouse, arranging and rearranging the furniture as well as naming, manipulating, and talking for the characters. Many children set up elaborate scenes, either individually or with a friend, and then play out stories, accompanied by words and sound effects.

A second type of pretending in which 4-year-olds engage is maxi-pretending, or role play. Usually, a group of children gather together and the play begins with the assignment of roles. A group of girls is most likely to play out a domestic theme such as cooking dinner, planning a party, going shopping, or going to a restaurant. Boys are likely to gather in large groups. Their favorite themes revolve around team sports, outer space, monsters, cowboys, cops and robbers, astronauts, soldiers, firemen, and superheroes.

A third type of pretend play is putting on a performance. Boys may organize a baseball game on the playground with pretend balls and bats and may gather up enough players to form a team, or they might decide to be disc jockeys, television stars, comedians, or sports announcers. Girls are more likely to put on shows—singing, telling jokes, dancing, doing acrobatics, cheerleading, or modeling the latest fashions. Frequently, girls will invite boys to take part in their shows.

The fourth type of pretending is dramatic play in which children act out a familiar story or put on a puppet show. It differs from role play or performing in that children reenact a series of events in a predetermined and logical sequence, with a beginning, a middle, and an ending. Dramatic play is often planned and initiated by the teacher and is likely to be a reenactment of a favorite story or book.

Recognizing the Many Benefits of Pretend Play

Pretend play is the hallmark of early childhood. It creates and sustains friendships, promotes intellectual growth, and encourages language development. It enables children to cope with bad or sad feelings and to feel good about themselves. Pretend play is the most effective and most delightful way to foster emergent literacy.

Pretend Play Supports Friend Making

Young children use pretending as a way to invite other children to play with them or initiate group interaction. Children recognize that a good way to recruit new friends is to engage them in an activity such as building a block structure, making a pile of sand-cakes, or putting out a forest fire. Children with good play ideas are sought after by other children and are likely to assume high-status roles in the pretend-play scenarios—roles such as mother of a family, teacher of the class, captain of the pirate ship, or leader of a danger-packed exploration. Children who are new to a preschool may use their skill at pretending to enter a closed group of players. In the following scenario, Theresa uses pretending to help herself fit in:

Theresa was a new student at the Academy Preschool. On her first day, she went out on the playground with the other children, who immediately dispersed into groups. Theresa went over to the jungle gym but was told by a group of boys that she better not stay around because they were pirates. Anybody who boarded their ship would be thrown into the ocean. Next, she went over to the slide. The astronauts had climbed onto the space shuttle and there was no room for her. Finally, she approached the sandbox. She watched the chief chef showing the kitchen staff how to make tortillas. Theresa picked up a sand toy, filled it with sand and brought it to the chef. The chef informed her that it needed more salt so she sprinkled some loose sand on top of her tortilla. From that point on, Theresa was a part of the group.

Pretend play not only helps a child gain status in the group but also supports prosocial behavior. When children decide to put on a performance, set up a role play, or act out a story, they begin by making plans. The planning process involves sharing ideas, negotiating conflicts over who is going to play which role, dividing responsibility, and working cooperatively to carry out their plans. As they play out their roles, children have the opportunity to see the world from someone else's point of view. The "mother" whose pretend children keep vying for her attention and the "teacher" who cannot quiet her pretend class feel more empathetic toward their actual mothers and teachers.

Pretend Play Supports Intellectual Growth

Pretend play is a symbolic activity that helps children develop and define their capacities to use symbols as representations of experience and to construct imaginary worlds. Children create symbols based on the materials that are available in their environments. If children have access to Tinker Toys®, for example, they may use a rod as a spoon for stirring the soup, as a baton for leading the orchestra, or as a gun for shooting the bad guys. If children have access to pencils and pads of paper when they are playing doctor, they are more likely to "write" a prescription or jot down some notes about their patient's condition.

Pretend Play Supports Language Development

Pretend play—whether it is miniature play, role play, dramatic play, or a performance—encourages children to communicate. In miniature play, children speak for the miniature characters. In role play, the children engage in heated discussions about who gets to play which role. Once the roles are assigned, each child invents the dialogue as the play progresses. In staging a performance, each performer communicates with the real or imagined audience in words, gestures, facial expressions, and actions. In dramatic play, the dialogue is spontaneous. Sometimes, children repeat some of the words of a familiar story, and at other times, they ad lib. The big bad wolf may threaten to "huff and puff and blow your house down" and then tell the pigs to stop oinking. Goldilocks may talk about being hungry and then complain that the porridge is "too hot" or "too cold."

McLane and McNamee (1991) suggest that pretend play becomes increasingly elaborate, complex, and abstract during the preschool years:

> With development, pretend play becomes less dependent on physical props, gestures, and actions, and relies increasingly on ideas, imagination, and language. An increasing proportion of the time devoted to pretend play is spent on talk as children discuss the setting, the characters or roles, and the plots they will reenact in their play . . . . As pretend play becomes increasingly dependent on language to create possible worlds and to express and communicate meanings, it comes closer to the experiences of storytelling, writing and reading. (p. 3)

Pretend Play Helps Children Feel Good About Themselves

Pretend play is a way for children to replay happy events, assume a powerful role, master their fears, deal with tragic events, cope with anger and jealousy, and gain a sense of power and control. As we watch children playing alone or with other children, we can easily identify the emotional value of pretending. Consider the replaying of happy events that occurs in the following scenario:

The Happy Times preschool planned monthly field trips for the preschool children. Most of the field trips were within walking distance, but once a year, they took the children on a special field trip. One year, the children were taken to a farm with cows, pigs, chickens, a vegetable garden, and a roadside stand. For the next 2 weeks, the children pretended that they were farmers. They put on oversized shirts and big straw hats. They milked the cows, fed the pigs, gathered chicken eggs, and set up a roadside stand. Veronica remarked as she pretended to milk a cow, "Got to pull on the utter thing, the milk is coming out. See. It's just like the milk that comes out of a bottle!"

Children love to replay happy events such as field trips, birthday parties, and holiday parties. They also like to assume roles in which they are the power figure. Children love to climb to the top of the jungle gym and shout down to the other children—for example, "I'm the king of the castle, and you're the dirty rascal!"

Although children spend most of their time replaying happy events or inventing exciting exploits, they also replay troublesome events in an effort to come to terms with them. After Chad was in an automobile accident, he spent hours at school crashing the cars into each other. After Carmen's dog was killed when it ran into the street, she gathered up all the stuffed animals in the child-care center. "You not dead," she told each animal in turn. "I give you a big shot and then you be all better."

Pretend Play Supports Emergent Literacy

Pretend play provides children with opportunities to develop a range of literacy skills and abilities. These can include storytelling skills, book-handling skills, and abilities to interpret signs and symbols as well as opportunities to practice actual reading and writing and to expand their language skills.

As children engage in role play, they may act out a series of events in a logical sequence. For example, they might write out a shopping list, go to the supermarket, pay for their purchases with play money, return home, and put the groceries away. They may plan an exciting adventure, pack up their gear, trudge around the playground, chase away the wild animals, jump across the river, discover the hidden treasure, and return home triumphant. In the course of these activities, children challenge themselves to create rich narratives with increasingly complex story scripts. The stories that they play out often reflect their understanding of the underlying structure of stories that they have heard (stories that have been either read to them or told to them) about real or imaginary events.

Pretend play can also familiarize children with printed words. As they play grocery store, for example, children may look at labels on packages and numbers on prices, play money, and cash register keys. They may incorporate pretend writing as they play out a restaurant scene in which the patrons are given menus with pretend writing, the waiter pulls out a pad and writes down the order by scratching random squiggles on a pad, and the waitress presents a bill at the end of the meal. The children are motivated to "write" because writing serves a real purpose for the grown-ups they are imitating.

This print-rich block corner invites children to use street signs, maps, and directions in their pretend play.

Reading and writing can also serve a real purpose for the children themselves. Children who are putting on a show may ask the teacher to help them write the program, create a billboard, or make signs that they can hold up at the appropriate times during the performance (e.g., "*GOLDILOCKS AND THE THREE BEARS*," "APPLAUSE," "INTERMISSION," and "THE END"). Children who are playing pirates may want to make a treasure map or invent a secret code.

Children who enjoy being read to are often motivated to "read" themselves. As they pretend to read to themselves or to a doll, they have an opportunity to demonstrate and practice book-handling skills. These skills include turning the pages from left to right, holding the book so the "audience" can see what they are reading, or pointing to an illustration or a word that they expect their audience to look at. Placing dolls or stuffed animals in the reading corner is one way to foster this behavior. As children pretend to read books whose words or storylines they have memorized, they sometimes slide over into real reading as they associate words on the page with words that they are saying.

Activities and Techniques for Supporting Pretend Play and Emergent Literacy

With all of these benefits, pretend play should have a central place in any toddler, preschool, or mixed-age classroom. The following suggestions provide ways to ensure that pretend play is highlighted in your classroom:

- Make pretend play a central part of your curriculum, not just something the children do in their "free" time or while you are busy with other tasks.

- Plan for pretend play. Use storybooks, group discussions, costumes, and props to suggest play ideas. Let the children help you set up classroom environments that reflect your curriculum themes—for example, a play farm in the block area, a post office or print shop in the writing center, a TV weather studio on the stage, or a Mexican restaurant and bodega in the house corner.

- Observe children's spontaneous play to get ideas for curriculum themes and story time selections.

- Look for natural opportunities to introduce new ideas and vocabulary words into children's play or to enrich favorite play themes through field trips, classroom visitors, storybook selections, and science activities.

- Look for opportunities to introduce a variety of print materials as play props and supports. For example, you can use real (empty) food packages in the play store, leave old newspapers or magazines in the house corner, help children make treasure maps for the pirates and blueprints for the house builders, and purchase or make traffic signs for children to use on the playground or with their miniature cars and trucks.

- Get into the act yourself. If the children are studying transportation, for example, you can pretend to be the engineer on a train and shout "All aboard!" when it is time for the class to line up to go out to the playground. Instead of simply going to the playground, your "train" might go on a trip over the "mountains" or around the "zoo." Similarly, you can use a puppet to encourage the children to help at cleanup time or to elicit their questions about a new curricular topic.

- Coach children who are having difficulty pretending alone or joining others in play. This coaching will help them develop pretend-play skills.

As a teacher can support pretend play in several different ways, you can set up the environment so that it is conducive to pretend play with a collection of props appropriate for playing out different themes. You can create a classroom schedule that allows flexible time for engaging in pretend play. You can also play an active role in inspiring and initiating pretend play. You can serve as an active participant in the children's pretend-play scenarios and can be an appreciative audience when children stage a performance.

Setting Up Environments That Support Pretend Play and Emergent Literacy

Indoor and outdoor environments that support pretend play give children opportunities to explore new ideas, invent new situations, play together in small or larger groups, practice newly acquired skills, and have fun. Environments must be preplanned to provide adequate space for pretend activities, and the space must be easy to rearrange as shortcomings are discovered or as new ideas are generated.

In setting up a classroom environment, create discrete centers or areas for role play, dress-up play, or miniature play as well as for putting on a performance. The circle time area can double as a place for performing, especially if you provide a play microphone and a CD player. If children want to perform "on stage," then bring in a mat or suggest that the performance might work out better on a playground structure.

For role play or thematic play in the classroom, set up play structures with a counter that can be used for various kinds of play. Such structures can encourage children to stage a puppet show. At other times, they can be used for playing store, post office, repair shop, or travel agency. Also set up areas for dress-up, housekeeping, block play, and miniature play. Setting up two imaginative play settings side by side—for example, a fire station and a hair salon—not only encourages boys and girls to play together but also tends to foster creative play and rich conversations.

You can also set up a play environment that relates to a curriculum theme and evolves as the children learn. For example, one preschool class had an opportunity to visit the circus, and their teacher built a unit around the event. After reading several circus books, the children turned their meeting area into a "ring" where they staged circus performances. A tour of the circus following the show prompted them to add a ticket booth, concession stands, a backstage area for putting on costumes and make-up, a stable for the elephants and horses, and their own "circus posters."

The selection of appropriate props makes each environment come alive. The teacher may want to set out props that represent the theme of the month, that relate to a story they read to the children, or that connect with a special event or classroom visitor that the children enjoyed.

One teacher described how a visiting parent showed the class her collection of seashells. After that visit, the children decided they wanted to create a classroom museum. The teacher supplied a collection of seashells, a picture book of seashells, old raffle tickets to use as admission slips, small display boxes, and stick-on labels for naming the different shells. The museum kept expanding as children brought in a variety of objects from home, including rocks, stamps, buttons, and postcards.

Many teachers create theme boxes, or collections of props that relate to their curriculum units or to the children's interests and experiences. They put out the theme boxes at appropriate times and store them away when it is time to introduce a new theme or when the children seem to need new play ideas. Common theme boxes include the following items:

- *Doctor or veterinarian:* doctor's kit, bandages, prescription pads, and pencil

- *Restaurant:* menus, order forms, paper placemats that children can decorate, packaging from fast food restaurants

- *Train ride:* whistle, engineer's cap, tickets, hole punch

- *Beach:* shells, pebbles, starfish, shovel, pail, towel, picnic basket and play food, empty sunscreen container

- *Birthday party:* invitations, hats, wrapping paper, cards, candles, favors

- *Travel agency:* plane tickets, travel brochures, souvenirs, postcards, maps

- *Store:* cash register or cash box, play money, calculator, sticky notes for marking prices, bags

As you put together theme boxes, think about how you can also include print materials such as catalogs and packaging that inspire pretend reading and writing.

Setting Up a Flexible Schedule That Provides Opportunities for Pretending

Make sure that the schedule you develop for the class includes plenty of time for spontaneous pretend play and is flexible enough to allow you to prolong the spontaneous playtime when children are engaged in a pretend role play, drama, or a performance that cannot be ended abruptly. Teachers need to develop schedules that provide a predictable sequence, ensure an appropriate mix of active and quiet play, and allow time for clean-up, lunch, and rest time; however, schedules should never be controlled solely by the clock.

Participating in Children's Play to Extend the Play and Support Emergent Literacy

As a teacher or caregiver, you can play an active role in children's pretend play by initiating pretend-play themes, making suggestions to children that extend the theme; taking a role in a pretend-play scenario; or helping children review their role plays and turn them into performances, puppet shows, or dictated stories. Consider the following vignettes.

Miss Politically Correct was disturbed by the fact that the girls always played in the housekeeping area and would seldom include the boys. She decided that the best solution was to set up the structure next to the housekeeping area as a fix-it shop and invite several of the boys to play in it. She then went over to the house-keeping area and told the girls that the toaster in the kitchen was broken and they better take it to the fix-it shop. The girls complied with her suggestion. For the next 15 minutes, the girls kept bringing their broken appliances to the fix-it shop and the boys had a great time hammering on the appliances as they made various repairs and collecting the play money that the girls offered in payment.

Miss Playful loved to see the children engrossed in pretend play. She set up a veterinarian's clinic in one of the play structures. Unfortunately, the play got too repetitive and the children started losing interest. She decided to join in. She brought an armful of stuffed animals to the clinic and demanded immediate service. Her camel was losing its tail and she needed to have it sewed on. Her white poodle had been swimming in a muddy pond and he was not white any more. Donald Duck had a bad cough and must be given a dose of cough syrup. Before she took the animals home, she insisted that the vet write out a prescription for more cough medicine. After Miss Playful's departure, the veterinarian's clinic was swarming with activity. Several children brought in their stuffed animals and demanded immediate service, asking for a dose of medicine and insisting on getting a "prescription." Miss Playful had succeeded in expanding not only their play but also their vocabulary.

Miss More-Than-One-Way-to-Skin-a-Cat was pleased that the children in her group had fun playing, but she was worried that they were not spending enough time on activities designed to promote literacy. At the end of the day in circle time, she asked the children to tell her what they had been playing. One group talked about building a block fence to keep in their runaway animals. Another group talked about dressing up their dolls because they were going to a party. Miss More-Than-One-Way-to-Skin-a-Cat wrote down each group's story. The next day, she read the stories back to the children and asked them to draw pictures to illustrate the stories. She helped them make books by combining the pictures with the text she had written, and she put the books in the reading corner. The children loved the idea of reading their homemade books to each other.

Each of these teachers had her own reasons for getting involved in the children's play and her own style of playing. Their stories illustrate just a few of the strategies that you can use and the benefits to children in terms of storytelling, vocabulary, reading, and writing, as well as creativity and cooperation.

Reflection

Think about your own classroom.

What could you do to enhance your children's pretend play?

How would this enhancement foster emergent literacy?

References

Dyson, A. H. (2001). Writing and children's symbolic repertoires: Development unhinged. In S. B. Neuman & D. K. Dickinson (Eds.), *Handbook of early literacy research* (pp. 126–141). New York: Guilford.

Gibson, E. J. (1975). Theory-based research on reading and its implications for instruction. In J. B. Carroll & J. S. Chall (Eds.), *Toward a literate society: The report of the Committee on Reading of the National Academy of Education with a series of papers commissioned by the committee*, p. 293. New York: McGraw-Hill.

Gurney, J. S. (1992). *Over the river and through the woods*. New York: Cartwheel Books.

Jalongo, M. R., & Ribblett, D. M. (1997). Using song picture books to support emergent literacy. *Childhood Education, 74*(1), 15–22.

Langstaff, J. (1955). *Frog went-a-courting*. Fairbanks, AK: Gulliver Books.

McLane, J. B., & McNamee, G. D. (1991). The beginnings of literacy. *Zero to Three, 12*(1), 1–8.

Ringgenberg, S. (2003). Music as a teaching tool: Creating story songs. *Young Children, 58*(5), 76–79.

Schickedanz, J. A. (1999). *Much more than the ABCs: The early stages or reading and writing*. Washington, DC: National Association for the Education of Young Children.

Snyder, J. (1981). [Untitled poem]. In R. Lewis (Ed.), *Miracles: Poems by children of the English-speaking world*. New York: Simon and Schuster.

CHAPTER 11

Assessing Children's Progress

The Little Elf

I met a little elf man once
Down where the lilies blow.
I asked him why he was so small
And why he didn't grow.

He slightly frowned and with his eye
He looked me through and through.
"I'm quite as big for me," said he,
"As you are big for you."

—JAMES KENDRICK BANGS (1959)

Whenever we decide to measure something, our first concern is finding an accurate or valid instrument with which to measure it. An instrument is valid when it measures what it claims to measure. The elf man complained because the human boy used height as the measure of normal growth and as a stand-in for maturity—without taking into account the typical heights of adult humans and elves. This measure, the elf pointed out, was simply not fair. "I'm quite as big for me," said he, "As you are big for you."

In addition to being valid, a measure must be reliable. Many of us, when we are asked to estimate the square footage of a room, will walk heel to toe down and across the room, figuring that our shoes are about a foot long. This technique can be a reliable way to measure square footage, but only if our shoes are not too long or too short and we walk in straight lines. Otherwise, pacing the floor heel to toe is not a reliable way to measure the length and width of the room because each time the room is measured this way, the answer is likely to be different. If a measure is not reliable, then it certainly cannot be valid.

DEFINITIONS |

Reliability: Reliability refers to the degree to which an assessment will produce consistent measurements across different raters and contexts. Contexts include where and when the assessment is done as well as differences in the ways evaluators may interpret the evidence.

Validity: Validity refers to the accuracy of a test in measuring what it is designed to measure and the extent to which the data can be supported by independent evidence. If, for instance, a test is designed to determine school readiness, then the content of the test should reflect the critical knowledge or competencies a child is expected to master to be ready to enter kindergarten or first grade.

PURPOSES OF ASSESSMENT AND EVALUATION IN EARLY CHILDHOOD PROGRAMS

For many of us, the term "assessment" suggests report cards and state-mandated tests—not the kinds of observations and progress reports that we consider appropriate for young children. Early childhood teachers know that young children develop at different rates, that their behavior changes from day to day and from situation to situation, that they are not always very good at following instructions, and that sometimes even people who know them well cannot understand what they are trying to say. Early childhood teachers also know that the little elf had it right—each child is "big" in his own ways, and no standard test could reliably or validly capture them all.

Thus many early childhood educators view assessment and evaluation with understandable skepticism. They worry about whether a very young child will be upset about being tested, whether assessments can honestly reflect what a young child knows or can do, whether testing requires paperwork that takes away from teaching time, or whether test results will be used to judge how well a teacher is performing. These concerns are reasonable, but they should not prevent us from doing assessments. Assessing young children, if done appropriately, can provide valuable information to teachers, parents, and policymakers that can enhance young children's educational experiences.

In a comprehensive review of school readiness assessment practices conducted for the National Education Goals Panel, Lorrie Shephard, Sharon Lynn Kagan, and Emily Wirtz (1998) describe four major purposes of early childhood assessment, which are briefly detailed in the following overview.

Assessments to Support Learning. Standardized tests measure a child's performance in one or more domains of competency and describe what a child already knows or can do as well as what he needs to learn. Assessments conducted on an ongoing basis by classroom teachers monitor a child's ongoing progress, inform teacher planning, and provide teachers with information that can be shared with parents.

Assessments for Identification of Special Needs. Screening tests are short assessments that determine whether there is a need for further testing. Diagnostic testing identifies areas of concern and determines whether there is a need for intervention within the classroom, outside the classroom, or both.

Assessments for Program Evaluation. These assessments determine whether a program is meeting its objectives and where change or modification is needed. These assessments are usually conducted using a standardized instrument but can also be conducted by a supervisor, director, or program consultant who makes an informal evaluation.

Assessments for Accountability. These assessments are based on standardized instruments and are used to measure the relative effectiveness of a program. The outcomes of these assessments are shared with funders or sponsors and may affect the future support of the program.

The following vignette shows how doing assessments on very young children can enhance children's educational experiences:

L eonardo was a gentle and compliant 2-year-old, but he seemed to be oblivious to questions or suggestions. His teacher, Mrs. Check-Again, was uncertain about what to do to help Leonardo. When she would ask him to come to circle time, he would smile and stare at the other children, but he would not move. If she took his hand and led him to the circle, he would comply willingly, then sit in the circle and copy the movements of the other children. He appeared to be very observant and was especially good with doing finger plays. When circle time was over, he would wait patiently until she led him to one of the play centers. He loved building with the unit blocks and would have stayed there all day if Mrs. Check-Again did not remember to take him somewhere else. He seemed to enjoy being with the other children, but he never spoke to anyone. During story time, he would look at the pictures but would never join in when the children repeated a refrain.

Because she was puzzled about his lack of participation in story time and his complete disregard of any directions or requests, Mrs. Check-Again decided to spend 20 minutes observing Leonardo during play time. She watched him stack the blocks, complete a four-piece knob puzzle, and make neat circles on a piece of paper with a felt-tipped marker. She was amazed at how carefully he put the toys back on the shelf, always checking the pictures to make sure that he put each toy in its proper place. Yet he made no effort to start a conversation and stared blankly when the children told him what to do. After reading her own notes, Mrs. Check-Again decided to refer Leonardo to the learning specialist. She was not the least bit surprised when she read the report: Leonardo had a hearing impairment.

Principles of Effective Assessment Systems for Preschool Children

As pressures to assess have mounted, professional groups have convened panels of experts to make recommendations. Rather than recommend specific instruments, these groups have delineated the quality criteria that should guide the development of an effective assessment system for young children.

The following criteria have been synthesized from position papers of the National Association for the Education of Young Children and the National Association of Early Childhood Specialists in State Departments of Education (2003), the National Education Goals Panel (Shephard et al., 1998), and the American Educational Research Association (1985):

- Assessments should bring about benefits for children.

- Assessments should be tailored to a specific purpose, and all measures used should be reliable, valid, and fair for that purpose.

- Assessments should involve multiple sources of information and multiple components.

- Parents should be not only a valued source of assessment information but also an audience for assessment results.

- Decisions that have a major effect on children—for example, those related to enrollment, retention, or assignment to remedial or special classes, should never be based on a single test score. (A single measure used in this manner is often referred to as a "high-stakes test.")

- Assessments should be age appropriate in both content and method of collection.

- Assessments should be linguistically appropriate (recognizing that, to some extent, all assessments are measures of language) and free from cultural bias.

- Testing of young children must be conducted by knowledgeable individuals who are sensitive to the developmental needs of young children and who are qualified to administer the tests they use.

Special care must be taken in assessing infants and toddlers. Especially for very young children, assessment should be a collaborative process in which parents, teachers, and professionals such as early intervention specialists share their observations, concerns, and perspectives. The child's relationships and interactions with parents and trusted caregivers should form the cornerstone of the assessment; evaluators should observe the parent and child together and also talk with the parent about their observations and concerns. In order to get an accurate picture, it is important that the child be assessed in the presence of a trusted parent or caregiver, in surroundings in which she feels comfortable. Children should never be separated from people they trust or be assessed by strangers without the benefit of parental reassurance and input.

Assessment should cover all domains—physical, social, emotional, and cognitive, with special attention to the child's functional capacities and ways of relating to others. Structured tests should be used as one of many sources of information, as most are not designed to bring out the unique capabilities of children with atypical developmental patterns. Using timetables and sequences of typical development as one organizing framework, the process should identify the child's current competencies and strengths as well as the competencies that will constitute developmental progression. Reassessment of a child's developmental status should occur in the context of day-to-day family, child-care, and early intervention experiences (Greenspan & Meisels, 1994; Meisels & Fenichel, 1996).

After we are familiar with the different purposes of assessment and the principles or criteria that should guide our assessment decisions, we need to become familiar with the different types of measures used for assessment with preschool children. These tools include both standardized measures and systems for tracking individual work and performance.

STANDARDIZED TESTS

> **DEFINITIONS**
>
> **Standardized Tests:** A standardized test refers to a performance test that is administered according to a prescribed procedure and is measured against the average scores of a comparable population. Standardized tests are an efficient way to compare the performance of a group of children with the performance of other children from a state or national sampling.

Tests That Assess Group Performance

Tests of group performance are used to determine the effectiveness of educational programs or interventions. A preschool whose graduates consistently score well on standardized tests can advertise to parents that it provides an effective program for the population it serves, at least in terms of the dimensions that the tests measure. An intervention that raises children's scores on a standardized test of an ability or skill set that the intervention is designed to improve—and raises those scores more than would be expected by typical growth and development—is judged to be effective in meeting its goal. Similarly, an intervention whose graduates score significantly higher as a group than similar children who have not had the intervention can be judged as effective for that population.

Policymakers often insist on standardized tests as "proof" that the programs they fund are meeting their intended goals. Early childhood educators have generally responded with caution, noting that these types of tests often lack reliability for young children or fail to meet other criteria for an effective assessment system. Nevertheless, tests of this type can be useful for research and program improvement purposes when they are properly administered at appropriate ages and when their results are interpreted in terms of a "theory of change" or "logic model" that links particular inputs or practices to expected results.

In addition to the roles that tests play in program evaluation and accountability, tests of group performance can also inform instruction. If a teacher's students consistently fall behind in a particular area, she may decide either to devote more time to teaching those skills or to consider alternative strategies. Note, however, that, although the practice of "teaching to the test" may be effective in bringing up scores, it is likely to be ineffective in the long run. Nevertheless, if a standardized test is a good measure of important skills, it can help teachers and administrators to judge the effect of their efforts.

Standardized tests can measure either *aptitude* (learning ability) or *achievement* (learning mastery) in a particular domain. These tests can be scored according to whether a particular *criterion* has been met (e.g., Can the child identify the front of a book?) or on a scale that compares a child's performance with group *norms* (e.g., the child reads at a second-grade level or scored above average for his age).

DEFINITIONS |

Aptitude test: An aptitude test is a standardized test for measuring abilities or characteristics that are related to a child's ability to learn in a particular area.

Achievement test: An achievement test measures a child's mastery of specific skills or information that has been taught.

Criterion-referenced measurements: Criterion-referenced measurements are tests designed to measure how well the learner has mastered specific skills. A criterion-referenced test for emergent literacy would determine whether the child has mastered a set of skills that are components of emergent literacy.

Norm-referenced tests: Norm-referenced tests are used to compare the performance of a child or a group of children with the performance of a representative group of children. Tests can be either age-normed or grade-normed. Age-normed tests are normed on a sample of children at each of several age levels, and an individual child is expected to perform at age level. Grade-normed tests are normed on children at different grade levels, and an individual child is expected to perform at grade level.

Tests to Determine the Need for Intervention

Some standardized tests are designed to identify individual children's strengths and weaknesses. These tests are used as part of a process to determine which children might benefit from special intervention and what kinds of interventions are likely to be successful. Among these kinds of tests are *readiness tests*, *screening tests*, and *diagnostic assessments*.

DEFINITIONS |

Readiness tests: Readiness tests measure the extent to which an individual possesses the basic skills and knowledge necessary for more advanced study of complex subjects such as reading, writing, or arithmetic. Commonly used readiness tests include the Brigance Diagnostic Inventory of Early Development (Brigance, 1991), the Metropolitan Readiness Test (Nurss & McGauvran, 1976), and the Stanford Early School Achievement Test (Madden, Gardner, & Collins, 1984).

Screening tests: Screening tests are brief test batteries that are designed to determine the need for more in-depth individual evaluations. A good screening test selects children who are at risk and neither screens out children who are truly at risk (false negatives) nor screens in children who are not at risk (false positives). Screening tests that are frequently used in early childhood programs include the Denver Developmental Screening Test (Frankenburg, Dodds, Fandal, Kazuk, & Cohrs, 1975), Developmental Indicators for Assessment of Learning (Mardell-Czudnowski, & Goldenberg, 1998), the Early Screening Inventory (Meisels & Wiske, 1983) and the McCarthy Screening Test (McCarthy, 1980).

Diagnostic assessments: Diagnostic assessments are used to determine whether a child has special needs. In most cases, diagnostic testing is prescribed when a child is identified by a screening test as being at risk. Diagnostic testing should be based on multiple types of data derived from multiple sources, over a reasonable time period, with the child's parents providing information and participating in the interpretation of test results. Diagnostic tests that are frequently used for diagnosing individual needs include the Bayley Scales of Infant Development (Bayley, 1993), the Kaufman Battery for Children (Kaufman & Kaufman, 1983), the McCarthy Scales of Children's Abilities (McCarthy, 1972), and the Stanford–Binet Intelligence Scale (Thorndike, Hagen, & Sattler, 1986).

The following vignette shows how screening tests and diagnostic assessments help determine the need for intervention.

Three-year-old Jin Hee was not speaking in sentences yet, and her parents were worried. At school, Jin Hee excelled at puzzles and drawing, participated eagerly in group activities, and loved to play with the dress-up costumes. She was good at sharing and taking turns and could follow multistep instructions. Her hearing and vision seemed fine, and, apart from her delayed speech, the screening tests had not picked up any real problems. Still, Jin Hee's parents and teacher worried that she was not able to participate in conversations or verbal pretend play. They decided that it was time for a thorough diagnostic assessment.

Jin Hee's teacher referred the family to the local Early Intervention program for a full workup. The results showed that Jin Hee's nonverbal intelligence was in the superior range and that she was on target in most developmental areas, including language comprehension. Her lack of speech was related to a weakness in her jaw muscles. The evaluator recommended speech therapy, and also gave Jin Hee's parents some exercises to do at home and to share with her teacher. Six months later, Jin Hee was speaking in full, complex sentences and was a leader in the classroom.

Although children often "outgrow" problems, it is always a good idea to explore further when a delay or difficulty seems to be interfering with current learning or full participation. Early intervention—especially in the areas of speech and language—can make the difference between a child who fully benefits from his educational experiences and one who continues to struggle academically and socially. Indeed, it is quite common for a short course of early intervention to eliminate the need for special education or ongoing therapy.

TOOLS USED BY CLASSROOM TEACHERS FOR ONGOING ASSESSMENTS

As a teacher, you share the concerns of administrators, parents, and policymakers about how the children in your care are doing as a group and how their levels of achievement compare to those of other children their age. But your most pressing concern relates to the individual assessment of each child's day-to-day progress. In addition to telling you how each child is doing, individual assessments help you to reflect on the effectiveness of your teaching strategies and to plan appropriate challenges for each child and for the group as a whole.

You will want to select a set of assessments that

- Capture each child's accomplishments and show her family what she has learned;

- Inform your intentional teaching by helping you to see where each child may need extra practice and what she may be ready to learn next;

- Help you to monitor the progress of individual children and the group as a whole in meeting the goals of your curriculum or program;

- Help you identify areas in which your program is successful and areas in which it may need to be strengthened or supplemented in order to build a strong foundation for all aspects of oral language, reading, and writing; and

- Are easy for you to use on an ongoing basis.

RESEARCH FINDINGS AND RECOMMENDATIONS

Johnston and Rogers (2001) provide a strong rationale for supporting the use of informal, teacher-administered assessment measures, rather than standardized group testing, for recording children's progress in acquiring emergent literacy skills. "When group assessment is used to predict individual performance in the future, it is risky and can be a self-fulfilling prophecy" (p. 381). The authors insist that there is "no reason for high-stakes literacy testing in early childhood and that accountability testing has unfortunate side effects, including a focus on deficits and a lack of sensitivity to cultural differences and home environments" (p. 381). The alternative to "formal assessment," the authors point out, is informal or documentary assessment that "explicitly depends on the human expert, a sensitive observer or kid-watcher" (p. 381). The most capable "human expert," the authors assert, is the classroom teacher, who should always be considered the primary assessment agent.

Salinger (2001) agrees that the classroom teacher is in the best position to monitor and track a child's progress in emergent literacy. He points out, however, that this is a complex undertaking that requires professional expertise. In addition to acquiring an in-depth understanding of the underlying constructs of emergent literacy, teachers must know what data to collect, how and when to collect the data, how to record and track them, and how to extract and summarize key data from the monitoring process. When teachers recognize that classroom data must be collected in a systematic, standardized way, their assessments can serve the dual purpose of informing instruction and ensuring accountability. Salinger asserts that with focused, ongoing support of teachers,

(continued)

"classroom-based assessment of literacy fulfills its role as the agent of reform that both enhances teaching and learning and replaces more traditional measures of literacy growth" (p. 402).

A major benefit of teacher-based assessment is that assessing and teaching can go hand in hand. The importance of maintaining this linkage is described by Bowman, Donovan, and Burns (2000) in *Eager to Learn: Educating Our Preschoolers,* a research review conducted by the National Research Council:

> There is great potential in the use of assessment to support learning. The importance of building new learning on prior knowledge, the episodic course of development in any given child, and the enormous variability among children in background and development all mean that assessment and instruction are inseparable parts of effective pedagogy. What preschool teachers do to guide and promote learning needs to be based on what each child brings to the interaction, cognitively, culturally and developmentally. (p. 11)

In some cases, your assessment system will be predetermined either by the curriculum you are using or by a system that has been put in place by the program director. In many cases, however, the teacher is expected to develop her own assessment system. Given this responsibility, you will need to develop an assessment system that (a) includes information from different sources (e.g., observing the child in different kinds of play and learning situations, talking to parents, and looking at the child's drawings and attempts at writing) and (b) provides for ongoing assessment.

Teacher-Developed Assessment Systems

Teachers who are seeking to develop an assessment system that promotes emergent literacy should begin by reflecting on the skills that they would like the children in their charge to acquire. These skills will depend on the children's ages and special characteristics, of course. In this process, teachers need to look broadly across key domains of development that affect emergent literacy—physical, intellectual, social, emotional, and language–communication— while recognizing that these domains are interrelated. The following subsections describe how this broad focus applies to typical age groupings.

Assessing Infants. A teacher of infants will want to focus on the skills and behaviors related to emergent literacy that most babies are likely to acquire in the first 12 to 14 months. During this period, each infant, ideally, will acquire concepts and develop skills that are the roots of literacy, including recognizing and responding to their primary caregivers, tuning in to the sounds and cadences of language, learning self-regulation, engaging in back-and-forth babble conversations, grasping a rattle and passing it from hand to hand, picking up small bits using thumb–finger opposition, and discovering that he is an agent who can make things happen.

Assessing 1- and 2-Year-Olds. A teacher of 1- and 2-year-olds who is seeking to foster emergent literacy will also focus on emotional development and self-regulation. In addition, she will be interested in tracking the child's development of receptive and expressive language and small-muscle skills; the child's interest in books, storytelling, singing, and writing; the emergence of pretending and other symbolic representations; and the acquisition of real-world concepts.

Assessing 3-Year-Olds. A teacher of 3-year-olds would continue to monitor the children's social and emotional development and their acquisition of phonological skills, including the ability to repeat rhythms and recognize as well as create rhymes. She would also be interested in tracking the language skills that each child is gaining, including conversational skills, ability to pose and respond to different types of questions, an expanding vocabulary, and ability to speak in longer sentences. The teacher would also want to track the level of the child's pretend play, drawing skills, recognition of symbols, conceptual development, and real-world knowledge base. Finally, the teacher would track the child's development of book-handling skills and the progress that he is making in comprehending stories, in participating actively during shared reading, and in retelling or reenacting familiar stories.

Assessing 4-Year-Olds. A teacher of 4-year-olds would continue to track social–emotional development, small-muscle development, language and drawing skills, book handling, concept development, and real-world knowledge. The teacher also would measure children's concepts of print and their inside-out skills, including phonemic awareness, alphabet skills, and beginning writing.

Measurement Tools

To record the progress of individual children, teachers can use a variety of measures—such as checklists, rating scales, anecdotal records, portfolios, recorded conversations, work samples, and work sampling systems—to assess a child's progress and establish goals and strategies for reinforcing acquired competencies and introducing new challenges.

Developmental Checklists

A developmental checklist is a list of dimensions, characteristics, or behaviors that are typically scored as yes–no ratings. A checklist typically describes either a scope and sequence of skills or a typical progression of skills in a developmental area such as drawing, symbol–sound correspondence, letter naming, or the recognition and writing of words. Developmental checklists can be used both to inform instruction and to demonstrate mastery. The following vignette shows one way to use a developmental checklist:

> The staff at the Ready-Set-Grow Child Care Center had been working together for 2 years to strengthen their language and literacy program. Working with a local university, they had all taken classes in promoting literacy and were working toward their CDA, AA, and BA degrees. They had worked as a team to put their new knowledge into practice. Their classrooms were full of displays that showed the parents—and the children themselves—all the great things that the children were doing. In the hallway, a display of children's art work and "writing" helped parents see how the 2-year-olds' scribbling became 3-year-olds' squiggles, which eventually turned into the 4-year-olds' attempts to make "real" letters and the 5-year-olds' attempts to write words. But the teachers realized that they needed something more.
>
> They could show that children were learning, but how did they know whether each child was on track? How could they be sure that they were covering all the bases, or recognize the parts of their program that still needed to be strengthened? Working together, the teachers came up with some checklists that reflected what they had learned about emergent literacy.

The checklist on page 295 was developed by Dr. Lorraine Breffni at the request of teachers she had been mentoring.

LANGUAGE–COMMUNICATION OBSERVATION FORM

Name of Child: _____ **Date of Birth:** _____

Age	Skill Developed	Date Observed	Comments
0–1	Notices and attends to sound in the environment (*e.g., turns head toward person talking*)		
	Uses language (sounds) to get attention (*e.g., coos and/or babbles*)		
	Understands words and/or simple commands (*e.g., waves when caregiver says "Wave bye-bye"*)		
1–2	Develops single-word vocabulary		
	Understands names of familiar people and objects (*e.g., points to the car when you say the word "car"*)		
	Uses two-word sentences		
	Responds verbally and/or nonverbally to simple questions (*e.g., "Where is your shoe?"*)		
2–3	Uses two- to five-word sentences		
	Begins to ask simple questions (*e.g., "What's that?"*)		
3–4	Participates in conversations (*e.g., describes events, tells imaginary stories*)		
	Follows simple two-part commands (*e.g., "Go to Joey and give her the brush."*)		
	Uses language for different purposes (*e.g., asks for help, talks about something that happened*)		
	Can retell the basic sequence of a story (*e.g., tells the basic storyline of Goldilocks and The Three Bears*)		
4–5	Asks "why" and "how" questions (*e.g., "Why is the sky blue?"*)		
	Follows directions with two or more steps (*e.g.," Finish your book, put it away, and wash up."*)		
	Follows directions on a tape or CD (*e.g., "Now wave your hands in the air!"*)		

PRE-READING OBSERVATION FORM

Name of Child: _____ **Date of Birth:** _____

Age	Skill Developed	Date Observed	Comments
0–1	Enjoys listening to/looking at books		
	Selects books for caregiver to read		
	Holds board books		
	Points to pictures in book		
1–3	Holds books right side up		
	Recognizes a favorite book by its cover		
	Recognizes and repeats rhymes (e.g., repeats verses from "Row, Row, Row Your Boat")		
3–4	Fills in a "missing" word and/or repeats a chorus (e.g., "Brown Bear, what do you . . . ?")		
	Recognizes that text represents spoken words		
	Recognizes print/signs in the environment (e.g., STOP, McDonald's®, Target®)		
	Retells story using flannel board pieces		
	Recognizes first letter of own name		
	Knows that books are read front to back		
	Recognizes own name from a group of words		
	Participates in story time (e.g., asks questions, comments on story)		
	Can clap out the syllables in own name		
4–5	Recognizes letters in own name		
	Has basic knowledge of terms "author" and "illustrator"		
	Recognizes words from environmental signs, food containers, and television commercials		
	Identifies some letter sounds		

PRE-WRITING OBSERVATION FORM

Name of Child: _____ Date of Birth: _____

Age	Skill Developed	Date Observed	Comments
0–1	Develops fine-motor skills (*e.g., picks up Cheerios® using finger and thumb*)		
1–2	Does random scribbling—explores with a crayon (around 18–24 months)		
2–3	Does controlled scribbling—repeats certain marks intentionally (*e.g., circles, dots*)		
3–4	Understands that print can tell stories and represent ideas		
	Makes scribbling letter-like marks to represent words		
	Asks teacher to write down dictated comments		
	Attempts to print own name		
4–5	Copies words (*e.g., may ask teacher to write a specific word and copy it from example*)		
	Writes own name from memory		
	Pretends to write stories and can "read" them when requested to		
	Uses invented spelling when attempting to write (*e.g., "I LV U" means "I LOVE YOU"*)		

Source: Lorraine Breffni, Mailman Segal Institute for Early Childhood Studies, Nova Southeastern University, 2004.

Rating Scales

Rating scales are used to describe the degree to which a particular behavior or trait is manifested. They are often used to measure traits that cannot be measured on a yes-or-no basis and that are not easily described by other assessment procedures. The following vignette shows one context in which using a rating scale would be appropriate:

M r. Cortez, who was teaching a class of 2-year-olds, was inter- ested in helping the children learn and practice behaviors that would help them to acquire emergent literacy skills. He realized that the behaviors he was looking for could not be described by a yes–no checklist. To keep a record of the children's progress in exhibiting those behaviors, he decided to develop a rating scale (shown in the following table), which could be used both to guide his teaching and to keep the children's parents informed. Periodically, Mr. Cortez asked the parents to complete the same scale so he could learn from what they were seeing at home. He found that parents enjoyed sharing examples of their children's new achievements as they discussed their ratings with him and helped him set goals for the children.

EMERGENT LITERACY RATING SCALE: 2-YEAR-OLDS

Name of Child: _____ **Date of Birth:** _____

	Never	Sometimes	Frequently	Always
Child is able to complete a simple task.				
Child is willing to come to circle time.				
Child listens to a story being read.				
Child follows a one-step directive.				
Child follows a two-step directive.				
Child enjoys playing with other children.				
Child comes to me when she needs help.				
Child selects a book and pretends to read it.				

Anecdotal Records

Anecdotal records are brief narrative descriptions of specific events. These in-depth portraits provide insights into a child's behavior that are difficult to capture with other kinds of assessment (Gullo, 1994, p. 72). The following vignette shows one way to use anecdotal records:

M rs. Baby-Lover was in charge of a group of four infants of working parents. Mrs. Baby-Lover realized that these parents were eager to know how well their babies were doing, even though they had very little time to talk with her and always seemed to be in a hurry to get to work or to get home after work. She decided to write anecdotal records to give to the parents so they could read about the good things that were happening with their babies. (The following box shows one example of Mrs. Baby-Lover's anecdotal records.)

Anecdotal Record of Theresa Blank, 9 Months Old

September 14

Theresa awakened from her nap today full of smiles. When I went over to her crib, she started babbling away and I, of course, babbled back. She had already learned to make d-d sounds, so I decided to try something new. When she began her babble conversation, I responded with "b-b-b bumblebee, b-b-b bumblebee." You know, she pursed her lips and made perfectly audible b-b babbles. I was delighted. Then, after I changed her diaper and fed her a bottle, I put her on her mat and gave her a rattle to play with. She started shaking her rattle vigorously, so I picked up another rattle and banged it on the mat. She watched me for a couple of seconds and then began banging her rattle on the mat. I held out my rattle. She immediately opened her hand, dropped her own rattle, and grasped mine. I could not believe how well she is imitating and how many new things she is learning to do!

Portfolios

Portfolios are collections of a child's work that document a child's progress. They may include a series of dated drawings, audiotapes of a child's conversations, photos of children's play constructions or crafts, videotapes of a child engaging in pretend play or reenacting a story, anecdotal records, or writing samples. Portfolios are used to help the teacher make decisions related to the child's program and to demonstrate the progress that the child is making to both the child and her parents. The following vignette provides an example of one way to use a portfolio approach:

M rs. Haughton, a family child-care provider, was taking care of a mixed-age group of children ranging from 3 to 5 years old. She felt that the best way of monitoring their progress was through portfolios of their work, which she could share with their parents. She did not have enough time to do much writing, but she did have a digital camera and a tape recorder. She had attended a workshop on portfolios and decided to collect a portfolio for each of the children in her home.

When Mrs. Haughton shared Emily's portfolio (described in the following box) with her father, he was pleased to see that his daughter was making friends and was doing so many different things. He loved looking at the photos and was delighted when Mrs. Haughton told him that he could keep the portfolio.

Description of the Portfolio of Emily Gonzalez, 3 Years Old

Drawings: The portfolio included eight drawings collected over a 4-month period. Each drawing was dated. The earliest drawing was a two-colored scribble that covered most of the paper. The next two drawings were quite similar except that they were more colorful. The fourth drawing was different. Emily seemed to be experimenting with form, and her scribbles looked more like circles. In the eighth drawing, Emily had not only made complete circles but also had put dots and a line inside each circle. She had called the drawing "My Mama," and Mrs. Haughton had written "Mama" underneath the picture.

Conversations: Mrs. Haughton had recorded three different conversations and had dated each tape. She recorded each conversation while Emily and her friend, Moses, were playing in the housekeeping area. Although the same play episodes were replayed on each tape, Emily's language was becoming easier to understand. She continued to introduce new ideas and new vocabulary words into the play. For example, Emily said that her doll couldn't have pancakes for breakfast because the doll's tummy was sick. She told Moses that they had to "go to the Seven-Elemon because we don't got no pasgheti."

Photos: Mrs. Haughton included six photos. One photo was a picture of Emily playing in the sandbox by herself, a second photo showed her holding Moses's hand on a walk to the park. A third picture showed Emily and Moses washing their tricycles with a hose. The last three pictures showed a block structure that Emily had built with two friends; Emily, dressed up as a Mommy, holding a book upside-down and reading it to her doll; and a long snake that Emily had made out of play dough.

Purchased Assessment Systems

Assessing young children's emergent literacy progress is an art that requires orchestrating children's individual accomplishments with curriculum goals and age-related expectations. Researchers often spend years fine-tuning systems so that they are reliable and valid and can provide teachers, parents, and program administrators with the information they need. The systems are then made available through commercial publishers, who also provide training in their use. Two of the best such systems are the Work Sampling System (Meisels et al., 1995) and the Early Language and Literacy Classroom Observation (ELLCO) Toolkit (Smith, Dickinson, Sangeorge, & Anastasopoulos, 2004).

Work Sampling System

The Work Sampling System tracks children's progress from age 3 through fifth grade in seven domains: personal and social development, language and literacy, mathematical thinking, scientific thinking, social studies, the arts, and physical development. The system includes three elements, which work in concert:

- **Developmental Guidelines and Checklists:** The guidelines set forth appropriate expectations for children, based on national standards and child development knowledge. Teachers fill out the checklists three times a year.

- **Portfolios:** These include student work that demonstrates growth and quality on "core items" in each domain and also examples that reveal a student's unique characteristics and engagement in classroom activities. Students and teachers work together to design and evaluate the portfolios.

- **Summary Reports:** Teachers complete these reports three times a year, using information from the other two components and their own knowledge of the child and of child development. The reports include ratings and brief comments that highlight the child's strengths and flag any areas of concern.

The Work Sampling System has many advantages for school systems, Head Start programs, and other early childhood programs that are willing to make the commitment to its use. It is comprehensive, covering seven curriculum domains and eight age or grade levels. It is based on children's daily learning activities and also reflects state and national learning standards. The Work Sampling System involves all children and their families, including children with special learning needs. Finally, it is designed to help teachers make instructional decisions that build on children's strengths, interests, and emerging capacities and also to provide an effective, easy-to-understand means of reporting children's progress to families, other educators, and the community.

ELLCO Toolkit

Rather than assessing individual children, the ELLCO Toolkit looks at the overall educational environment. Designed for pre-K (4-year-olds) through second grade, it assesses the availability, frequency, and quality of experiences that promote critical aspects of emerging literacy. The ELLCO Toolkit consists of three parts:

1. The Literacy Environment Checklist helps observers to scan the classroom environment and note the availability, content, and diversity of reading, writing, and listening materials.

2. The Classroom Observation and Teacher Interview rates the quality of literacy support, using age-specific items. These items cover the overall classroom environment and the formal and informal instruction program.

3. The Literacy Activities Rating Scale is used to record the frequency and length of time with which teachers engage children in specific literacy-promoting strategies during book-reading and writing activities.

The underlying assumptions of the ELLCO Toolkit are similar to those in this text:

- Children learn through play.
- Literacy emerges over time and builds on an oral language foundation.
- Both outside-*in* and inside-*out* skills are important.

- Every aspect of a classroom setup and curriculum can provide fuel for emergent literacy.

- Family and community also play important roles.

- Skilled teachers facilitate emergent literacy through intentional teaching that builds on children's interests, abilities, relationships, and cultural backgrounds.

For teachers of 4- and 5-year olds, the ELLCO Literacy Environment Checklist is a useful self-assessment tool. Parents will also be reassured to know that their children are in a classroom or family child-care home which incorporates literacy-promotion practices that are backed by up-to-date research.

Which Language (or Languages) to Use When Conducting Assessments

Determining which language (or languages) to use when conducting assessments is critical for programs serving a multilingual population or offering instruction and conversation in more than one language. A child's language and phonemic awareness skills as well as his understanding of test directions are likely to be strongest in his first language. Alphabet and writing skills are likely to be strongest in the language in which those skills were taught. Book-handling skills and concepts of print will reflect the types of books with which the child has experience; children who do most of their reading in Arabic or Chinese, for example, may have developed sophisticated concepts of print in their home language but may not realize that English writing flows in a different direction.

Tracking a child's emergent literacy is best done on an individual basis and in the language in which a child is most comfortable. However, to determine whether or not a child is being prepared adequately for the expectations of an English-only kindergarten or first-grade classroom, you may need to do this tracking in English, although additional tracking could be done in another language. Knowing the child's strengths and knowledge gaps in both languages will enable you to help the child transfer what he has learned from one language to another. It will also help you to know where differences in language and writing systems may be causing confusion. Similarly, if your goal is to foster bilingualism and biliteracy, then you will need to assess children in both languages.

In most places in the United States, teachers will have difficulty doing standard assessments in languages other than English. Even if tests and appropriately trained testers are available in the child's home language, the test norms or criteria may not be equivalent to those on a similar test in English. Extreme care must be taken (a) in interpreting the results of tests that rely on a child's knowledge of a language in which he is not yet fluent and (b) in comparing children's skill levels based on tests that were developed for different populations.

SUMMARY

Assessment fulfills several important purposes for early childhood programs and, in particular, for those that seek to foster emergent literacy. Assessments play essential roles in identifying children who would benefit from special programs or interventions, in informing instruction, and in keeping parents abreast of their children's progress. They also provide data on groups of children, which can be used for program improvement and accountability purposes.

Assessing young children accurately for these various purposes is not easy; it must be done with skill, care, systematic attention, good tools, and the collaboration of parents in both providing input and interpreting results. Data from any single test or source should not be used in a "high-stakes" manner either (a) to place a child in a program or deny services or (b) to determine whether a program is funded. Although the assessment waters are still muddy, administrators, directors, and teachers agree that every early childhood program must establish assessment systems that can inform program decisions and benefit young children and their families.

Tests, checklists, portfolios, and progress-tracking systems sharpen teachers' eyes and ears. They reveal and organize information that can help teachers provide children with experiences in all of the domains that support emergent literacy—experiences that are challenging but not frustrating. These tools provide fuel for a dialogue with parents and colleagues on how best to support learning for individual children and for the group as a whole. Finally, they provide evidence of achievements that parents, teachers, and program administrators can celebrate together.

M s. Record-Keeper was delighted. She had just finished her end-of-the-year reports, and every child had made important progress! Looking back over her records, even she was amazed at how far they had come. At the beginning of the year, Alicia could only grasp a crayon in her fist and make random marks—now she was drawing faces with eyes, mouths, arms, and legs! Angelo had only been able to say a handful of words—now he was routinely using two- and three-word sentences and was beginning to ask simple questions. In November, Ms. Record-Keeper had been so pleased when Andrew was finally able to sit through a whole song at circle time. Now, he was singing the songs on his own, listening intently when she read a story, and even, on occasion, asking her to "read it again."

Before the children left for their 2-week summer vacation, Ms. Record-Keeper gave each family a small book of captioned photographs showing some of the things that their child had enjoyed during the year. She also listed a few of their proudest accomplishments: "I learned to draw pictures." "I learned all the letters in my name." "I ask lots of questions!" "Allie and I put on a puppet show and everybody clapped." She ended each book with a well-earned smiley face.

Reflection

Think about ways in which you are evaluating your own teaching and the progress that children are making in your class.

- What are you accomplishing through your assessment efforts?

- How do the assessment tools that you are using guide you in planning your curriculum and in meeting the needs of individual children?

- How successful are you in involving parents in the evaluation of their children and in keeping parents abreast of the progress that their children are making?

- What additional tools do you need to guide your decision making, strengthen your partnerships with parents, and help you individualize your curriculum?

- How much time are you spending on paperwork that does not seem to serve a purpose?

- If a team of emergent literacy experts agreed to help you design an assessment system for your classroom, what would you ask them for?

REFERENCES

American Educational Research Association. (1985). *Standards for educational and psychological testing.* Washington, DC: Author.

Bangs, J. K. (1959). *The golden treasury of poetry.* New York: Golden Press.

Bayley, N. (1993). *Bayley scales of infant development* (2nd ed.). San Antonio, TX: Psychological Corp.

Bowman, B., Donovan, S., & Burns, M. S. (2000). *Eager to learn: Educating our preschoolers.* Washington, DC: The National Academy Press.

Brigance, A. (1991). *Brigance diagnostic inventory of early development.* North Billerica, MA: Curriculum Associates.

Frankenburg, W. F., Dodds, J., Fandal, A., Kazuk, E., & Cohrs, M. (1975). *Denver developmental screening test.* Denver, CO: Denver Developmental Materials.

Greenspan, S. I. & Meisels, S., with the ZERO TO THREE Work Group on Developmental Assessment. (1994). Toward a new vision for the developmental assessment of infants and young children. *Zero to Three, 14*(6), 1–8.

Gullo, D. F. (1994). *Understanding assessment and evaluation in early childhood education.* New York: Teachers College Press.

Johnston, P. H., & Rogers, R. (2001). Early literacy development: The case for "informed assessment." In S. B. Neuman & D. K. Dickinson (Eds.), *Handbook of early literacy research* (pp. 377–389). New York: Guilford.

Kaufman, A. S., & Kaufman, N. L. (1983). *Kaufman battery for children.* Circle Pines, MN: American Guidance Service.

Madden, R., Gardner, E., & Collins, C. (1984). *Stanford early school achievement test.* Cleveland, OH: The Psychological Corporation.

Mardell-Czudnowski, D. D., & Goldenberg, D. S. (1998). *Developmental indicators for assessment of learning* (3rd ed.). Circle Pines, MN: American Guidance Service.

McCarthy, D. (1972). *McCarthy scales of children's abilities.* Cleveland, OH: The Psychological Corporation.

McCarthy, D. (1980). *McCarthy screening test.* Cleveland, OH: The Psychological Corporation.

Meisels, S. J., & Fenichel, E. (Eds.) (1996). *New visions for developmental assessment of infants and young children.* Washington, DC: ZERO TO THREE.

Meisels, S.J., Jablon, J. R., Marsden, D. B., Dichtelmiller, M. L., Dorfman, A. B., & Steele, D. M. (1995). *The work sampling system: An overview.* Ann Arbor, MI: Rebus Planning Associates, Inc.

Meisels, S. J., & Wiske, M. S. (1983). *Early screening inventory.* New York: Teachers College Press.

National Association for the Education of Young Children & National Association of Early Childhood Specialists in State Departments of Education. (2003). *Early childhood curriculum, assessment, and program evaluation: A joint position statement of the National Association for the Education of Young Children and the National Association of Early Childhood Specialists in State Departments of Education.* Approved November 2003. Washington, DC: National Association for the Education of Young Children.

Nurss, J., & McGauvran, M. (1976). *The metropolitan readiness test.* New York: The Psychological Corporation.

Salinger, T. (2001). Assessing the literacy of young children: The case for multiple forms of evidence. In S. B. Neuman & D. K. Dickinson (Eds.), *Handbook of early literacy research* (pp. 390–418). New York: Guilford.

Shephard, L., Kagan, S., & Wirtz, E. (1998). *Principles and recommendations for early childhood assessments.* Washington, DC: National Education Goals Panel.

Smith, M. W., Dickinson, D. K., Sangeorge, A., and Anastasopoulos, L. (2004). *Early language and literacy classroom observation toolkit, research edition.* Baltimore: Paul H. Brookes.

Smith, M. W., Dickinson, D. K., Sangeorge, A., and Anastasopoulos, L. (2002). *Early language and literacy classroom observation toolkit.* Baltimore: Paul H. Brookes.

Thorndike, R. L., Hagen, E. P., & Sattler, J. M. (1986). *Stanford–Binet intelligence scale* (4th ed.). Riverside, CA: Riverside Publishing.

Partnering With Families

My Grandmother's Stories

Every single evening, before I go to bed
My Grandma tells me stories that come right out of her head.
She tells me many stories about relatives she knew.
And what's best about her stories is that all of them are true.

She tells me about her mother, who knew Martin Luther King
And followed him on a freedom walk on a beautiful day in spring.
She tells me about her children and the great things they have done.
She put them all through college, every single one.

When Grandma tells me stories, I listen very well.
She has such wonderful things to say, such beautiful things to tell.
And when she tells me stories, her voice is like a song
It makes me feel all warm inside. I know where I belong.

—Marilyn Segal

Every family has stories, and storytellers. Some of the stories are about people who play key roles in a child's life, some are about people who have passed on, and some are about the children themselves. Whether they are funny, or instructive, or just ordinary, these stories help children know who they are and where they come from. From family stories, children learn what matters to the people who matter most to them. They also learn language, rhythms, story-telling patterns, and life lessons that connect them with their families and with their larger heritage. Even quite small children can recognize and cherish the stories that are important to their families. As they grow, they will remember and retell the family stories that were told to them.

As teachers and caregivers of young children, we face the challenge, privilege, and obligation of building partnerships with families. Parents and other family members are children's first and most enduring teachers. They are the base from which children venture into the wider world. They provide the encouragement to learn new things, the appreciative audience for discoveries and accomplishments, the support to keep trying when tasks are challenging, the watchful eyes that notice when something is wrong, and the advocacy for change when a child's needs are not being met. They engage children in ongoing conversations and ask and answer questions that extend their learning. They share stories, books, and activities with children; they also teach children which stories, ideas, and activities are worthy of attention and pursuit.

Families count on professionals as sources of expertise about how children learn; we count on them as experts on their own children. They count on us as partners who will care for and about their children; we count on them as partners who will reinforce and extend the lessons we teach.

BUILDING RELATIONSHIPS WITH FAMILIES

Connecting with a young child is a whole lot easier if you also connect with her family. Young children, especially babies and toddlers, look to trusted family members for reassurance when a new person enters their lives. When a baby senses a continuity between the way a new adult holds, feeds, and cares for her and the kinds of care she receives from family members with whom she already has a strong relationship, then she feels secure and is ready to take in new learning experiences. When a toddler sees his mother talking comfortably with another adult, the child is likely to relax as that adult approaches him, and he will likely warm up to her overtures. When a young child senses that his parents feel good about various teachers, then the child, too, becomes eager to play with those teachers.

Appreciating Parents as Resources for Teachers and Establishing Two-Way Communication

Knowing about a child's home life helps a teacher build a relationship and engage the child in conversation. For babies, that teacher will want to know the following:

- What is the child's usual schedule?

- Who lives in the child's home? Who else is important in the child's life?

- What languages are spoken in the child's home? What language do the parents use with the child?

- What activities does the child enjoy? Does she have favorite toys, games, or routines?

- What kinds of activities get the child excited? If she tends to get overexcited, what are the warning signs?

- What kinds of things upset the child, or make her wary or on edge?

- How does the child like to be soothed or comforted? How does she comfort herself?

- What lullabies and nursery songs do family members share with the child?

- How does the baby go to sleep at home? Does she have her own bed, or is she used to sleeping with others?

For toddlers, the teacher will have some additional questions:

- What language (or languages) is the child learning to speak? Does she frequently hear another language as well?

- What words and gestures does the child use frequently? What tips do family members have to help you understand what the child is saying?

- Who are the child's pets, frequent playmates, extended family members, and neighborhood and family friends?

- Does the child have a special toy, blanket, or "lovey" that provides comfort and security?

- What places does the child like to go with family or friends?

- What kinds of music does the family enjoy? What are the child's favorite songs? Does he like to sing or hum along, dance, or play an "instrument?"

- Does the child enjoy being read to? What are his favorite books?

- What kinds of pretend play does the child enjoy? Does he have favorite props, costumes, or themes?

- Does the child have any special interests?

Preschoolers will be able to answer many of your questions with their own words. Still, information from family members will help you know what questions to ask, what sorts of environments and activities to set up, and how to begin conversations.

- Who are the important people in the child's life? Where do they live? Does the child's family include pets?

- What language (or languages) does the child hear, understand, speak, and see in written form? What are the family's desires and plans with respect to language learning?

- Does the child have any pretend friends, such as dolls, stuffed animals, or other toys? Does she have favorite television or storybook characters? Does she have "invisible" or imaginary friends?

- What are the child's favorite books? Do parents read those books in a special way?

- Does the child have any fears? What kinds of things do parents do to reassure the child or to prepare him for a potentially scary experience?

- What are the child's favorite themes in maxi and in mini play? Which ones are played out alone, and which ones are enjoyed with siblings or with special friends?

- What kinds of adult involvement does the child appreciate in his play?

- What are the child's special interests and talents? Is there something he is particularly good at or knows a lot about?

- What questions has the child been asking lately?

The questions listed above are not one-time questions, of course. You, the teacher, will not find out the answers all at once. You will probably find that some of the answers change weekly, although others might remain stable for quite a long time. Inevitably, the routines of school or child care will differ from those of home, and children will carry back new interests, skills, words, and behaviors that may sometimes surprise their families. Young children are not very good reporters, so family members will need ongoing information about what is happening at school to be able understand the context of their child's words and behaviors. Similarly, you will need ongoing information about out-of-school experiences and significant family events.

Little things—such as getting a new pair of shoes, falling into a mud puddle, going to a birthday party, or losing a favorite stuffed animal—can loom large in the life of a young child. Significant changes in the family and world events that preoccupy family members can have major effects on a child's behavior and general emotional well-being—even if the child is not directly involved or does not seem to understand. Knowing about events that are anticipated or that have occurred in the family—for example, the birth of a baby, illness, death, divorce, or moving to a new home, allows you to anticipate or cope with a child's behavior at school.

An open-door communication policy is critical to the success of any partnership between families and early childhood education providers. Parents need to feel welcome at any time; they also need to be able to call with brief questions and to set up appointments for longer conversations. Teachers and caregivers need to know that they can reach families in emergency situations and with routine messages; they also need to be attuned to what goes on at home that shapes the child's interests and behaviors.

Reflection

What do you know about the children in your class, and about their home and family experiences? What have you learned recently that you would not have guessed or predicted? What else do you wonder about?

Activities That Promote Home–School and School–Home Communication

Most early childhood programs include some kind of intake or orientation interview or parent questionnaire, an open-door visiting policy, informal exchanges at drop-off and pick-up, and regularly scheduled parent–teacher conferences with optional telephone conversations or face-to-face meetings in between. Announcements, notes, and children's work go home on a regular basis. In some programs, parents regularly help out in the classroom and work with teachers to maintain and enhance the environment. The following list includes some other techniques that teachers and providers have found useful; some of them also have the advantage of sparking conversations with children, which promote emergent literacy:

- Home notes. Many teachers make a habit of sending home brief notes on a weekly basis or whenever a child does something new or special.

- Joint Journals and Scrapbooks. Just as some parents keep baby books, teachers can keep journals or scrapbooks that show children's activities, interests, and progress in child care. These resources can be especially rich supports for emergent literacy when parents are invited to contribute on an ongoing basis and to share the books with their children.

- My Book About Me. Following the model of Dr. Seuss's *My Book About Me* (1969), children can make all sorts of drawings, books, murals, and even mobiles or other displays that tell about their families, friends, pets, homes, favorite activities and places, or things that they have learned to do at school and at home.

- Portfolios. Portfolios are collections of children's typical or best work, including artwork, photographs of construction projects or pretend play, teacher observations, memorable quotes, and "firsts." Parents also can be invited to contribute. Portfolios serve as records of a child's learning and as springboards for parent–teacher dialogue.

- Home Visits. Home visits serve many purposes, from simply getting to know one another to exchanging specific information to helping a parent incorporate classroom techniques and activities at home.

- Parent Bulletin Board. A parent bulletin board can be hung near the entrance to the building or classroom. It can be used to post public notices from teachers to parents, parents to teachers, or parents to other families. Individual folders, children's cubbies, an inbox, or a suggestion box can be used for individual communications.

- Family Fun Activities and Parents' Nights Out. Family fun activities such as pizza parties, potluck suppers or picnics, and literacy-focused events give teachers a chance to get to know parents in an informal setting and to see them interact with their children. They also give children the chance to introduce their parents to "their" school as well as to their friends and teachers. Parents' Nights Out, with other teachers or volunteers providing child care, give teachers and parents a chance to play and learn together. Both kinds of events help build bonds among families and provide opportunities to share information and address common concerns.

- Parent-to-Parent Links. Many parents are frequent visitors to their children's classrooms or to parent meetings and family events. Others, for various reasons, can come only on rare occasions. Some teachers enlist parent volunteers to help keep other parents in the loop or to serve as buddies who can help another family get to a school event or share in some way even if they cannot attend.

- E-mail. As more and more families and teachers get on line, e-mail is becoming an efficient way to arrange meetings, provide updates to a group or to individuals, send out reminders, share routine information, and get quick answers to questions.

- Project Displays. Classroom displays that show the process of children's learning and products that they have created provide a visual record for parents and spark conversations among parents, teachers, and children.

UNDERSTANDING WHERE PARENTS ARE COMING FROM

Stephen Covey, author of *The Seven Habits of Highly Effective People* (1990), teaches habits of mind and negotiation strategies that help people reach their goals. One of his slogans is "Seek first to understand, then to be understood" (p. 235). This habit of listening to another's perspective before asserting your own is especially useful when working with families whose backgrounds are different from yours.

Parents' values, concerns, and expectations are determined—at least in part—by their own cultural background and the way they were raised. These beliefs and attitudes are also influenced by the community that the family identifies with, by the people they trust, and by what they hear in the media and in the world around them. In some families, there may be strong disagreements between the parent or between generations about key child-rearing issues. Sometimes, one parent's choices are constrained by the other's strong beliefs or dominant voice.

When parents do not do the things that we, as professionals, have learned are good for children, we sometimes assume that they are ignorant and need to be taught "the right way." At other times, we may back off, feeling as if it is not our place to speak. Similarly, parents may insist that we discipline or educate their children in ways that make us uncomfortable, or they may not be assertive because they do not feel comfortable telling teachers what to do.

Most of the time, dialogue is a better approach. When your own belief system clashes with the belief system of the parent, it is important not only to talk with the parent about the areas in which you agree and the areas in which you differ but also to work together to negotiate a solution that you both can accept. At a deeper level, conversations about differences in beliefs, values, and caregiving styles help you to understand the meaning behind behavior patterns. For example, you may discover that a parent feeds and dresses a child who is capable of greater independence because, in that parent's culture, those gestures are important signs of love. You may learn that a parent considers it impolite for children to initiate eye contact with adults or to make eye contact when they speak; the parent may be surprised to learn that you interpret the same behavior as shyness or discomfort. Conversations such as these, when engaged in with genuine curiosity and respect, help you to see the strengths that each family brings and the resources on which each child draws in her journey toward literacy.

Building bridges across culture, class, language, or child-rearing philosophy takes time as well as interest and commitment. For educators seeking to foster children's emergent literacy, this commitment is essential. Fortunately, many excellent resources are available that can help providers and parents build these bridges. In particular, we recommend the following resources:

- *Looking In, Looking Out: Redefining Child Care and Early Education in a Diverse Society,* by H. Chang, A. Muckelroy, and D. Pulido-Tobiassen. California Tomorrow (Oakland): 1996.

- *Foundations: Early Childhood Education in a Diverse Society,* by J. Gonzalez-Mena. McGraw-Hill: 1998.

- *Bridging Cultures Between Home and Schools: A Guide for Teachers,* by E. Trumbull, C. Rothstein-Fisch, P. M. Greenfield, and B. Quiroz. WestEd (San Francisco): 2001.

- *How Culture Shapes Social-Emotional Development: Implications for Practice in Infant-Family Programs,* by M. Day and R. Parlakian. ZERO TO THREE: 2004.

As you build relationships with parents, you are likely to find that different families have different expectations of you as a child development professional and partner. Some parents will look to you as the authority with respect to how their child learns and what they should be doing to help him. Others will draw a sharp line between education and parenting and expect you to do the educating while they do the parenting. Still others will see you as one of many experts and will put equal or greater credence in the messages they get from other parents, pediatricians, community elders, the clergy, or the books and Internet sites they consult. Knowing where parents are coming from helps you to share information about how families support children's language and literacy in a way that they can hear and can put to use.

Some parents, for example, will welcome or even solicit your ideas on how they can support their children's language and literacy learning. For these parents, handouts, one-on-one conversations, and minilectures are all likely to be well received. Other parents will politely acknowledge your authority as teacher but ignore your messages unless other authorities in their families and communities also support these messages. You will need to enlist allies who can help you understand how to present your messages, what the parents understand and agree with and what they question, and what they want to know from you but may be uncomfortable asking. Many parents will be most comfortable in a group setting where they can ask lots of questions and share their own beliefs or where they can listen to other parents' questions and suggestions. Some are likely to be shy in a large group and will be most receptive when they can share ideas with a small group of people who speak their language and understand their culture and current circumstances.

Bringing Family Stories Into the Classroom

In the early days of Head Start, writers collected stories and folktales from children's families and other adults in their communities and turned these stories into books that teachers could read to young children. This practice served several purposes:

- It preserved stories that were important to the community and passed them down to children.

- It provided children with authentic stories that were important to their families and communities.

- It affirmed the value of those stories and of the people who told them, thus strengthening children's sense of identity and cultural connection.

- It helped children to develop concepts of print as they saw the oral culture of their communities reflected in books.

- It provided children with well-written stories that used the dialect, cadences, folk sayings, and literary devices of their home cultures.

- It provided teachers (most of whom came from the same community as the children they taught) with stories that they could read with enthusiasm and could use as springboards for conversation.

The Funds of Knowledge Project (Moll, Amanti, Neff, & Gonzalez, 1992) took these ideas a step further. Teams of teachers and anthropology students visited families to collect oral histories and uncover "funds of knowledge" about work, caretaking, growing things, arts, family and community history, local ecology, and other areas of interest. This information was then used to shape a classroom curriculum that drew upon the expertise that families could provide.

Alma Flor Ada (1988), a noted children's author who has published books in Spanish and English, created a multigenerational literacy program by helping parents and grandparents who had low levels of literacy turn their own experiences into simple picture books that they could share with their children. Even parents who had difficulty reading felt confident reading stories that they had written themselves.

On its Hollywood, Florida, reservation, the Seminole Tribe commissioned a storyteller to come to each Head Start classroom on a weekly basis to share traditional tales in the Seminole language with the children, who spoke mostly English. The storyteller often brought traditional crafts and natural objects that served as props for her stories. She taught children to name these objects in her language as they taught her the English words. She left recordings of the chanted stories so that the children could hear them again and practice the repeated refrains. She also taught the children their traditional Seminole names and the names of their clans. Through song, story, visual arts, and conversation, children learned the language and culture of their ancestors as they also increased their literacy in English.

Of course, very few child-care programs and family child-care homes have the resources to hire anthropologists, professional writers, or tribal storytellers. Still, creative teachers have found many ways to enhance their curricula with family stories:

- Hand Clapping and Jumping Rhymes. Ask parents to teach you hand clapping games, jump-rope rhymes, finger plays, and baby games that they enjoy with their children or remember from their own childhoods.

- Sing Along. Invite families to join you for circle time at the beginning or end of a day or on special occasions. Sing songs that the children know and ask your guests to teach others. Have parents help you make tapes of songs and rhymes from their childhoods and accompanying songbooks that you can share with the children.

- Celebrations. Invite parents, grandparents, and friends to help celebrate children's birthdays, cultural and seasonal holidays, and school traditions. Provide opportunities for them to share favorite books, songs, crafts, special foods, and memories with the children and with one another.

- Costume Collection. Ask parents to send in old clothes, hats, shoes, satchels, and accessories as well as remnants and recycled items for your costume collection. Find out the stories behind their contributions and share them with the children. Help the children dictate thank-you notes telling the parents how they used their gifts.

- Star of the Week. Give each child a turn to be "star of the week." Let parents sign up their child for a particular week, and remind them when it is their child's turn. The Star gets her name and picture on a special poster. She brings in an artifact or book from home and tells the class about it. A parent or family member may also come to your morning meeting and share a family story or tell about how the child got her name or nickname. During the week, children may make pictures or collages about things the Star likes or the activities she likes to do, say nice things about her, or cut out pictures that begin with the first letter in her name. These can be collected in a book for the Star to take home.

- Out and About. Ask parents to suggest field trips, visitors, or classroom resources that can enhance your curriculum themes or help children see how adults use reading, writing, and math in their daily lives. For example, you might be able to take the children on a trip to a parent's workplace, visit a nearby store owned by a family friend, or invite a grandparent with a special hobby into your classroom.

- Recipe Book. Create a class book of recipes for foods that children like to eat or like to help make. Ask parents to contribute recipes for their family's favorites and also to tell brief stories about why these foods are special for them.

- Folktale Variations. Keep parents informed about the stories that you are using in the class, especially traditional folktales and alternate versions. Ask parents about other versions that they are familiar with or about comparable stories or songs that they learned as children.

- Growing Together. As you get to know parents, you are likely to discover that they bring a wealth of skills and knowledge that will intrigue the children in your class and that can help you enhance your indoor and outdoor environments. Invite parents' advice, contributions, and participation in activities such as gardening, building forts, making books and toys, cooking, nature walks, art and woodworking projects, and setting up pretend-play environments that relate to classroom themes. Welcome parents into your classroom to read favorite books; to tell stories; to teach songs, games, or important words from their home languages; or to talk about their jobs, hobbies, or family traditions.

Building a Supportive Community

"It takes a village to raise a child" is an African proverb whose wisdom echoes through the ages and around the world. The village to which this proverb refers is a cohesive community with strong cultural traditions. This village provides support and guidance for families; companionship, adventure, education, and discipline for children; rituals and celebrations that bring people together; and a rich oral, artistic, and spiritual heritage.

Family child-care homes and child-care centers can be the village greens of today. They can be places where families of young children come together to meet friends, share information, exchange ideas, and provide mutual support. They can also be places where families find support and guidance and where they join with others to create new celebrations and traditions. For example, consider the following scenario:

The Developmental Preschool was holding their monthly Parent Support Program (PSP) meeting. The Parent PSP chairperson, Violet Gardens, was conducting the meeting.

Violet: Welcome everyone. What a great turnout! Would the secretary please read the minutes of the last meeting. (*The minutes are read.*)

Parent 1: (*Raising her hand*) I move that the minutes be approved.

Violet: Is there a second?

Parent 2: I second.

Violet: Everyone in favor say, "Aye." (*"Aye" is said.*) The minutes are approved. How did you all enjoy the picnic at the park last Saturday? (*Several parents raise their hands.*)

Parent 3: I thought it was great. Next time I'm bringing my husband.

Parent 1: You'll never get him to come. Men hate picnics.

Parent 5: (*A father*) What are you talking about? I was there and so were three of my buddies. Who do you think did the barbecuing?

Parent 2: You know, we should have another one real soon. My kids had a ball.

Violet: Good idea. We'll talk about it, but the next thing on our agenda is the toy-making night. Constantine, you are in charge of it. Tell us how it's going.

Constantine: Well, so far, I have gotten a donation of paint and some wood, and Steve, the custodian at the school, has agreed to help out.

Parent 3: He's good. I remember last year he showed us how to make blocks for the kids. Angeline still plays with them.

Constantine: Who can volunteer to bring in some tools? We will need some hammers, nails, a couple of saws, and a couple of screwdrivers.

The meeting continued for more than an hour. The group discussed the plans for setting up a General Educational Development (GED) course and a baby equipment auction. They also agreed to take $50 out of the kitty for a parent who just had a premature baby and was having trouble paying her bills. The meeting ended on a high note when one of the parents brought out a sweet potato pie that she had made for the meeting.

HELPING PARENTS TO FOSTER THEIR CHILD'S ORAL LANGUAGE DEVELOPMENT

M any parents do not realize that language is the foundation for success in school and that they play a critical role in providing their children with a strong foundation. The scientific evidence that supports this concept is strong, but it is not widely known. This thinking also goes against the grain of traditional beliefs such as "Children should be seen and not heard," "It's no use talking to babies who can't understand what you're saying or can't talk back," and "Children will learn what they need when they get to school."

The following list includes key messages that you can share and discuss with parents.

- Parents should talk to their child from the very moment of birth. A parent's voice is soothing to a baby and can also compel the baby's attention and help him tune in to the outside world.

- Babies' first "conversations" involve exchanges of glances, grimaces, smiles, and sometimes coos. When a baby first learns to coo or make babble sounds like *da-da* or *ba-ba*, the parent can engage him in a back-and-forth conversation by imitating the sounds that the baby makes.

- As the baby grows older, parents can engage in conversations with their child that use gestures and words instead of babbles.

- Parents' natural way of speaking to babies, slowly and in a high-pitched voice, helps babies realize that someone is talking to them. The babies listen to their parent's language and attend to key words.

- Speaking to babies and young children in your home language will not make it harder for them to learn English; in fact, the concepts children learn in their first language provide a strong foundation for English language comprehension.

- Current research demonstrates that holding conversations with children promotes language development. When parents spend most of their time telling children what to do and how to do it rather than engaging in back-and-forth conversations with their child, they are missing opportunities to improve their child's language skills.

- Children who take part in frequent conversations with their parents learn to "use their words" to express their desires and opinions, solve problems, and find out about the world around them. These skills prepare them to do well in school.

- Children whose parents engage them in frequent, interesting conversations develop good vocabularies.

- Children who have good vocabularies are likely to be successful when they are taught to read in school.

- Children who do well in reading in the first and second grade are likely to be successful all through their school years.

Many parents will be eager to learn tips and techniques for supporting their children's language. The following list includes suggestions you can offer specifically to parents of infants and toddlers:

- Talk with your baby or toddler as you engage in daily activities. Point out things that you think will interest him. Give him names for the things he points out to you. A young baby will connect conversation with pleasure and will tune in to the rhythms and sounds of language. Long before he can talk, an older baby will attach meaning to your words and begin to develop an extensive receptive vocabulary.

- Engage your child in back-and-forth conversation, even if her part consists mostly of babbles, grunts, gestures, and actions. Eventually, she will use more and more words to hold up her end.

- Include your child in adult conversations. With babies, a parent can talk to another adult while looking at the baby, using a sing-song to engage the baby's attention. The baby will respond to the sounds, rhythm, and inflection, while the adult attends to the meaning of the words. With toddlers, the parent can help the child participate by bringing up something that is relevant to the child. For example, a father might ask his daughter to tell his friend what they got at the store yesterday or what they saw at the construction site on their way to school. Being part of adult conversations makes young children feel important; it also gives them opportunities to hear and practice new words.

- As your child begins to put words together, elaborate her language to keep the conversation going. For example, if she pulls you over to the car and says "Go car," you might say "You want to take a ride in the car? Would you like to visit grandma?"

- Show your child books or photo albums with large, clear pictures of familiar objects or of people she knows well. Give your child a chance to touch the picture as you name each object or person. After a while, she will name one or two of the objects or people before you do.

The following suggestions for parents of toddlers and preschoolers are based on extensive research (Hart & Risley, 1995; Dickinson & Tabors, 2001).

- Use interesting words with your toddler or preschooler in ways that make their meaning clear. For example, you can talk about *sunflowers, roses,* and *chrysanthemums* rather than just *flowers;* describe a food as *crunchy, tart,* or *delicious;* or point out the *ripples* when you throw a *pebble* into a puddle. You will be expanding the child's vocabulary and, at the same time, helping him develop an interest in words and a deeper understanding of how words work.

- Talk with your child about past events. Help her retell or replay a recent experience. This type of activity develops memory, sequencing, and storytelling skills that will help her be a successful reader and writer.

- Talk with your child about what is going to happen. This type of activity helps her to cope cheerfully and successfully with new experiences. It also gives her practice in understanding and conveying meaning from words alone, without relying on the shared context of what the speaker and hearer can see. Researchers such as Dickinson and Tabors (2001) have found that lots of practice with this kind of "decontextualized talk" prepares children to follow the language in books and to get more out of what they read.

- Give your child choices instead of directions. "Would you like to help me set the table?" "Do you want to wear your red pants or your blue ones?" Your child will be hearing and using more complex language as she listens to your questions, figures out what she wants, and lets you know her decisions than if she just followed your orders.

- Ask your child open-ended questions that do not have right or wrong answers. This type of interaction will prompt him to think through ideas and to put his thoughts into his own words.

- Encourage your child to ask you questions. Answer the child's questions in words that the child understands, but do not be afraid to introduce new words, as well. If you do not know the answer to a child's question, talk about how, together, you could find out the answer from a book or from another person.

- Do not be surprised if your preschooler asks the same question over and over. Children learn by repetition and may get more out of your answer each time.

- Engage with your child in pretend play. Talk for her dolls, action figures, or stuffed animals; be the customer in her store or the patient at her hospital; help her build a castle for a knight or a princess; or make a tent for her camping trip. Extend the play with new twists, both reasonable and fantastic. As you and your child have fun together, you will be expanding your child's ability to create a world with words.

- Engage your child in word play. Jokes, riddles, tongue twisters, proverbs, silly sayings, nursery rhymes, and clever names for pets or toys all help children to tune in to the sounds and meanings of words and of word parts. Children who enjoy word play and have had lots of practice with it generally have an easy time learning to read.

- Build on your child's interests. If you take him to the zoo and all he wants to do is collect stones in the path, then help him make a rock collection. He can sort the rocks by color, shape, or size, can arrange them in pleasing patterns, and can learn words such as *rough, heavy, crystal*, and *sandstone*. If he loves toy trains, take him to see a real one, then get some books and learn all about trains together. You will do more than help your child build an impressive vocabulary; you will kindle a lifelong love of learning.

Some parents will be concerned about their children's pronunciation and grammar. If a child is having difficulties with speech or hearing, or if his receptive language is markedly delayed, it is important to refer the child for further screening and possible early intervention. However, in most cases, you will be able to guide and reassure the parents by sharing what you have learned:

- Adults should expand a child's early language attempts rather than correct them. When the child says, "Dat a big dog," answer, "Yes, that is a big dog." If a child mispronounces a word, say the word correctly in your response but do not make the child repeat it. It is more important, and more effective, to respond to what the child is trying to say than to teach him to say it correctly.

- It takes a while for children to learn fully correct grammar. It is normal for 4- and 5-year-olds to make pronunciation and grammatical errors; in fact, some of their errors (e.g., *heared* for *heard*) show how much they know about language. With many opportunities to hear language spoken correctly, children will master both the rules and the exceptions.

- Children who hear not only another dialect but also Standard English will learn both, and they will eventually learn which to use where and with whom. The same is true of children who hear more than one language.

FOSTERING FLUENCY AND LITERACY IN MORE THAN ONE LANGUAGE

For many families, fluency and literacy in more than one language is a priority. Some parents who face the challenge of learning English as adults want their child to be secure in that language but also to be able to converse with them in their home language or to act as translators. Some English-speaking families want their children to learn a language that is a vital connection to grandparents and other relatives or an important part of their heritage. Regardless of whether they are able to speak more than one language themselves, increasing numbers of parents feel that it is vital for their children to be both fluent and literate in at least two languages to succeed in a global economy.

Children throughout the world grow up with more than one language. Some children learn two or more languages simultaneously; others develop a strong foundation in one language before adding another. Research does not provide a clear map of the best route to multilingual

(continued)

**FOSTERING FLUENCY AND LITERACY IN MORE THAN ONE
LANGUAGE** (*continued*)

fluency and literacy. Yet the evidence is clear that (a) early childhood is
a time when languages are easily learned and (b) many of the underpin-
nings of literacy are the same regardless of language, even when there
are major differences in how the languages are written. The evidence is
also clear that (a) children learn complex concepts most easily when
they are presented in a language with which they feel comfortable and
(b) that being able to express themselves effectively is key to children's
emotional and social well-being as well as to academic learning.

Working together, parents and early childhood educators throughout
the country are creating programs that provide strong support for two or
more languages and that prepare children to read and write effectively in
all of the languages they speak. In these kinds of programs, children play
with peers who speak their home language and with peers who speak a
different one. Teachers respond to children's use of their home language
and use children's home languages to provide comfort, praise, and reassurance. Stories, songs, games, pretend play, and instruction are offered
in more than one language, either by teachers who are fully bilingual or
by a staff that includes speakers of multiple languages. We recommend
the following resources for developing these kinds of programs:

- *One Child, Two Languages: A Guide for Preschool Educators of
  Children Learning English as a Second Language,* by P. O. Tabors.
  Paul H. Brookes (Baltimore): 1997.

- *Looking In, Looking Out: Redefining Child Care and Early Education in a Diverse Society,* by H. N.-L. Chang, A. Muckelroy, and
  D. Pulido-Tobiassen. California Tomorrow (Oakland): 1996.

- *And Still We Speak . . . Stories of Communities Sustaining and
  Reclaiming Language and Culture,* by L. Olsen, J. Bhattacharya,
  M. Chow, C. Dowell (Ed.), A. Jaramillo, D. Pulido Tobiassen, and
  J. Solorio. California Tomorrow (Oakland): 2001.

ENCOURAGING PARENTS TO READ
TO THEIR CHILDREN

I n some families, adults read to children many times each day,
beginning well before a child's first birthday and continuing past
the time when children can read by themselves. In other families,

children are read to only at bedtime. Many parents read to their children only once or twice a week, and some do not read to them at all. Some of these parents may think that reading is not important before children get to school. Some may be unable to read easily themselves or may not have appropriate children's books in a language they feel comfortable reading. For some families, reading time may be crowded out by more pressing concerns. Some parents may figure that their children are getting enough reading in child care and that they should use their limited time with their children in other ways.

Researchers have concluded that reading to a young child daily is the single most important thing that parents can do to prime that child for school success (International Reading Association & National Association for the Education of Young Children, 1998). Daily reading supports language development, helps children learn book-handling skills and concepts of print, strengthens the bond between parent and child, develops concentration and listening skills, and fosters a love of books and learning. When a parent makes reading with a child a priority, it shows the child that reading is important. It also shows the child that he is important. But it is not just the fact that parents read with their children that matters; it is also *what* they read and *how*.

Encouraging Parents to Read With Their Children on a Daily Basis

Although many parents will need no encouragement to read with their children, others will need help to make it part of a daily routine. In particular, you can help parents and other family members to do the following:

- Realize the benefits of reading with young children.

- Overcome barriers that prevent them from reading with their children on a daily basis.

- Establish routines and rituals devoted to book reading.

- Use libraries.

- Select books with and for their children that their children will love.

- Share books with their children in fun ways that support their learning.

- Read (and write) in front of their children so children can see that literacy is a fun and important part of life.

Realizing the Benefits

Rather than lecture parents on the benefits of reading with their young children, you might want to solicit their ideas. One way to generate ideas is to start a list of two or three benefits and invite parents to expand it. Here is an example:

- It's fun.

- It keeps my child from watching too much television.

- It gives me a chance to sit down and cuddle my child.

- It will help her learn to read when she goes to kindergarten.

- It lets her know how much I love her.

- It lets him know how important I think reading is.

- It lets him know that we are a family and we do things together.

Overcoming the Barriers

Why don't some parents read regularly with their children? The following subsections describe some of the most commonly cited reasons—and possible solutions for overcoming each barrier. Brainstorm with your colleagues and with the families you serve to see whether you can find solutions to the barriers that pose a challenge in your community.

They Do Not Have Access to Books. In some neighborhoods, high-quality children's books are not easy to obtain. The library is far away, is open at inconvenient times, or does not have an up-to-date collection. Bookstores are far away, or their offerings are either too few or too expensive. Convenience stores may sell cheap books, but they are not of high quality. Here are some possible solutions:

- Talk to the people who own the convenience stores or grocery stores in the neighborhood. Suggest that they begin to sell books for young children. Bring them a list of book titles that parents might want to buy.

- Call the main library. Find out whether they have a bookmobile that they could send around to your community.

They Do Not Have Books That They Can Read.   Many parents lack literacy skills themselves, feel uncomfortable reading aloud, or cannot find books in their own language. Here are some possible solutions:

- Find children's books that parents can buy or borrow and that are written in their home languages. Your local librarian, your school district's bilingual education coordinator, or a community-based agency that serves a particular linguistic community may be able to help. Your school district or resource and referral agency may have a teacher resource center with a multilingual lending library of children's books.

- Give picture books without words to parents who are concerned about their own reading skills, and show them how to "read" the pictures.

- Encourage parents who have trouble reading to tell the story in their own words.

- Suggest that parents show their children the pictures in a book and encourage their children to make up their own story.

They Do Not Own Books.   Families who get into the library habit give their children important advantages in school and start them on the road to lifelong learning. But young children also benefit from owning books. When a child owns the book he is reading, parents are less apt to worry about his enthusiastic exploration than when the book has to be returned to the library. Also, owned books can be read over and over and over again until a child finally tires of them.

When children have had a favorite book that they listened to over and over again, they begin to memorize the words in the book and will be quick to notice if a parent changes a word or two or leaves out a few pages. Later on, when children are learning to read on their own, they are likely to go back to a favorite book and read it out loud by themselves.

Owning a shelf full of books means that a child always has choices of reading material. The books that he comes to love are often the first ones that he learns to "read," whether "reading" means pointing out or naming pictures, turning the page and retelling the story, or actually reading the words on the page.

The first books that children own are often treasured through life. Favorites can be put away for a time and then brought out again. As they reach new stages on their journey toward literacy, many children love to go back to the books they enjoyed when they were younger and read them "all by themselves," recite their favorite lines, find new meanings in the words and pictures, or just enjoy reconnecting with "old friends."

Here are some possible solutions for families who do not own books:

- Hold a book fair. Book publishers such as Scholastic are often willing to sell books in bulk at reasonable cost.

- Encourage parents to join children's book clubs that offer reasonably priced, high-quality books on a monthly basis. Local service clubs may be willing to donate memberships for families who cannot afford them.

- Call book vendors that you know or local service clubs and encourage them to donate books or contribute to a book fund.

- Go to a preschool in a high-income area and ask them to put out a book box where parents can donate books in good condition that their children have outgrown.

- Help parents make books for and with their children.

- Books are a perfect present for a birthday or a holiday. Encourage parents to give and request books as presents.

They Do Not Like Reading the Same Story Over and Over Again. Many parents feel that their child should be finished with a book after a few readings, so they stop reading to their child until they can get new books. Here are a few possible solutions for parents who do not like reading the same story over and over again:

- Explain to parents that hearing a well-loved story over and over and over again is a wonderful way to learn to read. As the child becomes familiar with the book, his questions may become more elaborate, and he may get more and more out of the story. At the same time, becoming familiar with and even memorizing the text enables the child to tune in to the print and even begin to recognize some of the words. As long as the reading is at the child's request, you cannot read a book too many times.

- Encourage parents to use favorite books to help children make books of their own. They might draw their own illustrations and dictate or attempt to write some of the words. In their own books, children can include only their favorite parts, change the ending, or even write themselves into the story.

They Do Not Have Time. Many parents are working full time or at more than one job. Some also have long or complicated commutes, are responsible for older or ill family members, or are facing otherwise challenging life circumstances. At the end of a long day, parents and children may be tired or stressed and desperately in need of "down" time. Here are some possible solutions for parents who say they do not have time to read to their children:

- Suggest to parents that they read a book to their child while she is in the bathtub or just before she goes to bed.

- Parents can recruit an older sibling or other family member and ask them to find a time when they can read to the child on a regular basis.

- If a child is an early riser, parents can keep books by his bed for him to look at independently or bring to them to read. They can also keep books for the child near their own beds and read to him before they get out of bed in the morning.

- Parents can get books on tape from the library and listen to them during car or bus trips.

- Some parents like to spend a few moments reading with their child when they arrive at child care or before they depart. When it fits into a family's schedule, this practice can help ease transitions for a child.

Their Child Does Not Seem to Be Interested. Some young children, especially toddlers, hate to sit still for more than a minute or two. They want to play with toys, run around, do whatever the big kids or doing—or they are interested in staying still only if they can watch television. Here are some possible solutions for parents whose children do not seem to be interested in reading:

- Assure parents that children have their own personalities, interests, and timetables, and that a child who rejects books at one point may show great interest at another time. Encourage them to offer book-sharing activities regularly, at times when the child has few distractions.

- Help parents develop realistic expectations about their child's attention span so that they keep book-reading time short and fun.

- Encourage parents to chose sturdy books for toddlers that give them things to do—holes to poke or peep through, flaps to lift, animals to pet, and pages they can turn by themselves.

- Encourage parents to choose reading time carefully and talk enthusiastically about reading time. "Before you go to sleep tonight we are going to read a special book together."

- Help parents find books that match their children's interests.

- Remind parents that, with young children especially, "more is caught than taught." If children see parents and other valued people showing an interest in reading, then they are likely to want to join in.

They Think Their Child Is Too Young. Many parents think that reading is for school-age children, certainly not for babies. Here are some possible solutions:

- Explain to parents that a child is never too young to listen to a book being read. Even a baby who has not yet acquired language will learn and remember the sounds of the words and the rhythm of the sentences.

- Take parents on a brief tour of your classroom or family child-care home and show them the range of ways in which you share books and other literacy activities with the children. Point out the activities and books that their child particularly enjoys, and talk with them about what he is learning.

They Do Not Think of Their Literacy Activities as "Reading."
Some families do a lot more reading with their young children than they give themselves credit for. Although they do not sit down to read a book with each child every day, they may be supporting their children's language and emergent literacy in other important ways. Here are some ways to validate and encourage those activities.

- Remind parents that we read to children in many different ways. We let them listen with us to story tapes. We show children pictures in a catalog and talk about what we are going to buy. We read a letter out loud. Even when we go to the grocery store and read the list of what is sold in an aisle, we are teaching our children about the importance of reading.

- Remind parents that oral language is also important. Singing, storytelling, interesting conversations, and participation in cultural or religious events all can help children develop foundations for literacy.

- Remind parents of preschoolers of the many ways that they can support their children's early attempts at writing. Help them to understand that, when children "read" their own scribbles, they are both demonstrating and practicing emergent literacy skills.

- Encourage parents to engage frequently in the literacy activities that they and their children enjoy together.

Establishing Routines and Rituals

In child-care programs that intentionally promote literacy, reading takes place throughout the day and at special times. Children look at books on their own and also ask adults to read to them. Adults regularly read books at a story time that children can expect and look forward to; they also share books with children when children have questions, need comfort or distraction, or are engaged in explorations, pretend play, and other learning activities that can be enhanced by reading.

The same is true at home. Reading can be woven into the fabric of daily life, taking place whenever a child or parent wants it. For busy families, reading can be squeezed into spare moments—for example, while waiting for an appointment or while the child is taking a bath. Regardless of the situation, setting aside a special time for reading ensures that it will happen on most days.

Young children enjoy routines and are happy to follow them most of the time. When reading is part of a daily ritual, children can look forward to reading time. They learn to participate by choosing a book, climbing into their parent's lap, and helping to turn the pages. Eventually, they will participate in the reading by telling part of the story, pretending to read, and actually reading some of the words and pages. They also look forward to the special closeness of reading with a parent and to the way their parent says the words, embellishes the stories, and engages them in book-related conversation. These rituals become so special to many children that they ask to be read to long past the time when they can read themselves.

Because reading to a child before bedtime is such a good way of helping her relax and fall asleep, many parents make reading a part of the bedtime routine. Some families with older children set aside a special time for homework, either right after school or right after dinner, and then either read with their young children during this time or give them books to look at and paper to scribble on.

Reading rituals can also help children to turn potentially stressful situations into pleasant times. Bringing books to restaurants or appointments, for example, can ease the wait for a young child. Bringing books—or books on tape—on a long trip can help make the journey special instead of a chore. Reading a book before leaving a child in child care or with a baby-sitter can be a special way of saying, "Goodbye—I'll be back."

Using Libraries

Today's public libraries are more than just places for reading or for borrowing books. Many of these libraries offer special programs for young children and their parents, including toddler story hours,

Regular family visits
help children feel at
home in the library.

playgroups, seasonal celebrations and family fun days, and opportunities to learn about other community resources. Most have specially
trained children's librarians who can help parents select books with
their children and who can also help them find resources for themselves. Some libraries have toys, audio- and videotapes, CD-ROMs,
and children's magazines that can be either used at the library or
checked out. Many have computers with Internet access that both
parents and young children can use. Some also have community
bulletin boards where families can post notices and find out about
events and resources.

If it is feasible, you may want to take your group on a visit to a
school or community library and invite parents to come along if
they can. Or, you may be able to persuade a children's librarian to
visit your class and bring along resources that the children can borrow. In addition, you can introduce parents to the libraries in your
community in the following ways:

- Many parents do not realize that libraries are places where toddlers are welcome. Talk with parents about the programs that your library provides. Explain that the library can be an important source not only of children's books that have been given the stamp of approval by experts but also of other resources that can help them foster their young children's language and literacy.

- Post library notices on your parent bulletin board and alert parents to special events that their families might enjoy.

- Invite a librarian to a parent program to describe existing services and hear about family needs and concerns.

- Make sure parents know where libraries they can use are located, when they are open, and how to get there. If parents need help getting to the library or applying for a library card, organize a group visit or enlist volunteers who can serve as guides.

- Create your own lending library in your classroom, center, or family child-care home.

Selecting Books

As you help parents become aware of the many sources of books for their children, you may be called upon to help them make choices. You will also want to involve parents in selecting books for your classroom and in sharing books that their children particularly enjoy. You can share the following guidelines with parents as you choose books separately and together.

For all children, choose books that

- Have won a children's book award

- Have illustrations that are bright, beautiful, or playful

- Are not too wordy

- Represent the cultures and families of the children in the class

- Do not stereotype people on the basis of gender, race, language, age, or disability

- Are well written and are pleasant to read and repeat

- Have features that are particularly appropriate for promoting early literacy. These books are likely to

  —Be fun to read and repeat

  —Have distinct and easily recognizable illustrations

  —Be written in rhyme or include rhyming verses

  —Have an easily discernible rhythmic pattern

  —Highlight letters and their sounds, using illustrated ABCs or alliteration

  —Include a chorus or other repeated words and lines

  —Use words that are familiar to preschool children

  —Use some rare words, in contexts that children can understand

  —Have large print and a simple font.

For individual children, choose books that

- Reflect their individual interests—for example, trucks, kittens, or dinosaurs

- Represent the child's culture and family

- Can help the child prepare for an upcoming event such as a family trip or move or the arrival of a new baby

- Can help a child cope with a challenging issue such as a problem with eating, sleeping. toileting, or sharing

- Appeal to *you* (If your child falls in love with a book, you may find yourself reading it several times a day.)

You will also want to encourage parents to involve their children in the selection process. Children will not always choose books of the highest quality, but they will feel good about being given a choice. Their literary tastes will grow over time if they have access to a diverse collection.

Sharing Books in Fun Ways That Support Learning

Parents can enhance the fun and educational value of reading with their children by using some of the techniques that work in child-care settings. Welcoming families into your classroom during story-reading times and including story-reading as part of Family Fun Night programs can give you opportunities to model these techniques. Here are some tips and techniques that you might want to share with parents:

- Preview a book yourself before you read it to children. That way, you can decide which parts to read word for word and which parts to paraphrase or skip. In addition, when you are familiar with the story and the words, you can concentrate more on the child's reactions to the reading and focus less on your own reading. You will also have a sense of how long the story is and what will hold the child's interest.

- Tailor your reading to the child's age and interests. A baby may be happy to listen to anything you read—even an adult book—but a toddler may want to get into the act by turning pages (often before you can read all the words) and pointing to pictures. Preschoolers may insist that you read every word of stories they have memorized or that strike their fancy. At other times, they may be impatient to find out what happens or want to skip to their favorite parts.

- Read with expression and enthusiasm, varying your pitch, volume, and inflection to maintain the child's interest.

- Use book reading as an opportunity to develop book-handling skills and an understanding of how books work.

  —Let your toddler or preschooler help hold the book and turn the pages.

  —Point out words and letters to a preschooler who shows interest (e.g., "Here's where it says 'Happy Birthday.'" "Jeep has a *J* at the beginning, just like your name.").

- Use book reading as an opportunity for conversation.

  —Encourage your child to talk about the book, ask questions, and choose when it is time to turn to the next page.

  —Give your child things to do (e.g., "Search really hard and see if you can find the kitten who is hiding in the picture.").

  —Encourage your child to interrupt the reading with questions or comments.

—Ask your child questions about the illustrations or the stories (e.g., "How many candles does she have on her cake?" "What's the little boy doing now?" "Can you guess what will happen next?").

—Help your child make connections between the story and pictures in the book and real-life experiences (e.g., "Look, the doctor is using a stethoscope just like Dr. Sherry does when he listens to your heart.").

• Use book reading as an opportunity for children to show off and practice their emerging literacy skills.

—Encourage children to follow along and to say the words they know.

—Encourage children to "read" books themselves and to read aloud to a doll, stuffed animal, baby brother or sister, or appreciative parent.

—Listen approvingly when your child attempts to read or when she retells a story from memory and says she is "reading." Provide help on a difficult word (or provide a correction when words are left out or changed) only if the child asks for it.

Showing Children That Reading Matters to You

Children who grow up in homes where parents read and write for pleasure and for a variety of other purposes have a distinct advantage when it comes to literacy. They see grown-ups reading and writing for a variety of purposes and are likely to imitate their actions. Children's natural desire to be included in grown-up activities leads to questions such as "How do you know how much flour to put in?" "Can you help me write a letter?" and "What does that say?"

Similarly, children growing up in families and communities where reading and writing are connected with religious devotion learn early that these are valued and important activities. As they see adults reading the Quran or the Bible, copying or memorizing sacred texts, using hymnals and prayer books, and quoting or discussing religious writings, they know without being told that something special is happening.

When children see their parents reading and writing—whether it is for work, pleasure, worship, learning, or routine purposes—they recognize these activities as things that they, too, would like to learn to do. If parents and other important people in a child's life spend most of their time watching television, then children will want to spend most of their time watching television and will be less interested in reading.

In *Other People's Words: The Cycle of Low Literacy*, Victoria Purcell-Gates (1997) describes the troubles of a child whose parents do not read. Purcell-Gates points out how resourceful the parents are: They have learned to memorize complex directions and instructions that they cannot write down, to get around by using landmarks instead of street signs, to recognize the products that they regularly buy in the supermarket and remember where they are located, to cook without recipes, and to perform a job by following oral instructions or taking cues from coworkers. They tape educational television shows and watch them over and over with their children, using them as a basis for family discussions. Yet their inability to read often makes them feel like second-class citizens and makes it hard for them to support their children in schools where reading is key and where most school-to-home communication is in written form.

The child Purcell-Gates describes is caught between two worlds—a school that demands he learn to read and write well and to use literacy as a dominant mode of learning, and a home that neither models nor values these activities but, instead, promotes learning through oral language, television viewing, and the development of strong memorizing skills.

Parents who read and write extensively as part of their jobs and their daily lives at home will probably need little support to include their children in literacy activities and show them that reading and writing are important. Those for whom reading and writing are less frequent activities may be helped by suggestions such as the following:

- Read signs and labels aloud when you go places with your child.

- When you are making a grocery list, clipping coupons from the newspaper, following a recipe, checking the dosage on medication, or reading the instructions for assembling a new purchase, explain to your child what you are doing. Show her the words that you are reading or writing and explain what they tell you. Let her help by suggesting items to add to the list, finding and measuring ingredients, or helping you locate the parts you need to attach.

- Talk to your child about something that you have read in a newspaper or magazine that would interest her. Show her the pictures and read aloud some of the words.

- When you receive cards and letters that are appropriate to share, read them aloud to your child. Help him to compose a reply or draw a picture that you can include with your response.

- Turn off the television when you are reading to yourself or to your child.

- Share with your child the pleasure you get from reading or the kinds of information you learn.

Parents who do not read can still give their children the benefits of participation in a culture of literacy and access to its tools. They can

- Take their young children to public events that involve reading—for example, church services, library story hours, school plays, and community literacy celebrations.

- Take their children to the library to borrow books whose pictures the parent or child can "read."

- Tell children stories, sing songs, and listen to story tapes together.

- Join a family literacy program such as the Even Start Family Literacy Program.[1]

- Let their children see them studying and enjoying learning.

---

[1]The Even Start Family Literacy Program aims to help break the cycle of poverty and illiteracy by improving educational opportunities for families. This is done by integrating early childhood education, adult literacy and adult basic education, and parenting education into a unified literacy program. Even Start is implemented nationally through cooperative projects that build on existing community resources, creating a new range of services for children, families, and adults. For more information, go to www.evenstart.org.

Encouraging Parents to Engage in Home Activities That Foster Emergent Literacy

In addition to language and reading, parents can also support emergent literacy through the games they play with their children; through conversations about words, letters, and books; and through drawing and writing activities. Here are just a few suggestions that you might give to parents who feel that their children are ready to enjoy alphabet and word recognition games:

- When you are fixing a meal, talk about the words you are reading. "This jar says 'peanut butter.' We need peanut butter for your sandwich." "This carton says, 'milk.' You need milk for your cereal."

- When you go to a store with your child, point to letters and words. "Look at the big *M*. We are at McDonalds." "See that sign? It says 'Stop.'"

- Play games with children that introduce sounds and letters. "I spy an *A*. Who can find it?" "I spy something big and yellow that rhymes with *mouse*."

- When you are writing a letter or paying bills, give your child a crayon and sheet of paper and let him pretend that he is writing. You may notice that his scribble is beginning to look like writing.

- Teach your child nursery rhymes or alliteration ditties such as—

Little Tommy Tucker,
Sang for his supper.
What did he sing for?
White bread and butter.

BUILDING A CLASSROOM LENDING LIBRARY

A classroom or program lending library can be a wonderful way to build children's excitement about books and to help families make reading a habit. For families who do not have easy access to high-quality books, using this type of lending library can make it easier for them to read to their children daily. In addition, families who want to get books that relate to the themes you are studying in the classroom, that reflect their children's interests, or that are written in the languages that are spoken in children's homes will appreciate this resource.

The first task, of course, is to build a collection of books that families can borrow. Families can help in this task by donating books, holding fundraisers, soliciting gifts from grandparents and from local businesses, and making simple books or tapes. They might also help you create a partnership with a local or school library, a service program for older children who could serve as book donors or library volunteers, a community book drive, or a service club or local business that may want to "adopt" your library.

Next, you will need a checkout system, with policies that are easy for you as well as for the children and their families to follow. A simple way to set up this system is to put the title of each book on a separate page of a loose-leaf notebook and divide each page into two columns titled "Borrowed by" and "In." That way, a teacher, a parent, or even a child who can write her name or initials can "sign" the book out in the *Borrowed by* column and put a check in the *In* column when it is returned.

Finally, you may want to do some things that enhance the lending library experience for children and their parents. The following activities take a bit more work and planning, but they help to make the library a vital resource for families:

- Encourage parents to write a note to the class or attach a picture drawn by their child to the last page of a book that they donate or one that their family checked out and particularly enjoyed. The note or picture will help make the book special for its next reader.

- Make cards containing simple suggestions for parents that can go along with some of the books. These suggestions can include questions to ask children while reading the book or fun activities to extend the learning. You can produce a few samples yourself and then encourage contributions from parents.

- Provide parents with a coupon every time they bring back a book that they have borrowed from the parent lending library. At the end of the school year, present parents who have collected 25 coupons with a certificate or a "Diploma," or hold an auction in which parents can use the coupons to bid for children's books that have been donated to your school.

- Make a "bookworm" display for your classroom or for the library, featuring a bookworm with colorful body segments, which grows with each book that children check out and read with their families. When the child returns a book, he gets to help put its title on a piece of colored paper that gets added to the worm's body.

CREATING A CULTURE OF READING

The best way to prepare children to become adept readers is to establish a strong foundation of emotional security, language learning, book reading habits, and real-world knowledge in the early years. Sharing books with infants and toddlers establishes physical closeness that is important for social and emotional development. Sharing books enhances language-listening skills and language learning in infants and toddlers, which in turn helps children learn about objects and people. In addition, sharing books helps infants and toddlers learn to focus their eyes on the page and become familiar with the way written words look. Sharing books with preschool children fosters emergent literacy by enhancing pre-reading skills—for example, helping children learn that a written word stands for a spoken word. Sharing books also helps children learn what to expect from different kinds of books—books that tell stories, books that provide information, books that are funny and make you laugh. In addition, reading together helps children to recognize rhymes, alliterations, different rhythms, and repetitive lines, and to identify words that are repeated over and over again. Most important, reading with children lets them experience the joy of reading.

Child-care centers and family child-care homes are places where young families can connect with one another. The "culture" of the program and of the community of families that it supports shapes children's experiences both at the program and at home. Everybody wins when families and teachers work together to build a culture where rich conversations and frequent reading are the norm, where children's home languages and cultures are supported and celebrated, and where children and adults enjoy learning. Young children flourish in these kinds of communities as they build a love of learning and a strong foundation for lifelong literacy.

REFERENCES

Ada, A. F. (1988). The Pajaro valley experience: Working with Spanish-speaking parents to develop children's reading and writing skills through the use of children's literature. In T. Skutnabb-Kangas & J. Cummins (Eds.), *Minority education: From shame to struggle* (pp. 223–238). Philadelphia: Multilingual Matters.

Chang, H., Muckelroy, A., & Pulido-Tobiassen, D. (1996). *Looking in, looking out: Redefining child care and early education in a diverse society.* Oakland, CA: California Tomorrow.

Covey, S. (1990). *The seven habits of highly effective people.* New York: Simon and Schuster.

Day, M., & Parlakian, R. (2004). *How culture shapes social-emotional development: Implications for practice in infant–family programs.* Washington, DC: ZERO TO THREE.

Dickinson, D. K., & Tabors, P. O. (Eds.). (2001). *Beginning literacy with language*. Baltimore: Paul H. Brookes.

Gonzalez-Mena, J. (1998). *Foundations: Early childhood education in a diverse society*. New York: McGraw-Hill.

Hart, B., & Risley, T. (1995). *Meaningful differences in the everyday experience of young American children*. Baltimore: Paul H. Brookes.

International Reading Association & National Association for the Education of Young Children (1998). *Overview of learning to read and write: Developmentally appropriate practices for young children, a joint position statement of the International Reading Association (IRA) and the National Association for the Education of Young Children (NAEYC)*. Washington, DC: National Association for the Education of Young Children.

Moll, L. C., Amanti, C., Neff, D., & Gonzalez, N. (1992). Funds of knowledge for teaching: Using a qualitative approach to connect homes and classrooms. *Theory into Practice, 31*(2), 132–141.

Olsen, L., Bhattacharya, J., Chow, M., Dowell, C., Jaramillo, A., Pulido Tobiassen, D., et al. (2001). *And still we speak . . . Stories of communities sustaining and reclaiming language and culture*. Oakland, CA: California Tomorrow.

Purcell-Gates, V. (1997). *Other people's words: The cycle of low literacy*. Boston: Harvard University Press.

Seuss, Dr. (1969). *My book about me, by me myself*. New York: Random House.

Tabors, P. O. (1997). *One child, two languages: A guide for preschool educators of children learning English as a second language*. Baltimore: Paul H. Brookes.

Trumbull, E., Rothstein-Fisch, C., Greenfield, P. M., & Quiroz, B. (2001). *Bridging cultures between home and schools: A guide for teachers*. San Francisco: WestEd.

CHAPTER 13

Celebrating Literacy Together

The More We Get Together

The more we get together, together, together,
The more we get together, the happier we are.
For your friends are my friends
And my friends are your friends
The more we get together, the happier we are.

—TRADITIONAL

lthough each chapter of *Building Literacy With Love* focuses on a different facet of emergent literacy, the same basic themes permeate each chapter: Warm relationships with others are the basis of a child's motivation to learn. The early years provide a special window of opportunity for parents and teachers to build warm relationships with children. By reading to children, parents and teachers help children develop an abiding love of books. When children fall in love with books, they want to learn how to read. Children who become good readers are likely to be successful in school and in life.

STORY-TIME CELEBRATIONS

tory-time celebrations present a wonderful opportunity to create a community in which families, teachers, and children come together to celebrate the joy of reading. We invite you to come with us as we visit some story-time celebrations initiated

When David's mom came to school for Story Time, he asked her to read his favorite book: *No, David!,* by David Shannon.

by preschool teachers who work with children from low-income communities.

Our first stop is a celebration led by Miss Carminha, a teacher of 3-year-olds, and Miss Helen, a teacher of 4-year-olds, who work at Children's World South Preschool in Fort Lauderdale, Florida. The event celebrates families' diverse cultures and languages as well as their children's literacy achievements.

Miss Carminha and Miss Helen decided to have a potluck dinner for families as their first story-time event. They posted a sign at the entrance of the school announcing the event. Then, with the help of the children in their classes, they created invitations in Spanish and English that the children brought home to their parents. "Please bring your family to our story-time potluck dinner. If you would like, bring in your favorite dish to share with other families. Describe the dish on a card so that everyone knows the name of the dish and where it comes from. We will celebrate together the joy of reading."

The families arrived promptly at 6:00 p.m. All the children were there, and each child had brought at least one parent or grandparent. Miss Carminha arranged the buffet table while the children, directed by Miss Helen, sang multicultural songs for the parents in Spanish, English, and Hindi. As soon as everyone finished eating, Miss Carminha and Miss Helen asked the children to choose a favorite book from the classroom and ask their parent to read it to them.

One child, Devin, chose a book but he did not want his mother to read it to him. Instead, he got some crayons and paper and showed her how he was learning to write. Another child, Henry, gathered a whole stack of books. His parents, who are both deaf, watched as he read the first book word for word. Henry's mother was able to read his lips. When Henry missed a word, she put his finger on the word he missed. Henry understood her signal and corrected the word. Both parents clapped when he came to the end of each book.

Before the children went home, they each chose a book from the parent lending library and put it in their special carry-home bag. With a big smile on his face, Henry held up his book so that his teacher could take his picture.

Our next stop brings us to another story-time celebration at Children's World South Preschool—this time with Miss Adeline, a teacher of 4-year-olds, Miss Sherrie, a teacher of 3-year-olds, and Miss Rosina, a teacher of 2-year-olds.

The three teachers decided to plan a joint story-time celebration for their classes. They chose "Brown Bear" as their story-time theme, knowing how much their children loved to read the Big Book titled *Brown Bear, Brown Bear, What Do You See?* (Martin & Carle, 1967). The teachers cut out invitations in the shape of a bear, and the children "decorated" them with brown crayons and carried them home to their parents.

The evening began with a chicken dinner bought from a local catering service. After dinner, Miss Adeline read the Brown Bear story to the class. "Brown Bear, brown bear, what do you see?" she read, "I saw a—" "yellow duck," the children chimed in, "looking at me." Following the story, the teachers passed out brown paper bags, glue, scissors, eyes, pom-poms, and strips of colored paper. With the help of their parents, the children made brown bear puppets. Then, each child chose a book from the classroom and, with the help of their parents, read the book to their brown bear puppets. At the end of the evening, each family chose a book to take home from the lending library. Amazingly enough, every child in the three classes came to the event with one or two of their parents or grandparents.

We go now to a story-time celebration that has been organized by Miss Jackie, a teacher of 4-year-olds at Palmetto Beach Community Child Care in Tampa, Florida:

Miss Jackie also decided to use "Brown Bear" as the theme of her first story-time event, but she approached it differently. Before sending invitations, she helped each child create her own Brown Bear book. On each page of the book, Brown Bear saw a picture drawn by the child. When the children finished making their Brown Bear books, Miss Jackie put each book in a bag with the child's name written on it and put the bags on a high shelf. The children helped their teacher create invitations to the Brown Bear Story-Time Celebration. The invitations read, "Please come to our Story-Time Celebration. It is this Wednesday at 5:00 p.m. You will receive a special surprise that I made just for you." Miss Jackie told the children not to tell their parents what the surprise was. It was their special secret.

When the parents arrived on Wednesday evening, Miss Jackie explained the different activities that were set up on the tables. She told the families to select the activity they would like to begin with and to rotate to a different activity whenever they were ready. On one table, Miss Jackie had set out a variety of snacks that the children could make and eat. A second table was set up with paint, paper, and letter stamps. A third table had paint, paper, and letter-shaped sponges. The final table was set up with bookmaking materials. The families could also choose a book from the book corner, where the favorite Big Books and board books were displayed.

Angel immediately took her grandmother by the hand and brought her to the cozy hideaway inside the playhouse, where they read book after book together. Iris and her mother went right to the snack table, and Iris spread jelly on two crackers—one for her mother and one for herself. Gabrielle led her parents to the table with sponge letters. Colin and his friends brought their families to the bookmaking table so that they could make books to take home.

At six o'clock sharp, Miss Jackie announced that it was cleanup time. "And when everything is cleaned up," she announced, "the children can bring their families the special surprise." The children made sure that the cleanup was completed in 2 minutes flat. Then, one by one, the children presented the Brown Bear books they had made to their parents. The families "oohed" and "ahed" when they opened their surprise packages.

After the families received their surprises, Miss Jackie asked the children to sing the good-bye song. As they left the classroom, the children chose a book from the parent lending library and put it in a special bag with the Brown Bear book. Miss Jackie was delighted with the evening. Every child had succeeded in getting one or more family members to come to the story-time celebration.

We now move to another story-time celebration, this time with Miss Lisa and Miss Monica, each of whom teach a class for 4-year-olds at Little Scholars Preschool in Fort Lauderdale, Florida.

Miss Lisa and Miss Monica chose "Family Night" as their theme for the story-time celebration. Miss Lisa and Miss Monica created an invitation that had a picture of a child in a nightgown and a nightcap with the words, "You are invited" printed underneath the picture. On the inside of the invitation, Miss Lisa and Miss Monica wrote, "Family Night Celebration at Little Scholars Preschool."

When the families arrived at the school, they were served a "Chinese cuisine" dinner. After the dinner, each family was given a card with an animal drawn on the front and a short poem about an animal written on the back. Family members were told to read the poem out loud and to encourage their children to make animal sounds and move like the animal as they listened to the poem. After the poems were read, the children took part in an animal parade. Deborah, mooing like a cow, led the parade. She was followed by Francis, who was making loud quacking noises as he waddled behind her. Next came Colin, who was swinging his arms back and forth as if they were a trunk. The last child to join the parade was Carmen, who squeaked like a mouse as she scuttled behind the other "animals."

After the parade, the children went to their respective classrooms, taking their family members along. Miss Lisa and Miss Monica each read *One Fish, Two Fish, Red Fish, Blue Fish* (Seuss, 1960) to her group in a storytelling voice. Then each child was given a cutout blue fish, some crayons, sequins, wiggly eyes, confetti, and a container of paste. The families helped the children decorate the blue fish. Before they went home, the children helped their parents choose a book from the parent lending library. The teachers asked the parents to read the book to their children before they went to sleep that night.

Nearing the end of our tour, we reach a celebration led by Miss Deborah, who teaches 4-year-olds at Cradle Nursery in Fort Lauderdale, Florida.

Miss Deborah chose "Bedtime Stories for Preschoolers" as her theme. The invitations she sent to the parents were covered with stars. Inside the flap of the invitation was a drawing of a child in bed with the words of the theme written across it. At the bottom of the invitations, she wrote, "Please bring your child to the story-time celebration, dressed in pajamas."

When the parents arrived with their children, the room was darkened. Silver foil stars hung from the ceiling. The only illumination was from nightlights, which gave the room a dim glow. Miss Deborah then turned on the lights and served a light dinner with small sandwiches, chips, pickles, and punch. After dinner, Miss Deborah read *Goodnight Moon* (Brown, 1985). The parents and children made s'mores. Then the parents each read stories to their children for about 30 minutes. Before they left, each parent selected a book from the parent lending library. One parent commented as she left the room, "This was a wonderful evening. When are we going to have the next one?"

Finally, our tour ends with a story-time celebration led by four teachers at Toddler Tech in Fort Lauderdale, Florida. Miss Mamie teaches 1- to 2-year-olds; Miss Nicole teaches 2- to 3-year-olds; Miss Joey teaches 3- to 4-year-olds; and Miss Mary Ann teaches 4- to 5-year-olds.

The four teachers selected *The Very Hungry Caterpillar* by Eric Carle (1987) as the theme for their story-time evening. Their invitations were designed in the shape of a leaf, with a caterpillar pasted on it. The invitations were posted prominently throughout the center and also sent home to the parents. To make sure that everyone would come, Ms. Camille (the director of the center) also spoke with parents individually during drop-off and pick-up, encouraging them to come and to bring their entire families.

Most families arrived between 6:30 and 7:00 p.m. for a buffet dinner of roast chicken, rice, salad, and a variety of sauces. Tables were located around the perimeter of the large multifunction room and groups ate "family style," with teachers joining the families of their students. The atmosphere was relaxing. Books and toys were available for younger children, who were free to explore the room.

Books that children could take home after the event were displayed in the entrance hallway. As parents signed in, they reviewed the books with their children. Many children pointed out their favorite books. One child got very excited when she saw the book *Caps for Sale* (Slobodkina, 1947) on the table. She told her mom, "This is my *favorite* book." She picked up the book and carried it to her table. She refused to part with the book all evening. This little girl "read" her book to a visiting newspaper reporter and to her mom.

After dinner, Ms. Camille welcomed everyone and gave a short talk about the literacy program at Toddler Tech. She highlighted the active role that each teacher was taking to ensure that the children in their care had opportunities to develop early literacy skills. This brief talk was followed by an acknowledgment of parents' important role in creating a partnership for learning.

Then the nominated reader, Miss Joey, invited parents and children to gather around on the floor while she read *The Very Hungry Caterpillar*. Most of the children gathered around Miss Joey while the others sat next to their parents on cushions or low chairs. Miss Joey read the story in such an engaging voice that the parents and children applauded when she finished. She then engaged the children in talking about the book by asking both closed and open-ended questions: "What type of food did the caterpillar eat, can you remember?" "What is your favorite food?"

The families—including siblings—were then invited to participate in a story extension activity. Craft sticks, glue, and pom-poms of various sizes and colors were set out on each table. Moms, dads, and children were very involved in this activity and enjoyed creating their own unique caterpillars to take home.

When everyone had finished the activity, the teachers asked the families to select a book from the classroom and read it with their child. Before leaving, children selected "take-home" books. The event ended at about 8:30 p.m.

Tips for Planning a Story-Time Celebration

S tory-time celebrations are a marvelous way to include parents in your goal of supporting emergent literacy both in your program and in the children's home. Here are some tried and true

This child made his own "very hungry" caterpillar at Story Time—with the help of his very proud dad.

ways of increasing the likelihood that your story-time celebrations will be a resounding success:

- When you plan your yearly calendar, make sure to plan for at least four story-time celebrations per year.

- Story times do cost money. Find ways of securing funds for your story-time events. Different centers have gone about this task in different ways.

  —Some story-time coordinators have gotten support from local service programs such as Kiwanis Clubs.

  —Some story-time coordinators have been supported by their center director or owner, who viewed the story-time celebrations as a way of maintaining enrollment.

  —Some story-time coordinators have held fund-raising events such as bake sales or the sale of recipe books that include the parents' favorite recipes.

  —Some story-time coordinators have either charged the parents for story-time celebrations or asked each parent to contribute a dish for a potluck dinner.

- Before setting a date for a story-time celebration, talk with the parents about the time and the day of the week that would work best for them.

- Begin your preparations early. These include the following:

  —Choosing a theme for each story-time celebration

  —Getting the children excited about the event

  —Planning a performance with the children—for example, a song fest or puppet show that would entice the parents to come to the event

  —Planning a range of activities related to emergent literacy and gathering the materials that you will need for the activities

  —Creating and sending the invitations with the help of the children

  —Putting up a sign in your center announcing the story-time celebration

- Invite a local newspaper to take pictures at your story-time celebration.

- Tape record each parent as they read the book to their child and put the audiotape in your listening center so the children can listen to the tape as they read the book.

- Give each parent a classic storybook—one with which the children are already familiar—to take home and keep.

- At the event, take pictures with your own camera so that you can post the photos in the classroom or share them with the parents.

- If you have a parent lending library, make sure that each family chooses a book to borrow.

- Invite the parents to help you plan and carry out the next story-time celebration.

Reflection

Think about how you could develop a story-time celebration for your own classroom or program.

What theme would you use?

What would you do to ensure that *all* of the families would attend and that they would all have a meaningful, enjoyable experience?

REFERENCES

Brown, M. W. (1985). *Goodnight moon.* New York: Harper & Row.

Carle, E. (1987). *The very hungry caterpillar* (2nd ed.). New York: Philomel Books.

Martin, B., & Carle, E. (1967). *Brown bear, brown bear, what do you see?* New York: Henry Holt.

Seuss, Dr. (1960). *One fish, two fish, red fish, blue fish.* New York: Random House Children's Books.

Shannon, D. (1998) *No, David!* New York: Scholastic.

Slobodkina, E. (1947). *Caps for sale.* New York: Harper & Row.

Appendix A

Books That Build Literacy With Love

The following collections of books were selected for the PARITY program, a university/community partnership to support the emergent literacy of children birth through age 5. The letters after each book indicate special features that intrigue children and can foster particular aspects of emergent literacy. The code key is as follows:

A—actions, the text and illustrations encourage children to act out phrases or physically interact with the book; ABC—develops alphabet skills, including letter recognition, phonemic awareness, and letter/sound correspondence; C—colors; CH—cultural heritage; promotes positive identity and cross-cultural learning; may use dialect; CT—counting and number sense; H—humor; I—informative; provides science or social studies information; O—opposites; P—predictable text, with a pattern, sequence, or repeated refrain; M—music; children can sing or say the words to a favorite song; R—rhymes or poetry; RW—recognizable words, large type labels or photographs of common signs encourage children to "read" key words; S—sounds; encourages children to imitate sounds of animals, machines, or processes and to play with onomatopoetic words; SE—social/emotional; supports positive relationships; addresses issues likely to concern children; helps children name and express their feelings and deal with common conflicts in positive ways; V—vocabulary; introduces rare words that will stretch children's vocabularies

Infants (Birth–1)

Ain't No Mountain High Enough
(M, SE)
Charles R. Smith, Jr.

All Fall Down (R)
Helen Oxenbury

Baby Dance (A, R, SE)
Ann Taylor, illustrated by Marjorie
van Heerden

Baby Faces (SE)
Margaret Miller

Baby's World *Bathtime* (R)
Beth Landis

Baby's World *Goodnight* (R)
Beth Landis

*Brown Bear, Brown Bear, What Do
You See?* (C, P, R)
Bill Martin, illustrated by Eric Carle

Clap Hands (A, R)
Helen Oxenbury

Goodnight Moon (P, available in
Spanish)
Margaret Wise Brown, illustrated
by Clement Hurd

How Sweet It Is To Be Loved by You
(M, SE)
Charles R. Smith, Jr.

I Make Music (R)
Eloise Greenfield , illustrated by
Jan Spivey Gilchrist

My Girl (M, SE)
Charles R. Smith, Jr.

Say Goodnight (R)
Helen Oxenbury

Spot Counts From 1 to 10 (CT)
Eric Hill

Spot Looks at Colors (C)
Eric Hill

Spots First Words (R, W)
Eric Hill

Sugar Pie Honey Bunch (M, SE)
Brian Holland, Charles R. Smith,
Jr., Lamont Dozier, and Eddie
Holland

Tickle Tickle (R, S)
Helen Oxenbury

Toddlers (1–3)

Ain't No Mountain High Enough
(M, SE)
Charles R. Smith, Jr.

The Daddy Book (SE)
Todd Parr

Dinosaur Roar! (O, R, V)
Paul Strickland

Freight Train (C, V)
Donald Crews

From Head to Toe (A, R, V, available
in Spanish)
Eric Carle

Goodnight Gorilla (H)
Peggy Rathmann

Goodnight Moon (P, available in
Spanish)
Margaret Wise Brown, illustrated
by Clement Hurd

I Read Signs (RW)
Tana Hoban

Joshua James Likes Trucks (O)
Catherine Petrie, illustrated by Joel
Snyder

The Little Engine That Could
(SE, available in Spanish)
Watty Piper, illustrated by George
and Doris Hauman

Mama Do You Love Me? (CH, SE, V)
Barbara M. Joosse, illustrated by
Barbara Lavallee

Museum ABC (ABC)
Metropolitan Museum of Art

Mrs. Wishy Washy (P)
Joy Cowley, illustrated by
Elizabeth Fuller

My Daddy and I . . . (R, SE)
Eloise Greenfield, illustrated by
Jan Spivey Gilchrist

My Five Senses (I)
Aliki

Of Colors and Things (C)
Tana Hoban

On the Farm (no words)
Frantisek Chochola

Planting a Rainbow (I, C, RW, V)
Lois Ehlert

*Polar Bear, Polar Bear, What Do
You Hear?* (P, S)
Bill Martin, illustrated by Eric Carle

The Rainbow Fish (SE, available in
Spanish)
Marcus Pfister

The Runaway Bunny (SE)
Margaret Wise Brown, illustrated
by Clement Hurd

Ten, Nine, Eight (CT, R, SE)
Molly Bang

Tools (I, V)
Ann Morris, illustrated by Ken
Heyman

Truck
Donald Crews

Two Eyes, A Nose, and A Mouth (R)
Roberta Grobel Intrater

The Very Hungry Caterpillar (A, CT,
P, available in Spanish)
Eric Carle

The Wheels on the Bus (A, M, P, R, S)
Raffi, illustrated by Sylvia
Wickstrom

Where Does Brown Bear Go? (P)
Nicki Weiss

Preschoolers (3–5)

Abby (SE)
Jeanette Caines, illustrated by
Steven Kellogg

A Very Special House (R)
Ruth Kraus, illustrated by Maurice
Sendak

*Alexander and the Terrible, Horrible,
No Good, Very Bad Day* (H, SE)
Judith Viorst, illustrated by Ray
Cruz

Amazing Grace (CH, SE)
Mary Hoffman and Caroline Binch

Are You My Mother? (P, S, SE)
P. D. Eastman

Best Friends (SE)
Miriam Cohen, illustrated by
Lillian Hoban

The Big Box (R, SE)
Toni and Slade Morrison, illustrated
by Giselle Potter

Big Red Barn (C, R, available in
Spanish)
Margaret Wise Brown, illustrated
by Felicia Bond

Blueberries for Sal (P, S)
Robert McCloskey

Bread, Bread, Bread (I, V)
Ann Morris, illustrated by Ken
Heyman

Bright Eyes, Brown Skin (CH, SE, R)
Cheryl Willis Hudson and Bernette
G. Ford, illustrated by George Ford

Bringing the Rain to Kapiti Plain
(I, CH, R, V)
Verna Aardema, illustrated by
Beatriz Vidal

*Brown Bear, Brown Bear, What Do
You See?* (C, P, R)
Bill Martin, Jr., illustrated by Eric
Carle

Bus Stops (P, V)
Taro Gomi

Caps for Sale (A, C, P)
Esphyr Slobodkina

Carribbean Alphabet (ABC, CH, I, V)
Frane Lessac

The Carrot Seed (P)
Ruth Krauss, illustrated by
Crockett Johnson

Celebrations (I, R)
Myra Cohn Livingston, illustrated
by Leonard Everett Fisher

A Chair for My Mother (SE)
Vera Williams

Chicka Chicka Boom Boom (ABC, P, R)
Bill Martin, Jr. and John
Archambault

Children's Zoo (I, RW)
Tana Hoban

Corduroy (SE)
Don Freeman

Eating the Alphabet (ABC, RW, V, I)
Lois Ehlert

Eat Up, Gemma (SE)
Sarah Hayes, illustrated by Jan
Omerod

Even If I Did Something Awful (SE)
Barbara Shoot Hazen

The Feelings Book (SE, V)
Todd Parr

The Fox Went Out on a Chilly Night
(M, R)
Peter Spier

Go Away, Big Green Monster!
(C, P, SE)
Ed Emberly

Goodnight Gorilla (H)
Peggy Rathman

Goodnight Moon (P, available in Spanish)
Margaret Wise Brown, illustrated by Clement Hurd

Grandpa's Face (SE)
Eloise Greenfield, illustrated by Floyd Cooper

Hail to Mail (I, R)
Samuel Marshak, illustrated by Vladimir Radunsky

Harold and the Purple Crayon
Crockett Johnson

Hats, Hats, Hats (I)
Ann Morris, illustrated by Ken Heyman

A Hole Is to Dig (P)
Ruth Krauss, illustrated by Maurice Sendak

Honey I Love (CH, R, SE)
Eloise Greenfield

A House Is a House for Me (I, P, R, V)
Mary Ann Hoberman

Houses and Homes (I)
Ann Morris, illustrated by Ken Heyman

If You Give a Mouse a Cookie (P)
Laura Numeroff, illustrated by Felicia Bond

Is Your Mama a Llama (H, I, R, P, available in Spanish)
Deborah Guarino, illustrated by Steven Kellogg

It's OK to Be Different (P, SE, available in Spanish)
Todd Parr

Jamaica's Find (CH, SE)
Juanita Havill, illustrated by Anne Sibley O'Brien

Jumanji
Chris Van Allsburg

Just Us Women (CH, P)
Jeanette Caines, illustrated by Pat Cummings

Loving (I)
Ann Morris, illustrated by Ken Heyman

Mary Wore Her Red Dress and Henry Wore His Green Sneakers (C, M, P)
Merle Peek

Martin's Big Words: The Life of Dr. Martin Luther King, Jr. (I)
Doreen Rappaport, illustrated by Bryan Collier

Mean Soup (SE)
Betsy Everitt

Moja Means One: Swahili Counting Book (CH, CT, I, available in Spanish)
Muriel Feelings, illustrated by Tom Feelings

The Mommy Book (SE)
Todd Parr

Mrs. Wishy Washy (P)
Joy Cowley. illustrated by Elizabeth Fuller

My First Kwanzaa Book (CH, I, V)
Deborah Newton Chocolate, illustrated by Cal Massey

No, David! (SE)
David Shannon

On Monday When It Rained (SE)
Cheryl Kachenmeister, illustrated
by Tom Berthiaume

Over the Moon: An Adoption Tale (SE)
Karen Katz

Pet Show (SE)
Ezra Jack Keats

Peter's Chair (SE)
Ezra Jack Keats

Planting a Rainbow (I, C, RW, V)
Lois Ehlert

*Polar Bear, Polar Bear, What Do You
Hear?* (P, S)
Bill Martin, Jr., illustrated by
Eric Carle

The Rainbow Fish (SE, available in
Spanish)
Marcus Pfister

Runaway Bunny (SE)
Margaret Wise Brown

Tell Me a Story, Mama (CH, SE,
available in Spanish)
Angela Johnson, illustrated by
David Soman

There's a Nightmare in My Closet (SE)
Mercer Mayer

Tight Times (SE)
Barbara Shook Razen, illustrated by
Trina Schart Hyman

Tikki Tikki Tembo (P, SE)
Arlene Mosely, illustrated by
Blair Lent

Too Many Tamales (CH, SE, V)
Gary Soto, illustrated by Ed
Martinez

The Toolbox (RW, V)
Anne and Harlow Rockwell

Tools (I, V)
Ann Morris, illustrated by
Ken Heyman

The Trip (SE)
Ezra Jack Keats

The Very Hungry Caterpillar (A, CT,
P, available in Spanish)
Eric Carle

The Wheels on the Bus (A, M, P, R, S)
Raffi, illustrated by Sylvie
Wickstrom

Where Does Brown Bear Go? (P)
Nicki Weiss

Where Have You Been? (H, R)
Margaret Wise Brown, illustrated
by Leo and Diane Dillon

Where the Wild Things Are (SE)
Maurice Sendak

A Whisper Is Quiet (O, P, available
in Spanish)
Carolyn Lunn

Whistle for Willie (SE)
Ezra Jack Keats

William's Doll (SE, available in
Spanish)
Charlotte Zolotow, illustrated by
William Pene du Bois